Learning Race, Learning Place

The Rutgers Series in Childhood Studies

The Rutgers Series in Childhood Studies is dedicated to increasing our understanding of children and childhoods, past and present, throughout the world. Children's voices and experiences are central. Authors come from a variety of fields, including anthropology, criminal justice, history, literature, psychology, religion, and sociology. The books in this series are intended for students, scholars, practitioners, and those who formulate policies that affect children's everyday lives and futures.

Edited by Myra Bluebond-Langner, Board of Governors Professor of Anthropology, Rutgers University, and True Colours Chair in Palliative Care for Children and Young People, University College London, Institute of Child Health.

Advisory Board

Perri Klass, New York University
Jill Korbin, Case Western Reserve University
Bambi Schieffelin, New York University
Enid Schildkraut, American Museum of Natural History and Museum for African Art

Learning Race, Learning Place

Shaping Racial Identities and Ideas in African American Childhoods

ERIN N. WINKLER

RUTGERS UNIVERSITY PRESS

NEW BRUNSWICK, NEW JERSEY, AND LONDON

LIBRARY OF CONGRESS CATALOGING-IN-PUBLICATION DATA

Winkler, Erin N.

Learning race, learning place : shaping racial identities and ideas in African American childhoods / Erin N. Winkler.

p. cm. — (The Rutgers series in childhood studies)

Includes bibliographical references and index.

ISBN 978–0–8135–5430–3 (hardcover : alk. paper) — ISBN 978–0–8135–5429–7 (pbk. : alk. paper) — ISBN 978–0–8135–5431–0 (e-book)

1. Racism—Study and teaching—Michigan—Detroit.   I. Title.

HT1506.W56   2012

305.800710774'34—dc23   2012005047

A British Cataloging-in-Publication record for this book is available from the British Library.

Portions of this book appeared previously in the following articles:

Erin N. Winkler, "I learn being black from everywhere I go": Color blindness, travel, and the formation of racial attitudes among African American adolescents, in *Children and youth speak for themselves,* ed. Heather Beth Johnson, Sociological Studies of Children and Youth, vol. 13, 423–453 (Bingley, UK: Emerald Group Publishing, 2010). Copyright © 2010 Emerald Group Publishing Limited. Used by permission.

Erin N. Winkler, "It's like arming them": African American mothers' views on racial socialization, in *The changing landscape of work and family in the American middle class: Reports from the field,* ed. Elizabeth Rudd and Lara Descartes, 211–241 (Lanham, MD: Lexington Books, 2008). Copyright © 2008 Erin N. Winkler. Used by permission.

Visit our website: http://rutgerspress.rutgers.edu

Manufactured in the United States of America

In loving memory of Kamilah O. Neighbors, whose inspiring work on children and race was cut short too soon; Lynnéa Y. Stephen, who showed me I was ready to embark on this project; and Viola Suggs, who made it all possible. I miss you terribly.

CONTENTS

ILLUSTRATIONS

Map

Tables

ACKNOWLEDGMENTS

First, and most importantly, I thank the young people and mothers who so graciously and candidly shared their stories for this study. It goes without saying that there would be no book without their generous willingness to let me into their lives. Would it not breach confidentiality, I would thank each of them by name. I hope it will suffice to say how deeply grateful I am for their gifts of time, trust, and truthfulness.

This project began when I was a graduate student at the University of California, Berkley. I am indebted to the wonderful faculty in the Department of African American Studies there, none more so than my incomparable mentor Stephen A. Small, who repeatedly went above and beyond to encourage and improve this project. Ula Y. Taylor also deserves special thanks for her guidance, feedback, and encouragement and for miraculously offering these without ever seeming rushed (now that I am a professor, I marvel at her ability to do so!). I count myself very lucky to have been privy to the outstanding mentorship of the late Vèvè A. Clark and the late Barbara Christian, both of whom offered valuable wisdom. In the Department of Sociology, Arlie R. Hochschild provided unmitigated support and critical feedback. All these great scholars helped shape this work in important ways. I hope to honor them by passing on to my students the unparalleled guidance they gave me.

Several people at the University of Michigan offered significant help on this project. Beth Glover Reed taught me the humanizing art of the ethnographic interview, Alford Young Jr. helped me think about the contexts of my interviews, and Woody Neighbors introduced me to qualitative data analysis software for analyzing those interviews. Heather Ann Thompson's History of Detroit seminar provided a superb knowledge base. Larry Gant helped me with the practicalities of conducting community-based research in Detroit and introduced me to the singular Viola Suggs. Ms. Suggs, an active community member in Detroit, gave a great deal to this project and changed my life for the better in the process. This study would have been very different without her unceasing support and boundless enthusiasm. Although her passing in 2009 was a devastating blow, her generosity and good works for the children of Detroit live on.

In my postdoctoral year at Northwestern University, my wonderful colleagues in the Department of African American Studies gave me crucial support,
time, and space to develop my scholarship. I especially want to thank Sherwin
Bryant, Barnor Hesse, and Mary Pattillo for their important feedback on my first
attempt at conceptualizing place in relationship to children's developing
ideas about race, and Darlene Clark Hine, Dwight A. McBride, Mary Pattillo,
and Sandra Richards for their professional mentorship. I am truly grateful to
everyone in this outstanding department; my year there was invaluable.

At the University of Wisconsin–Milwaukee, Joyce F. Kirk and the
Department of Africology Executive Committee encouraged my writing and
helped me create time for it. Merry Wiesner-Hanks has been a magnificent
mentor, patiently tutoring me in the world of academic publishing and beyond.
I was lucky to have graduate student Stephanie Calloway as a superlative
research assistant, and I am grateful to former undergraduate student Bridget
Finnegan for checking my Spanish. Special thanks to Donna Genzmer, director
of the Cartography and Geographic Information Science Center, for producing
the demographic map in chapter 3.

As any writer knows, readers are priceless. I am exceedingly grateful for the
many colleagues and friends who read all or pieces of earlier drafts of this book,
including Daniel McClure, Lisa Ze Winters, and Marisa J. Fuentes (all of whom
gave shrewd and thorough feedback on tight timelines), and also Katie Mosack,
Elizabeth Rudd, Lara Descartes, Sandra Jones, Anika Wilson, and Nancy Konrad.
I would like to give special thanks to Rutgers University Press's anonymous
reviewers, whose critical feedback greatly improved the book. Karolyn Tyson
waived her anonymity as one of the reviewers, and I am grateful for her insight-
ful and expert feedback, which shaped the book in key ways.

Also vital were the many participants in the various conferences at which
I first floated these arguments. In particular, I would like to thank those at
Marquette University's 2008 conference, Who Claims the City? Thinking Race,
Class, and Urban Space, especially Roberta Coles and Evie Perry; those at the
New York Institute of Technology's 2009 Urban Childhoods Conference, espe-
cially Marta Gutman and Alan Feigenberg; and those at the 2011 Association of
American Geographers sessions on Race and Space, especially Anne Bonds,
Carolyn Finney, Marlon Bailey, and Rashad Shabazz.

Funding is essential to research, and I am indebted to the many entities
that have funded this project at various stages, including the American
Association of University Women; the Greater Good Science Center at the
University of California, Berkeley; the Berkeley Center for Working Families
(an Alfred P. Sloan Center); the Departments of African American Studies at the
University of California, Berkeley, Northwestern University, and the University
of Wisconsin–Milwaukee; and the University of Wisconsin–Milwaukee Research
Committee.

Peter Mickulas at Rutgers University Press is an extraordinary editor who believed in this project from the start. He deserves recognition for his patience and gracious guidance. I am very grateful to Karen Johnson for copyediting the manuscript and Marilyn Campbell for seeing it through production. Thank you to my sister Becky Winkler for the book cover design and to Anne Hegeman and her team at Rutgers University Press for its execution. I also thank Marlie Wasserman, director of the Press, and Myra Bluebond-Langner, editor of the Series in Childhood Studies, for their support and for sustaining a series dedicated to the experiences of children. I am truly honored to be a part of this series I have long admired.

Thank you to those who always make room for me when I am in Detroit, especially the late Viola Suggs and my sisters Eyvette and Stephanie Kidd. I am grateful for them and the many other friends and family members who put up with me as I wrote this book, including Rosie DeLuca, Marisa Fuentes, Shawna Gourdine, Laretta Henderson, Cara House, Emily Johnson, Kim Porco, Susie Squier, Anika Wilson, Lisa Ze Winters, Sara Zocher, my sister Becky Winkler, my brother-in-law Binod Dhakal, my nephews Ravi and Sunil, my parents, Chris and Noel Winkler, and my partner, Tim Turner. I could not have done it without you.

This project has been in the works for several years, and I fear I may have unwittingly omitted some of those who helped along the way. If so, please accept my sincerest apologies. Despite the wonderful help I have had throughout this process, any mistakes and omissions herein are, of course, my own.

Learning Race, Learning Place

1

Comprehensive Racial Learning,
Grounded in Place

"Show me the smart child. Why is he the smart child?" "Show me the dumb child. Why is he the dumb child?" "Show me the nice child." "Show me the mean child." So went the questions posed to black and white children in the recent, widely discussed series on CNN.[1] The series recalled Kenneth and Mamie Clark's 1940s doll studies, used to argue against racial segregation in the landmark 1954 *Brown v. Board of Education* decision. The children in CNN's 2010 study were asked to answer the questions by pointing to one of five cartoon children, identical except for their skin tones, which ranged from light peach to dark brown. Their responses, which shocked many viewers and brought at least one child's mother to tears, evidenced pro-white bias and showed what scholars have been arguing for years: children are not colorblind (Aboud 2008; Hirschfield 2008; P. Katz 2003; Patterson and Bigler 2006; T. Williams and Davidson 2009). Mistakenly, however, in the public commentary on the story—which CNN says "became one of the most discussed stories on the [CNN web]site, eliciting more than 4,500 comments"—parents bore the brunt of the blame, as explained in the story headline, "Kids [*sic*] views on race start at home" (CNN 2010b, 2010a). The problem with this regrettably common way of thinking is that it leaves out so much of the equation. Children develop their ideas about race in the context of systems, structures, institutions, government, and culture, all of which are racialized within the US context (Omi and Winant 1994; Van Ausdale and Feagin 2001). Not only their parents, but schools, media, religious institutions, neighbors, police, peers, place, and a whole host of other forces enter into the process. Finally, and perhaps most importantly for this book, this way of thinking paints children as undiscerning, empty vessels into which adults (particularly their parents) pour ideas, rather than as active, critical participants in making sense of ideas about race.

In an American society increasingly globalized and diverse, and at the same time increasingly segregated, the signals children receive about race are more confusing than ever. Over the course of their day, children are likely to encounter ideas about race from television, movies, music, advertising, books, magazines, schools, churches, community members, neighborhoods, public servants, peers, family members, and more. For African American children, this means receiving mixed messages about what it means to be black in the United States. Some messages are positive: for example, studies overwhelmingly show that most African American families actively work to promote pride in African American culture and heritage (e.g., Coard et al. 2004; Hughes et al. 2006; Suizzo, Robinson, and Pahlke 2008). Other messages are negative: for example, the disproportionate portrayal by mainstream media, schools, and the legal system of African Americans as deficient in areas such as intelligence, beauty, culture, and productive citizenship (Noguera 2008; Perry 2011; Tyson 2011). These negative messages are part of an insidious social script that serves to justify and rationalize disparities along racial lines (Bonilla-Silva 2003; R. Lewis 2010; Omi and Winant 1994; Winkler 2010).

Children confront these messages in a world in which race is increasingly blurred and intricate, in which we have a black president and prominent black figures in all areas of society, but also in which black men are incarcerated at rates of nearly seven times those of white men (US Department of Justice 2010, 21), and black children are seven times more likely than white children to experience persistent poverty (Ratcliffe and McKernan 2010). Furthermore, this is a society in which "blackness" is increasingly diverse, encompassing people with a wide range of cultural practices, appearances, languages, religions, ethnicities, parentage, and national origins. In this world, how do African American children develop ideas about race? How do they negotiate the various messages they receive? How do they process, rearticulate, and make meaning of them? *Learning Race, Learning Place* engages these questions using in-depth interviews conducted in Detroit, Michigan, with an economically diverse group of twenty-eight African American middle school children and their nineteen mothers over the course of several months in 2003 and 2004.[2] Using their stories, this book argues that current explanations of the process of racial formation are not sufficient for understanding the child's experience. Instead, this book explores the nuanced process through which children develop their ideas about race, positing it as an ongoing, active-learning process with the child at its nexus. Placing children at the center of the analysis and taking their voices seriously, this book shows how a wide range of factors and sources are negotiated by children throughout this process. It is also a story of place, positing that, while children's racial identities and experiences with racism are shaped by a national metanarrative of race, they are also specific to each particular place.

Race and Racism in Today's United States

By examining how children develop their ideas about race and racism, *Learning Race, Learning Place* engages key popular and academic debates around how we think about and use the concepts of race and racism. Social scientists agree race is not natural, but rather entirely constructed by human societies (Bonilla-Silva 1999; Flagg 1998; Mukhopadhyay et al. 2007; Omi and Winant 1994). This has led to an ongoing debate, both in academia and in society more broadly, as to whether it is possible to utilize the concept of race with integrity. One side of the argument—often called the "anti-essentialist" position—holds that by merely invoking the notion of race, one is necessarily reifying or substantiating race (Loveman 1999; Stubblefield 1995). The other side, sometimes called "anti-anti-essentialist" (Gilroy 1993), argues that this approach is faulty in that it disregards the sociohistorical construction of race as a central organizing factor in modern society that has real effects on people's lives (Bonilla-Silva 2003; Crenshaw 1995, 1997; Delgado and Stefancic 2001; Gotanda 1995; A. Johnson 2006; Omi and Winant 1994; Winant 1994). These scholars assert that, while it is positive to move away from notions of race as an inherent or biological trait, it is problematic to replace those notions with colorblind ideology which strips away the ability of racially oppressed groups to name and resist their oppression (Balibar 1990; Bonilla-Silva 2003; Crenshaw 1997; A. Johnson 2006; A. Lewis 2003; McIntosh 1990). In this book, although I do not use quotation marks around the word *race*, the reader should be aware I employ the term in a non-essential manner to examine how it works as a social fact in the lives of young people, placing me firmly in the latter camp. Following Omi and Winant (1994), I reject the dialectic of race as either an essence or an illusion, instead emphasizing that conceptions of race are based on social meanings, particular to place, and are constantly being redefined.

There are also debates—again, both popular and academic—as to the contemporary nature, reach, and import of racism. Some argue that legal and social changes have led to the end of racism in the United States, except in extreme cases. For example, Wilson (1980, 1) posits that, while racism was a historical cause of oppression against African Americans, it does "not provide a meaningful explanation of the life chances of black Americans today." Scholars in this camp hold that economic conditions now explain the persisting oppression of poor African Americans (Loury 1995; Sowell 1998; Steele 1991). They contend today only the "black underclass," in Wilson's language, face subordination, while the black middle class is free from racial oppression (Wilson 1980, 2).

Evidence in this book, however, supports those scholars who argue racism still impacts African Americans of all ages, even those in the middle class (Feagin and McKinney 2003; Feagin and Sikes 1995; Lacy 2007; Pattillo-McCoy 1999). While contemporary manifestations of racism are more covert than in the pre–civil rights era, racism still impacts the lives of people of color in very real ways (Feagin 2010; A. Johnson 2006; Omi and Winant 1994; Small 2002; Winant 1994). This newer "colorblind" racism maintains white privilege in a more coded manner through structures, ideologies, and images (Bonilla-Silva 2003; Perry 2011; Small 2002); and this only increased with the election of President Barack Obama in late 2008, when the concept of America as a "post-racial society" erupted in popularity (Wingfield and Feagin 2010).

The fact that racism is still very real and prevalent—but is more covert and accompanied by a public script of colorblindness—leads to denial and resistance among the public, especially white Americans (A. Johnson 2006). In studies conducted in the Detroit area over the past two decades, African Americans consistently cite the primacy of racism in their everyday lives, including its effect on their employment, housing, and police harassment (Farley et al. 2000; Welch et al. 2001). Conversely, whites living in the Detroit area feel racism and discrimination have "greatly decreased" (Welch et al. 2001, 158) and any racial differences in employment or education are due to a lack of initiative on the part of African Americans, as opposed to a lack of opportunities (Farley et al. 2000, 10–11). These opinions are mirrored in the nation as a whole, where "most whites believe that 'racism' is less relevant today than ever before as a factor in determining blacks' life chances," and a majority of whites believe "blacks complain too much" (Bonilla-Silva 2001, 89 and 121). Yet empirical evidence has laid bare the continued institutional racial discrimination in the United States (M. Brown et al. 2003; Feagin et al. 2001; Oliver and Shapiro 1995; Perry 2011). Recent studies clearly show racialized inequality persists in such areas as housing (MacEwen 2002; Squires and Kubrin 2006; Welch et al. 2001), employment (Farley et al. 2000; Pager 2003), health care (Smedley and Smedley 2005), education (Irvine 1990, A. Lewis 2003; Mickelson 2003; Wallace and Graves 1995; Zamudio et al. 2011), and wealth (Kochhar et al. 2011; Shapiro 2005). This reality of a new, more covert form of racism alongside a public script of colorblindness makes for mixed messages for children trying to understand race and racism, and what each will mean for their lives.

Defining a New Framework: Comprehensive Racial Learning

To this point, there has been no established scholarly term to describe how children develop racial identities, attitudes, and strategies, only the general term "socialization"—a passive term, indicating something that happens *to* children—or "racial socialization," which refers exclusively to how *parents* teach their children about race and racism. Indeed, over the past twenty-five years, literature on how African American children develop understandings of race has focused very heavily on the family. Racial socialization research emerged in the 1980s, with a focus on families of color, in response to the vast majority of socialization literature that presented the experiences of white families as normative or representative of "the American experience" (Bowman and Howard 1985; Boykin and Toms 1985; Harrison 1985; Peters 1985). Much of the racial socialization literature focuses on African American parents and the "messages and strategies . . . [they use] to teach their children about Black American culture, prepare them for potential experiences with racism and prejudice, and promote healthy mistrust of non-blacks" (Constantine and Blackmon 2002, 324). The last few decades have seen racial socialization research grow, addressing primarily *what* messages parents send (T. N. Brown and Lesane-Brown 2006; Caughy et al. 2006; Coard et al. 2004; Coles 2009; Harrison et al. 1990; S. Hill 1999; Hughes et al. 2008; Hughes et al. 2006; Hughes 2003; Hughes and Chen 1997, 1999; Lacy 2007; Neblett et al. 2009; Peters 1985; Scottham and Smalls 2009; Shelton 2008; Stevenson et al. 2005; A. Thomas and King 2007; A. Thomas and Speight 1999; Thornton 1997; Winkler 2008), *how* and *when* parents send these messages (T. N. Brown et al. 2007; Caughy et al. 2002; Hughes 2003; Hughes and Chen 1997, 1999), and *why* parents send the messages they do, including the impact of factors such as ethnicity, immigration status, socioeconomic status, gender, racial identity, and marital status on parents' practices (T. N. Brown et al. 2007; T. L. Brown et al. 2010; Coles 2009; Hughes 2003; Hughes and Johnson 2001; Lacy 2007; Lacy and Harris 2008; McAdoo et al. 2007; McHale et al. 2006; Scottham and Smalls 2009; Stevenson et al. 2005; A. Thomas and King 2007; A. Thomas and Speight 1999; Thornton 1997; Thornton et al. 1990; Winkler 2008). Racial socialization research also looks at how parents' racial socialization practices influence a variety of outcomes for children, including racial identity (Anglin and Whaley 2006; Bannon et al. 2009; Bennett 2006; Demo and Hughes 1990; Hughes et al. 2009; McHale et al. 2006; Neblett et al. 2009; Stevenson 1995; Supple et al. 2006; D. Thomas et al. 2003; A. Thomas and Speight 1999), self-esteem (Constantine and Blackmon 2002; Goodstein and Ponterotto 1997; Walker et al. 1995), mental health (Constantine et al. 2006; L. Scott 2003; D. Thomas et al. 2003), coping strategies and resiliency (D. Johnson 2001; Miller 1999; Miller and McIntosh 1999), cognitive development (Caughy et al. 2006), and academic engagement and achievement (T. L. Brown et al. 2009; Chavous et al. 2003; Grantham and Ford 2003; S. Marshall 1995; Neblett et al. 2006; Oyserman et al. 2003; Robinson and Biran 2006; Smalls 2009).

While racial socialization research is concerned specifically with parents' role in socializing their children, there also are important bodies of scholarly work that consider influences outside the family. Some scholars emphasize the central role played by schools in shaping black children's developing ideas about race (Davidson 1996; Ferguson 2000; A. Lewis 2003; Lynn and Parker 2006; Noguera 2008; Rosenbloom 2010; Staiger 2005, 2006; Stanton-Salazar 1997; Tyson 2011; Van Ausdale and Feagin 2001). Some work, including some of the research on schools, asserts the relative impact of peers in influencing developing racial identities and attitudes (Fordham 1996; Pahl and Way 2006; Rosenbloom 2010; Staiger 2006; Van Ausdale and Feagin 2001). Still other scholarship posits media as key to African American children's ideas about race (Bang and Reece 2003; Berry 1998; Brooks and McNair 2009; Graves 1993, 1999; Henderson 2008; Holtzman 2000). Much more limited attention has been paid to religious organizations and community members (Lesane-Brown 2006; Lesane-Brown et al. 2005; Wiggins 2005). Some scholars have argued that neighborhood factors like violence, crime, safety, racial composition, poverty, and social climate can independently influence African American children's developing racial attitudes, identities, and coping skills (Bennett 2006; D. Johnson 2005). Finally, Karyn Lacy and Angel Harris (2008, 173) found social class to have an independent impact on African American adolescents' racial identities, with "adolescents in higher social class categories demonstrat[ing] greater attachment to racial identity [and] . . . feel[ing] more positively about being black than . . . their less-advantaged counterparts despite their parents' beliefs or practices about race."

The literature is not in agreement regarding which of these sources is most influential. Literature on racial socialization, perhaps not surprisingly, cites the family as the most critical agent (Boykin and Ellison 1995; T. N. Brown et al. 2007; Demo and Hughes 1990; A. Franklin and Boyd-Franklin 1985; S. Hall and Carter 2006; Hughes 2003; Jackson et al. 1997; McHale et al. 2006; S. Marshall 1995; Miller 1999; Sanders Thompson 1994; Spencer 1990; A. Thomas and Speight 1999; D. Thomas et al. 2003; Thornton et al. 1990; Townsend and Lanphier 2007; Tyler et al. 2005; Wakefield and Hudley 2007). This school of thought claims the family is primary because it decides "what to filter out, [and] what to promote" (Boykin and Ellison 1995, 124). However, other scholars argue society—or, more specifically, the "mainstream" or "dominant" social realm in American society, including schools and media—has as much or more power and influence as the family (Billingsley 1992; S. Hall and Carter 2006; Irvine and Irvine 1995; Stanton-Salazar 1997; Wilkinson 1995). They argue that, although the family does act as an agent in children's learning, it cannot completely over-power the competing messages sent by American society at large. These authors assert that their findings "provide a useful corrective to theories that emphasize the power of parents in socializing youth" (Lacy and Harris 2008, 173).

The existing research is valuable not only for what it tells us about what, where, and how children learn about race, but also for helping us understand how these processes affect various outcomes for children. However, the current literature is limited in that it tends to be source-centered, meaning it is organized around those entities sending the racialized messages, or the "socializing agents," rather than around children and their interpretations of the messages they receive. As Barrie Thorne (1993, 13) reminds us, "children don't necessarily see themselves as 'being socialized,'" and research on children should "move beyond adult-centered" models. In this book, I address this issue in research on children and race by introducing a new framework, which I call *comprehensive racial learning*. Comprehensive racial learning is the process through which children negotiate, interpret, and make meaning of the various and conflicting messages they receive about race, ultimately forming their own understandings of how race works in society and their lives. The term *comprehensive* indicates attention to multiple influences—as opposed to the model of "racial socialization" that focuses solely on family, models focused on specific socializing agents such as schools or media, or social psychology models that focus on "significant or relevant others" such as teachers, family members, or peers. Using the term *learning* (as opposed to a passive term like *socialization*) suggests the centrality of the active, ongoing role of the child in developing his or her ideas about race. Although messages from many different sources figure prominently in this process, comprehensive racial learning is ultimately a child-centered rather than a source-centered approach. Utilizing this new framework does not mean that we ignore the role of other actors and influences, but rather that we examine them *at the children's prompting*, listening to the children's interpretations of their experiences and allowing them to direct the inquiry. In this way, comprehensive racial learning helps us rethink what, how, and from where children learn about race by looking at the process from children's points of view.

The Role of Place

Embarking on this study, I wanted to know how children sift through and navigate the various and often conflicting messages they receive about race on a daily basis. I was also looking to see if any factors held particular sway over this process. I thought specifically about factors such as media, schools, peers, families, religion and religious institutions, socioeconomic status, household structure, gender, and skin tone. I was not, however, thinking or asking about the role of place. I chose to conduct my study in Detroit for a number of reasons, including my familiarity with the city and working knowledge of its political, racial, and social history; personal emotional investment in the city; friends and contacts there; and the opportunity it provided to study racial learning across socioeconomic status while controlling for racial demographics of neighborhood and school.[3] I did not choose Detroit with the intention of studying its special role in how children develop ideas about race. Nevertheless, place emerged repeatedly in the interviews as a central and overarching factor in children's comprehensive racial learning.

Place has been left largely unexplored in the literature on racial socialization (Hughes et al. 2006, 760) and, some scholars argue, in literature on issues of racial identity, racial attitudes, and racism more generally (Lacy 2007; Lipsitz 2011; Wilkins 2007). Settings for ethnographic studies involving how children develop racial attitudes at school, among peers, or at home are often not deeply analyzed beyond demographics, but rather given fictionalized names and vague descriptions in the name of confidentiality (e.g., Hamm 2001; A. Lewis 2003; R. Lewis 2010; K. Scott 2003; Seaton and Yip 2009; Staiger 2006), although there are important exceptions to this norm (e.g., Bennett 2006; Caughy et al. 2006; Lacy 2007; Pattillo-McCoy 1999). In the tradition of the ecological perspective on child development (Bronfenbrenner 1979), a small body of literature has emerged addressing place as part of the ecology in which children develop ideas about race. However, this literature usually does not include children's own voices. As Nicole Schaefer-McDaniel (2007, 417) argues, children's own "perceptions of the neighborhoods and environments they occupy every day go largely unnoticed" in the burgeoning field of neighborhood research. Moreover, this literature mostly looks at how specific neighborhood factors influence parents' racial socialization practices (Caughey et al. 2006; N. Hill et al. 2007; Lacy 2007; Stevenson et al. 2005) or children's racial identity, attitudes, or racial coping skills (Bennett 2006; D. Johnson 2005). The neighborhood factors considered include violence, crime, safety, racial composition, poverty, concentration of socioeconomic resources, social climate, neighborhood cohesion, and social capital, but these factors are considered independently rather than in aggregate. Thus, when place is considered, it is usually as merely a collection of such independent variables.

In contrast, in this book I adopt a view of place as a combination of elements that "together shape the tone of local life" (Paulsen 2004, 245), and place becomes, itself, "an agentic player in the game—a force with detectable and independent effects on social life" (Gieryn 2000, 466). By *place*, I mean not only the location and geography, but also the material environment (buildings, vacant spaces, public spaces, and so on), the social character and cultural milieu, the history, the racial demographics, the economic identity, and the civic leadership, character, and control (Gieryn 2000; Paulsen 2004). As you will note throughout this text, participants in this study speak to each and every one of these things, as well as their combined effect (which one mother perhaps most succinctly summarizes in her statement, "Detroit is Blacktown"), to illustrate and describe children's comprehensive racial learning. Of course, it is important to avoid essentializing place; it is not static and is experienced differently by various people (Massey 1994), as we will see from the children's and mothers' testimonies throughout this book. Nevertheless, Krista Paulsen argues that what she calls "place character" does indeed "shape local fates" (2004, 243) by molding "the tone of local life, encouraging or discouraging different patterns of action" (245). John Hartigan (1999, 16) argues Detroit's place character creates a cultural context in Detroit in which "Blackness is locally dominant."

Perhaps one way in which Detroit is particularly unique is its racial demography. In the year 2000, among US cities with populations of at least 105,000 people, Detroit had the highest percentage black population, with 83 percent of its 951,270 residents reporting being either black or African American (US Census Bureau 2001). While residential segregation is the norm throughout the country, particularly in the Northeast and Midwest, in 2000 Detroit had the highest level of black/white segregation of any of the fifty largest metropolitan areas in the United States (Charles 2003). This ranking as the most hyper-segregated metropolitan area derives from the contrast between Detroit and its suburbs, which are overwhelmingly white, with only a 5 percent African American population (Farley et al. 2000).

But Detroit's place character is about more than just racial demographics. Significant to this study is Detroit's unique status as a large city in which civic and cultural life is largely governed by African Americans. Coleman Young became Detroit's first black mayor in 1974 and was instrumental in exponentially increasing the number of "blacks in positions of civic authority" (Thompson 2001, 211). This transformation from white to African American leadership and control was also mirrored in other arenas, such as the public school system, police department, city council, and city government as a whole (Welch et al. 2001). During his twenty-year tenure as mayor, Coleman Young was credited with making "genuine gains in racial equality" (Thompson 2001, 210), as well as rooting out racism in the police department and other public services (Thompson 2001, 205–206), and was admired for his blunt, public critiques of racism, particularly that practiced by white suburbanites (J. Thomas 1997, 204). This solidified Detroit's reputation as a city that did not kowtow to whites, and since Young's election, all of the city's mayors have been African American. This leadership, the political and civic transformation that followed, and the accompanying reputation as perhaps the one large city in the United States that does not defer to whites, all contribute to Detroit's place character, which inevitably influences the children growing up there. All these things have led to a feeling that, as one mother puts it, "We're running things." This distinguishes Detroit from even the two cities that have a larger numerical black population than Detroit—Chicago and New York (US Census Bureau 2001)—because the black populations in those cities still only constitute 26 to 37 percent of the population as a whole (US Census Bureau 2000c, 2000g), rendering them perhaps less powerful in citywide politics.

It is important to note that, at the time of this study, Mayor Kwame Kilpatrick had been in office just over a year and, as the youngest elected mayor of Detroit and the only African American mayor to have been raised there, was still seen as a role model for the children of Detroit—an example of what a successful child of Detroit could achieve. Because this study was conducted in 2003 and 2004—before Kilpatrick's 2005 reelection and well before his 2008 felony indictment—pride in the thirty-one-year-old son of Detroit, dubbed "the Hip-Hop Mayor," was still widespread. I note this because Kilpatrick's scandals and ultimate conviction, resignation, and imprisonment led to some highly problematic, but nevertheless widespread, racist rhetoric suggesting black leaders were incapable or corrupt. Not that racism toward Detroit as a black-run city was nonexistent at the time of this study, but the atmosphere within the city was more like that described above, of Detroit as a city in which black civic leadership was not only the norm, but a universal positive to which children could aspire.

Despite the shift to black civic control over the past four decades, economic control remained largely in the hands of the "Big Three" automotive companies; and this time period saw the automotive industry's recession, the elimination and relocation of blue-collar work, and the reorientation of local suburban jobs toward white-collar high-technology research (Darden et al. 1987; Sugrue 1996; Thompson 2001). These factors, along with dramatic white flight (Farley et al. 2000), created a stark contrast between the economic and racial compositions of Detroit and its suburbs. Detroit is located within a larger, "overwhelmingly white" tri-county metropolitan region of over four million people, which, in contrast to Detroit proper, "is among the nation's most prosperous" metropolitan regions (Farley et al. 2000, 2). June Thomas (1997) illustrates the animosity of the majority-white suburbs toward predominantly black Detroit by quoting an interview with a prominent elected official in Oakland County, a county that borders Detroit to the northwest and is one of the wealthiest in the United States, with a median income more than twice Detroit's. The official begins, "'In no sense are we dependent on Detroit. The truth is, Detroit has had its day. I don't give a damn about Detroit. It has no direct bearing on the quality of my life.' The interviewer asked, 'What about the quality of life for Detroiters?' The official responded, 'It's like the Indians on the reservation. Those who can will leave Detroit. Those who can't will get blankets and food from the government men in the city'" (J. Thomas 1997, 211).

This kind of ideology supports George Lipsitz's (2011, 29) concept of the "white spatial imaginary," which "promotes the quest for individual escape rather than encouraging democratic deliberations about the social problems and contradictory social relations that affect us all." It leads what Lipsitz terms "a disgruntled group of 'haves'" to support policies that are punitive toward inner-city residents and that ultimately heighten social problems (2011, 33). In this way, racial inequity is reproduced through place (Barraclough 2009; Pulido 2000). At the time of this study, Detroit's unemployment rate was America's highest, almost half of Detroit's children were living in poverty, and the powerful suburban lobby caused Detroit's concerns, including unemployment, poverty, and education, to become marginalized in state and national politics (Sugrue 1996; Welch et al. 2001). Within a decade, it had become even worse. In 2009, Michigan had the highest unemployment rate in the nation, at 14.1 percent (US Department of Labor 2009), and Detroit's unemployment rate, at 22 percent, was triple the national average (Gallagher 2009).

Nevertheless, alongside these economic struggles has occurred a clear empowerment of the black middle class, with an increase in African American political and social power (Thompson 2001; Welch et al. 2001; Widick 1989). Heather Ann Thompson argues that the sheer increase in African American "corporate executives, social welfare advocates, educational personnel, middle managers, and the professional staff of hospitals and city agencies" by the end of the twentieth century indicated "that the inner city had also become one of the very few places in the country where 'equal opportunity' finally had some meaning" (2001, 220). In fact, while Detroit has seen increased black suburbanization, it has not been to the extent of other major cities such as Atlanta, Los Angeles, Saint Louis, and Washington, D.C.; and there remains significant socioeconomic diversity within the African American population within Detroit's city limits (Farley et al. 2000). As the middle-class mothers in the study attest, they have made a concerted effort to stay in the city and have also felt and been confined there by structural racism (Lipsitz 2011; Pattillo-McCoy 1999). Regardless of its causes, the socioeconomic diversity of the city's black population shapes Detroit's place character in important ways and, in turn, shapes the ideas young Detroiters develop about race.

Material environment, too, is important to Detroit's place character. Detroit is a relatively large city. At 139 square miles, it could fit Boston, San Francisco, and Manhattan within its borders with room to spare (Gallagher 2010). All this space was necessary at mid-century, when the population was over two million and multiple and sprawling auto factories functioned within the city limits (Gavrilovich and McGraw 2000). By the time of this study, however, Detroit's population had halved and most of the auto manufacturing had been moved out of the city, leaving massive buildings to crumble or be razed. This extreme population and industry contraction, along with the resulting economic woes, led to what John Gallagher (2010, 24) calls "Detroit's striking emptiness." One expert labels the estimated forty square miles of vacancy, approximately 29 percent of Detroit's total area, as "the most significant vacant property problem in the country" (Gallagher 2010, 22, 28). "It's this scale of vacancy," Gallagher (2010, 22) writes, "these vast patches of rural landscape within a city of several hundred thousand residents, that defines Detroit's uniqueness among American cities." Although recent media reports have voyeuristically homed in on Detroit's abandoned buildings and urban decay in an oversimplified and sensationalized way—so much so, Gallagher (2010, 26) notes, that a local writer named Thomas Morton felt compelled to write a satirical commentary entitled "Something, Something, Something Detroit: Lazy Journalists Love Pictures of Abandoned Stuff"—such decay does hold meaning for the children in this study and, as you will find in this book, shapes children's understandings of what it means to live in a black city in profound ways.

Another consequence of a city abandoned by industry and full of vacant property is a low tax base, often insufficient to meet the public service needs of its citizens. For example, Detroit is notorious for not plowing the streets after snowstorms. In 1999, the *New York Times* reported that Detroit had only "59 snowplows, compared with 750 in Chicago, whose area is just slightly larger" (Bradsher 1999). If a street is not cleared after a large snowstorm, mail is not delivered, children cannot make it to school, adults cannot make it to work, and emergency services cannot pass. It is not uncommon for residents of a given block to actually shovel the entire street themselves, as I have witnessed more than once. Snow removal is just one example. In 2000, 35 percent of Detroit's roads were rated "poor" by a national nonprofit (Gavrilovich and McGraw 2000, 242). Finally, Detroit's emergency response times are abysmal, leaving residents with little sense of safety (LeDuff 2010). Some Detroiters dealing with burglaries or other problems considered "non-priority" by the police have resorted to reporting a shooting just to receive the "priority response" time of almost thirty minutes, rather than the more standard hour or more (S. Gray 2010).

Transportation is another issue. Part of Detroit's place character, of course, is its identity as the Motor City. Its automotive history and its notoriously unreliable and inadequate bus system have ensured it is a driving city. As one resident put it, "My feet are a lot more reliable than the transit system" (Crowell 2005). *The Detroit Almanac* (Gavrilovich and McGraw 2000) has a substantial section entitled "Transportation," detailing automobile, air, and rail transport in the city of Detroit. Tellingly, buses receive only one dozen words in this thirty-five-page section, signifying their tiny place in Detroit's transportation priorities (Gavrilovich and McGraw 2000, 230). To the one-third of Detroiters who do not have access to a car, this poses a serious problem (Crowell 2005; Lipsitz 2011). For the young people in this study, who have not yet reached driving age, whether or not they are able to access one of Detroit Public Schools' many charter schools or schools of choice often depends on their parents' ability to drive them an hour or more round-trip each day. Less importantly—although adolescents may beg to differ—this also impedes their access to social and leisure activities like going to the movies or the mall.

While Detroit is unique in many ways, the findings from this study can help us understand comprehensive racial learning for African American children nationwide. Like the families in this study, an overwhelming majority of African Americans live in metropolitan areas, most within the central city (US Census Bureau 2003b), where they remain "severely segregated" from whites (Charles 2003). Such segregation especially impacts children, who are less likely than adults to travel outside of segregated realms (neighborhoods, schools, houses of worship) as a part of their daily routines (Logan et al. 2001). The less real-life cross-racial contact children have, the more likely they are to depend on media and popular culture images as sources of reliable information about people of other races (Aboud 2008; Bang and Reece 2003; Fujioka 1999; Graves 1993, 1999; Pettigrew and Tropp 2006). These and other factors create parallels between Detroit and other urban contexts in which black children's comprehensive racial learning occurs. These parallels do not negate Detroit's specificity but remind us that local racialized spaces are still "productions of the United States" and therefore reflect and are shaped by national constructions of race (J. Brown 2005, 8). Moreover, my finding that Detroit's "place character" (Paulsen 2004) plays a large role in the children's developing ideas about race is broadly applicable in that it encourages us to better examine the role of place in all children's comprehensive racial learning. As Lipsitz observes of research on public opinion more generally, "Scholars . . . have long been cognizant that these views represent the experiences and opinions of different *races*, but they have been less discerning about the degree to which these differences in views stem from the experiences and opinions generated by life in different *places*" (2011, 69, emphasis in original). Heeding this criticism, this book seeks to properly situate the overarching role of place in children's comprehensive racial learning.

Doing the Research: Conversations about Race

Curiously, it is not the custom to devote much real estate to discussions of methods or methodology in scholarly books; or, when it is done, it is often relegated to an appendix. This may be because research methods are not considered interesting narrative reading, or because researchers are reluctant to discuss the messy ins-and-outs of research, lest it cause readers to question the study's findings (A. Lewis 2003). The truth, of course, is that no study is perfect, and readers must know how the study was conducted in order to decide what to think of its results. This is particularly the case in a study such as this one, in which the participants are black, the researcher is white, and the topic of study is racism, racial identities, and racial attitudes. So here I will devote substantive space to explaining the study—how it was done and why it was done that way, who participated, how they were chosen, what they knew about the study and were asked during interviews, and, finally, what is called "researcher effect," or the ways my own social identities (particularly my race) influenced the research process.

"I Can Talk about This Stuff for Hours": Open-Ended Interviews

Most studies on racial socialization, racial identity, and racial attitudes employ quantitative methods, using closed-ended interviews, questionnaires, and surveys as their primary data collection tools. Quantitative studies are useful to understanding these processes in that they allow us to survey larger, more representative samples, which permits us to then generalize the findings more broadly. However, because they usually have a predetermined set of questions and responses, studies relying on quantitative methods alone do not fully capture participants' voices nor the complexities and nuances of their experiences (Hughes et al. 2008; O'Brien 2011; Silverman 1993). In contrast, qualitative, open-ended interviewing, with a focus on understanding the intricacies of phenomena that have received limited research attention, is a particularly effective research method to capture African American children's experiences of comprehensive racial learning. Patricia Hill Collins (1991, 209) asserts, "Experience as a criterion of meaning with practical images as its symbolic vehicles is a fundamental epistemological tenet in African-American thought systems." Thus, as Carol Stack and Linda Burton (1994, 34) argue, instead of imposing "conceptual frameworks . . . derived from explorations involving white, middle-class families," it is critical that we develop theoretical models from the self-articulated experiences of African American families. Open-ended interviewing, more so than positivistic or closed-ended methodologies, allows us to do so. Through this method, the interviewees can identify what they see as key areas of discussion and address issues not covered by a preestablished set of questions and responses (Charmaz 2006; Gubrium and Holstein 2002; Rubin and Rubin 2005; Silverman 1993). In-depth qualitative interviewing "implies talk between two subjects, not the speech of subject and object. It is a humanizing speech, one that challenges and resists domination" (hooks, quoted in Collins 1991, 212). The models introduced in this book—about both children's learning and mothers' practices—are derived from the participants' experiences as they tell them.

In this study, children's experiences and perspectives are given parity with those of adults. This is in contrast to most existing research on how children develop ideas about race, which until recently elicited data only from adults (Lesane-Brown 2006). Indeed, Michael Zwiers and Patrick Morrissette note in social science research in general, "Few researchers have made a consistent effort to include the thoughts, feelings, experiences, and specific statements of children in their empirical investigations" (1999, 127). This may be because of the perceived challenges of working with children (Eder and Fingerson 2001), especially in terms of informed consent and Institutional Review Board approval (France 2004), or because of the disturbingly common "adultist" trend in research, which suggests children do not have much to contribute (Boocock and Scott 2005; France 2004; Hagerman 2010; Van Ausdale and Feagin 2001). In the past decade, however, an increasing number of studies on racial attitudes and racial socialization involve the collection of primary data from children and adolescents. Despite notable exceptions (Christerson et al. 2010; Connolly 1998; Davidson 1996; Elton-Chalcraft 2009; R. Holmes 1995; Hughes et al. 2008; A. Lewis 2003; R. Lewis 2010; K. Scott 2003; Tyson 2011; Van Ausdale and Feagin 2001), this most often takes the form of closed-ended questionnaires or surveys (Hughes et al. 2008, 229; e.g., Bennett 2006; T. L. Brown et al. 2010; T. L. Brown et al. 2009; Buckley and Carter 2005; Caughy et al. 2006; Constantine et al.

2006; Hughes et al. 2006; Hughes and Johnson 2001; Lacy and Harris 2008; S. Marshall 1995; McHale et al. 2006; Nagata and Cheng 2003; Neblett et al. 2006; Pahl and Way 2006; Smalls 2009; Stevenson et al. 2005; D. Thomas et al. 2003; Townsend and Lanphier 2007). This may at least in part be due to the paucity of methodological literature on how to best "elicit authentic kids' voices" (Hagerman 2010, 64; Docherty and Sandelowski 1999). The unfortunate result is that voices of children and youth are, as Heather Beth Johnson (2010, xiv) notes, "voices seldom heard in the arena of academe." This book joins the growing body of literature employing children's own voices in the study of racial identity and racial attitudes.

Considering children's voices on a par with those of adults, however, does not mean we do so to the exclusion of adult perspectives; in fact, adult voices are still an important part of the puzzle. As Alan France (2004, 179) argues, "While listening to young people and their perspectives is important, others may also have important contributions to make: for example, parents and professionals may have an alternative perspective that adds to our understanding of the broader social and cultural processes that help shape and impact upon the lives of young people." This does not mean, however, that adults' ideas are held in higher esteem or given more weight; they simply provide additional relevant perspectives. For example, listening to both children and mothers in this study allows us to look at the influence of place on comprehensive racial learning from a variety of angles, including place's direct influence on children's racial attitudes and identities, as well as its indirect influence vis-à-vis the ways it shapes mothers' racial socialization practices and messages. Listening to both also allows us to examine the interrelationship and gaps between what mothers say they are teaching and what children say they are learning. This concurrent consideration of data from children and their mothers also distinguishes this project from the overwhelming majority of the existing literature on the topic (D. Johnson 2001, 57; exceptions include Bannon et al. 2009; Byrd and Chavous 2009; Caughy et al. 2006; Hughes et al. 2008; Hughes et al. 2009; Hughes and Johnson 2001; S. Marshall 1995; McHale et al. 2006; Nagata and Cheng 2003; A. Thomas and King 2007). The importance of considering both children's and adults' voices on par is reflected in the equal reliance on each throughout this book: some chapters draw exclusively on children's interviews, others exclusively on mothers' interviews, and still others rely equally on each.

Description of Sample: Who Participated

Through their own words, you will get to know the participants in this study beyond simply their statistics. Still, it is important to give you a snapshot of the demographics of the research sample as a whole. This study included forty-seven participants—nineteen African American mothers and their twenty-eight middle-school-aged children—who were interviewed in Detroit, Michigan, in

TABLE 1.1

Type of school attended

Type of school	Number of child interviewees
Neighborhood	8
Charter	6
School of choice	12
Parochial	2

2003 and 2004. Although recruitment materials called for middle-school-aged children and their parents or primary caregivers, all of the adults who participated were mothers.[4] This is just one of the many ways in which gender entered into the discussion of comprehensive racial learning, which—as I will discuss in chapter 6—children and mothers alike argue is deeply gendered. However, although we do not hear the voices of fathers and male caregivers in this book, they clearly participate in children's racial socialization and play an important role in children's comprehensive racial learning. This is made clear throughout this book via the participants' evocation of messages sent by fathers, uncles, grandfathers, and other male caregivers.

Of the children, eighteen are girls and ten are boys. At the time of the interviews, they were ten to fifteen years old, with an average age of twelve and grade level of seventh grade. I focus on children in this age range because research indicates they are developmentally equipped to begin understanding complex, abstract constructions like race and racial identity (Lefrançois 1995; Murray and Mandara 2002; Stevenson 1995). Two of the children attended parochial school, while the rest attended Detroit Public Schools (DPS), including DPS-authorized charter schools (which require students to apply), schools of choice and magnet schools (which require students to apply and, in the case of a few "Gifted and Talented" schools, to also take an entrance exam), and neighborhood schools ("regular" schools, geographically zoned, where students end up if they enroll in DPS with no special applications or requests) (see table 1.1).

The families all resided within Detroit city limits and represented a range of incomes, educational backgrounds, family structures, and neighborhoods. In 2000, the median household income in Detroit was $29,526 per year. The median reported household income range for this study was $25,000–$35,000 per year—approximately equivalent to Detroit's overall median household income. Of the nineteen families, five reported household incomes below the city median, five were roughly equal to the city median, and nine were above the

TABLE 1.2

Household income

Income range	Number of families
Less than $15,000	4
$15,000–$25,000	1
$25,000–$35,000	5
$35,000–$45,000	2
$45,000–$55,000	3
More than $55,000	4

city median (see table 1.2). Of the seven families in the two highest income ranges in this study (see table 1.2), four were dual-income households. Of the five families reporting incomes below the city median, four were living below the poverty line.[5] Thus, the percentage of families in this study living below the poverty line (21.1 percent) is approximately equal to the percentage of families living in poverty in Detroit as a whole (21.7 percent) (US Census Bureau 2000d).

Twelve mothers were employed and seven were unemployed. Of the seven unemployed women, four had no household income sources beyond state assistance and were living below the poverty threshold, while the remaining three had employed spouses and household incomes above the poverty line. Reported occupations of the interviewed mothers included travel agent, teacher, substitute teacher, computer repair technician, telecom technical specialist, administrative secretary, nonprofit executive director, telemarketer, word processor, store clerk, retail assistant manager, attorney, nutritionist, and homemaker. All but two of the mothers graduated from high school, and a little under one-third held a college degree (see table 1.3).

The mothers had between one and four children, although only their middle-school-aged children were interviewed for this study. Using the family structure definitions of the National Survey for Black Americans, eight families have *simple nuclear* households, which consist of a married couple and children. One family has a *simple extended* household, which consists of a married couple, children, and a family member of a third generation (in this case, grandparents of the child interviewee). Seven families live in *attenuated nuclear* households, which are comprised of a single parent (in this case, all mothers) and children. Finally, three families live in *attenuated extended* households, which are comprised of a single parent (in this case, all mothers), children, and a family member or family members from a third generation (in this case, two families

TABLE 1.3

Mothers' educational attainment

Highest education completed	Number of adult interviewees
Some high school	2
High school diploma	2
Some college	7
Associate's degree	2
Bachelor's degree	3
Some graduate school	1
Graduate degree	2

have a grandparent or grandparents of the child living in the home, and one family has the grandchild of the adult interviewee/niece of the child interviewee living in the home).

The participants were drawn from seven (out of twenty-eight) different zip codes within the city of Detroit, three of which had poverty rates significantly higher than the city as a whole, two of which had poverty rates significantly lower than the city as a whole, and two of which had poverty rates roughly equal to that of the city as a whole. All of the families lived in predominantly African American neighborhoods, most in zip codes that were at least 95 percent African American. The twenty different schools attended by the children in this study were all predominantly black. In fact, only four children attended schools with African American enrollments under 95 percent; the average African American enrollment of all the schools attended was over 97 percent. These neighborhood and school demographics roughly reflect those for the city as a whole, which was 83 percent black in 2000 (US Census Bureau 2001), and in which the Detroit Public Schools overall were about 90 percent African American in 2005.[6]

Research Procedures: Recruitment and Interviewing

The interviewees were part of a purposive sample (Charmaz 2006; Strauss and Corbin 1998), drawn from a range of neighborhoods and socioeconomic backgrounds. Participants were recruited through neighborhood associations, posted flyers, a computer literacy program, and word-of-mouth of community members and existing participants. The purposive sampling allowed for comparison across socioeconomic groups, family structures, school types, and neighborhoods, while controlling for racial demographics of neighborhood.

All names used in this book are pseudonyms. Because naming is a powerful statement of racial socialization and can be an important part of children's racialized experiences (Figlio 2005), pseudonyms were assigned with attention to the nature of the participants' real names. For example, if a child was named after a biblical figure or a historical leader in the African diaspora, a pseudonym was chosen that reflected that name. Similarly, if participants' names were identifiable as traditionally African American, Latin, or European in origin, pseudonyms were assigned to reflect this aspect of their names. None of the pseudonyms used are names of actual participants in this study.

This study had Institutional Review Board (IRB) approval at every step of the way, and IRB protocols were strictly followed in interviewing both children and adults. Informed consent was obtained prior to each interview, and both child assent and parental consent were obtained for child interviews. Recruitment materials read, "Seeking: Participants for study about racial identity and African American families in Detroit," and consent forms indicated the study was about "ways in which African American children learn about racial identity and racism." Child interviews lasted an average of thirty to forty-five minutes, although a few lasted as long as an hour, and adult interviews lasted anywhere from forty-five minutes to over two hours. I conducted all of the interviews, which were done individually, so neither children nor adults would feel influenced by the presence of a family member. As both an incentive and a sign of gratitude and respect for their time and participation, mothers were remunerated twenty-five dollars, and children, ten.[7] This remuneration was given to each participant who began an interview, regardless of whether he or she chose to answer any or all of the questions asked, or whether the interview was truncated.

Mothers were asked very broad interview questions revolving around background, how they came to live in Detroit, and their family's everyday activities. The questions then moved on to what, if anything, they teach their children about racial identity and racism and how they do so; whether and how they believe racial socialization messages vary by socioeconomic status, gender, and skin tone; and what they remember of their own racial socialization as a child. Mothers were also asked to complete a very brief demographic questionnaire, asking for their zip code, number and ages of children, racial identity, household income range, occupation (if any), and educational background. With the exception of household income range, all of these questions were open-ended, allowing participants to answer in their own words, as opposed being forced to choose from predetermined options.

Children's interviews were broken down into three sections, the first of which had a "getting to know you" theme. There children were asked to take me through a day in their lives, to tell me about themselves and what they think is special about them, and to explain what they like best about themselves and why. I then asked them to describe themselves as if they were talking on the phone to a cousin they had never met who lived in another state (this was before the days of social networking sites like Twitter, Facebook, and MySpace, which likely would have made this question obsolete). I also requested that they explain, in turn, how their teachers, friends, and family would describe them and whether they would agree with those assessments (and why or why not). We then moved onto ideas of attractiveness. I asked them to talk about the best-looking person they could think of and explain why they chose that person. I then asked whether they think of themselves as attractive and why or why not. Finally, I asked them if there were any activities in their daily lives they found especially easy or difficult, and to discuss why they thought those particular things were easy or difficult for them.

The second section of the children's interview had a "favorite things" theme. Here, I asked them to tell me about their favorite television shows, books, magazines, musical artists, music videos, and activities to do in their spare time. I also asked them to tell me about what makes them laugh the most. The third and final section got to direct questions about racial identity, racism, racial socialization, and comprehensive racial learning, including whether or not their parents or primary caregivers talk to them about being black or African American (I used whatever term the child used), and if so, what they say. This was followed by a similar question, but oriented toward racism rather than racial identity. I then asked if their parents tell them and their siblings the same or different things about race and racism, in order to tease out the ways in which messages vary by age, gender, skin tone, or other variables. Next, I inquired whether they learn about being black from other people besides their parents, and, finally, what they consider most important out of everything they learn about being black.

At the very end of each interview, I always asked if they had anything else to add or if they thought there was something I should have asked. Most children said no, but one child suggested I ask, "Do [you] like living here in Detroit?" Consistent with grounded theory, I added this question to the end of the remaining interviews (Charmaz 2006, 16), and I followed up by asking them to tell me any good or bad things they could think of about growing up in Detroit. About one-third of the children were asked this question.

Racialized Context

Given Detroit's specific racial context, as well as that of the larger United States, it is important to talk about the research process in the context of race. Specifically, how does my own whiteness enter into this study, and how can I expect to conduct cross-racial interviews in Detroit—on the topic of race and racism, no less—and come away with reliable and valid results? The answer to this question is extremely complex and could fill an entire book, but it is important to consider here, albeit briefly.

Active, in-depth interviews are two-way conversations (Charmaz 2006), and the idea of the interviewer as the "co-author" of the narratives produced through interviewing (M. Young 1993, 72) is well established (C. Marshall and Rossman 2010). The results of an interview can never be assumed to be "basic truths" (Silverman 1993, 90) but must be understood in the context of the interview. Certainly, in a society as highly racialized as the United States, the context of a white researcher interviewing black participants about race, racial identity, and racism comes to bear on the resulting conversations. A lack of shared experience between researchers and participants of different racial groups can lead to both reluctance in sharing information and misunderstanding of the information that is shared (Duneier 2000; Edwards 1993; Morton-Williams 1993; Sieber 1993). Largely due to the historical misrepresentation and exploitation of black study participants by white researchers, a presumption took hold over the last several decades in qualitative, ethnographic research that "insiders" or "researchers who share membership in the same social categories as their respondents (the most common being race, gender, and class)" would produce the most accurate data and research results (A. Young 2004, 187). In response, cross-racial (and cross-gender and cross-class and so on) research did not cease, but researchers who were considered outsiders vis-à-vis their study participants worked either to attempt to become insiders in some ways or to adopt very careful reflexivity and analysis of the ways in which their position influenced their research (Creswell 2009; C. Marshall and Rossman 2010; Silverman 2010; A. Young 2004).

Recently some scholars have argued that this dichotomy (insider equals good data and useful results; outsider equals bad data and unusable results) is oversimplified and inaccurate (O'Brien 2011; A. Young 2004). For example, Alford Young Jr. (2004, 192) argues that there are ways in which outsider status can be helpful and even necessary "for stimulating important and revealing conversations in the field." He explores various ways his "extreme insider" status was limiting in his own research, like when the young black men he interviewed either believed "information simply went without saying" (195) or became frustrated that they would be asked to explain something they believed an insider should already understand. His insider status, Young believes, created a situation in which respondents often did not feel "obligated to elaborate upon that which they regarded as perfectly understandable to me" (197). Even taking into account the possible negatives of a cross-racial interview context, Young still believes: "It is . . . quite possible that men in my studies might have been prepared to explain more fully or further elucidate their views to an outsider such that a broader and more expansive narrative could have emerged around the topics that we discussed. Thus, a different, and in some ways potentially more comprehensive, insight into how these men take stock of themselves as social actors might have been produced from their having to speak to people who they construed as outsiders to their experiences and social environments. Instead, in these cases my insider status averted rather than extended the conversation" (2004, 197).

Eileen O'Brien (2011), too, questions the conventional wisdom that same-race dyads are necessary to produce the best data in in-depth interviews. "It is possible," she writes, "for cross-race interview dyads (as well as same-race dyads) to produce situations of candid self-disclosure across racial lines, violating social norms of colorblindness, when interviewers 'activate a racialized subject'" (88). In other words, O'Brien argues that interviewers, through the way they approach the interview topic, respond to interviewees' answers, and even reveal some of their own experiences and motivations, "in effect, give the respondent permission to speak more about his racialized experiences, without worry that his experiences would be questioned and second-guessed" (79). This means, O'Brien argues, "it is not as important for respondents to simply perceive a shared phenotype status with their interviewer as it is for them to know that their interviewer would validate and/or be open to their own experiences with race and racism" (78). Of course, in a racialized society like the United States, the former ("phenotype status") often serves as a shorthand signifier of the latter (a willingness to validate experiences with race and racism). O'Brien's argument, then, is that interviewers in cross-racial interviews can get past this shorthand through "mutual self-disclosure" in which the interviewer essentially shows herself to be validating of and open to the interviewee's racialized experiences (79–80).

I am a white woman, and the cross-racial nature of the interviews and the broader study is certainly an important contextual factor, as it is for all of my research and teaching as a graduate of and faculty member in various African American studies programs.[8] Although this context cannot be erased—and perhaps, as Young (2004) argues, may even have some research benefits as well as deficits—I designed this study to address, as much as possible, these racialized issues. First, in terms of methods, I chose open-ended, qualitative interviewing because it allows the interviewees to guide the discussion. In open-ended, qualitative interviews, unlike in closed-ended interviews or surveys, participants are not forced to select their answers from a set of predetermined responses. It follows, then, that I was also not forced to presuppose that I already knew all of the possible answers or even all of the possible questions. Instead, the interviews created a conversational atmosphere in which the participants had the space to discuss the topics they thought were most important. This kind of interaction shifts the interviewees' position from that of passive object to active subject (Silverman 1993, 94), empowering the interviewee through her ability to "talk back" (Rubin and Rubin 2005, 26). This is especially critical in the context of a cross-racial interview, particularly given the racially oriented topic of discussion. The open-ended interview allows participants not only to direct the conversation where they believe it needs to go, but also to challenge the interviewer and be sure their points are being understood and interpreted correctly. Indeed, various interviewees did so during this study, like Sarah, a mother who admonished me not to "put words into [her] mouth," or a mother named Audrey who advised me to "take [the cross-racial context of the interviews] into consideration when you write up your paper."

Second, in terms of recruitment and the interviewing process, the first few months I spent in Detroit, I just spent time on porches and in living rooms, getting to know people, discussing politics, family, sports, and current events, attending block parties, and working with an after-school program. Over time, I received the trust and endorsement of a core group of people who were respected in the community (one community elder in particular), and this group helped me with recruitment. Interviewees were therefore recruited through third parties whom they knew personally and who vouched for my credibility and intent. Having the approval of respected people within local neighborhoods did build confidence and trust and rapport in a particular way. Furthermore, interviews took place in homes in Detroit—either in the home of the participant, in the home of a neighbor or friend, or in the home of a local community leader or block club president. The participants were not driving out to the suburbs or being interviewed in some institution or unfamiliar place. I was meeting and talking with the women and children on their terms, inside the city of Detroit. Here again Detroit's place character comes into play. Its identity as a city of black control that does not pander to whites likely influenced the power dynamic of the interviews in some ways, at least with the adults.

The cross-racial context of the interview was discussed openly prior to the interviews, and while the children were likely to brush it off with a laugh or say they did not care, several mothers asked questions regarding my qualifications and intent and how this study would benefit the African American community. Some mothers said it was important to them that their perspectives were being solicited and used in academic research on racial identity and racism, much of which they saw as misrepresenting African American experiences. Several first vetted me on the phone or in an initial pre-interview meeting. During her interview, Audrey said she decided to do the interview only after being satisfied by our pre-interview conversation. "I asked you about [your approach to this project] the other day. Remember I addressed it? What was your theory, or what were you trying to support? And you said, 'No, the theory is going to come from the voices of the people that I interview.' So, I heard you say that." Some mothers expressed curiosity or surprise that a white person would be in the field of African American studies or would want to come into Detroit and hear black people's perspectives on issues of race. As one mother put it, "You are not the norm. I'm serious. What kind of community were you raised in?" This may be reflective of O'Brien's assertion: "Whether my interviewer is willing to openly engage in candid discussions about race and validate my racialized concerns and interpretations of my life's events may be more important to me as an interview subject than whether my interviewer shares my phenotypical race" (2011, 79–80). Of course, as O'Brien points out, this is not to say "that race does not matter" in the interview context, but simply that the interviewer's approach, response, and "mutual self-disclosure" during an interview can mitigate (or activate) some of the legitimate concerns and skepticism on the part of interviewees (79–80). On the other hand, Darlene Clark Hine's seminal concept of "dissemblance" or "the behavior . . . of Black women that create[s] the appearance of openness and disclosure but actually shield[s] the truth of their inner lives and selves from their oppressors" (1989, 912) may also come into play in these interviews. While it is impossible to know for sure the extent to which interviewer approach, "mutual self-disclosure," or "dissemblance" impacted their responses, you will see in this book that the mothers indeed shared a great deal. After thorough discussions of their concerns regarding theoretical and methodological issues, all of the mothers said that they accepted my research approach and agreed to participate in the interviews.

With the children, it was a bit more of a challenge to negotiate the cross-racial interview context. None of the children asked directly about my whiteness or how it would impact the study. When I asked if they had any questions about it, all replied in the negative. Although the children did not always acknowledge the racial context of the interview as openly as their mothers did, race was, of course, an underlying context of the interview process. In order to address this context, I piloted and modified the child interviews several times before data collection for this study began. When I first piloted interviews with children, I found that opening immediately with questions about race, before the children had time to decide what they thought of me and, therefore, how much they wanted to share, caused the children to answer questions strictly according to a mainstream cultural script, which, I am guessing, they thought I would see as the "right" answers. As Donna Eder and Laura Fingerson note, researchers working with children must be careful "to avoid creating situations that remind youth of classroom lessons based on 'known-answer' questions . . . [which may cause them] to provide the answers they feel are expected of them rather than stating what they actually think or feel" (2001, 184). After several rounds of pilot interviews, I settled upon a set of questions (outlined in the previous section) that seemed to best minimize, although certainly not erase, this effect. This interview structure served two purposes: First, the opening two-thirds of the interview, which did not include any questions about race or racism, revealed a great deal not only about their daily lives, but also (as we will see especially in chapter 2) about some of their thinking regarding race. Second, this structure allowed them time to converse with me and decide to what extent they trusted me, so when we finally did get to questions asking directly about race and racism, they had a better idea of how much they wanted to tell me.

All in all, the children were quite open. Although it is impossible to say conclusively, the racialized context of the interview did not seem prohibitive to communication. They tended to begin statements critical of white people with "no offense" or to use the word *Caucasian* instead of *white* as a way of formalizing or de-personalizing their statements. Even though children might insert a statement like "no offense," they were not, as a group, shy in sharing negative experiences they had with white people. There were some exceptions. About four children were less forthcoming overall, but this did not apply more to the questions about race than to the questions about school, friends, activities, and their everyday lives. It is possible such guardedness was related to the cross-racial context of the interview, but it is equally possible that it was related to other factors, such as age or personality. Three children did appear noticeably less vociferous in their responses to questions about race than the previous questions, although two did still share experiences with racism and ideas about race. One child, however, expressed that he felt he should keep to himself the things that his parents teach him about race and racism. While his parents did indeed, he said, talk to him about issues of race, Shaun felt he should not "get nosey into it" during his interview. While it is unclear whether his hesitancy was related to the cross-racial (and cross-gender) context of the interview, Rosalind Edwards suggests, "Black people, regarding their families as a haven from racism, may wish to keep their family lives especially private where white people and those in authority are concerned" (1993, 181). This may well have influenced what children and mothers alike chose to share. However, it should be noted that, despite the inherent power relationship based on age and race, children did assert their agency, choosing not respond to some inquiries, asking clarifying questions, and ultimately deciding to share a great deal of useful information regarding their thinking about and experiences with race and racism.

Adults and children alike expressed a sense of pride in being asked their opinions and experiences and being treated as experts. As several researchers who work with children have found, children often enjoy being interviewed (Davidson 1996; Hagerman 2010), showing delight in "taking on the 'expert' role for a change, and talking themselves rather than being talked to" (Staiger 2006, 17). While the children seemed less self-conscious about chatting, several mothers worried aloud they might even be "talking too much" (Audrey and Barbara), "fill[ing] in everything" excessively (Patrice), or "going off on a tangent" (Lena). Even though all of these women were quite forthcoming in their interviews, it is possible these particular comments had roots in the cross-racial context of the interview and their awareness of racialized-gendered notions of black women as either unintelligent or "too loud" and "outspoken" (Collins 1991; Lei 2003).

Nevertheless, most interviewees seemed to enjoy sharing their experiences, and a few were even disappointed when I explained that the resulting publications would use pseudonyms, not their real names. "I don't care [if you do use my real name]," a mother named Lena said; "In fact, this might be the only time my name will be on anything important." Others seemed surprised someone would come from California to study Detroit, and several mothers said they saw my interest in Detroit as a positive and deciding factor in their participation. (Kids were more likely to ask why I would come to Detroit during the winter and just be somewhat reverent toward California in general. Although, referring to what the US Forest Service [USDA 2005] called "the California Fire Siege of 2003," one girl named Nina declared, "California, you're cool, but all them fires burning. I don't know about that.")

Finally, although I no longer permanently lived in Michigan at the time of this study, I am originally from Ann Arbor, Michigan, which is about forty miles west of Detroit. People from both Ann Arbor and Detroit will be quick to point out that Ann Arbor and Detroit are very different cities. Ann Arbor is a college town of about 115,000 residents, about 9 percent of whom were black and 75 percent of whom were white in 2000 (US Census Bureau 2000a). Detroit, as you have read, is a large city of about 950,000 residents in 2000, 83 percent of whom are black and 12 percent of whom are white, and is surrounded by a ring of largely white suburbs (US Census Bureau 2000d, 2001). Ann Arbor is not considered a suburb of Detroit—it is outside of the suburban ring—but growing up in Ann Arbor, I heard about Detroit politics and events from the television and radio and major newspapers, all of which came from the city of Detroit. Much of what they had to say was both highly racialized and highly negative—Detroit as "Murder Capital of the World" and the annual arson of abandoned buildings on "Devil's Night" were among the headlines favored by the local news as I came of age. Luckily, my parents and some of my teachers were critical of such sensationalized reporting and taught me to be as well. When I was a teenager, I began to research Detroit's history and explore the city for myself. Growing up in the area and studying Detroit in high school, college, and graduate school (as well as earning three degrees in African American studies) contributed to the development of a considerable knowledge of the city's history, culture, and place character, as well as a familiarity with contemporary Detroit politics, local personalities and celebrities, parks, street names, restaurants and bars, local nicknames for things and places, and the physical geography of the city. All of this translated into both my deep personal investment in the city of Detroit (which some of the participants said was important to them) and a bit of cultural currency that allowed me to engage meaningfully in conversations about the city with study participants.

Having said all of this, let me be clear that I still believe that the cross-racial context of these interviews inevitably impacts their outcome and interpretation;

the deeply racialized nature of American society guarantees as much. Methods, research design, recruitment practices, personal experiences, cultural currency, demeanor, and other factors can mitigate, but not eliminate, researcher effect. The most important thing, I believe, is for researchers to always interrogate how our own identities impact our work, from design, to implementation, to data analysis, and beyond.

Book Overview

The following chapters rely on African American children's and mothers' voices to lay out a detailed exploration of children's comprehensive racial learning. I begin by exploring the tension between how children conceptualize versus experience race and racism. Although many of the children tend to conceptualize race and racism as things of the past, in giving accounts of their everyday lives they reveal that both impact them in important ways. I argue this tension is a result of the prevalence of colorblind ideology, which seeps into their consciousness through its ubiquity in mainstream media, curricula, textbooks, public policy, and popular culture, and which, when held up against everyday experiences, creates confusion and ambivalence for children.

I then move on to analyze the ways place emerges as influential in, and even responsible for, children's comprehensive racial learning. Here I look at place's direct role—the messages children draw directly from place—as well as its indirect role, the ways it influences their mothers' racial socialization practices. First, I lay out how children draw *directly* from their experiences of travel and place to develop their ideas about such things as how racism works and connections between race and behavior. This analysis reveals that, in various ways, Detroit's place character makes the burden of racism both heavier and lighter for the children in this study than for peers in other places. Next, I show how place *indirectly* influences children's comprehensive racial learning, this time through its influence on what their mothers choose to teach them about race and racism. Here I reveal that the mothers in this study rely on place (Detroit itself) to send positive messages about black history, leadership, creative expression, beauty, and culture. I then suggest that whether or not the mother herself grew up in Detroit influences how she engages in racial socialization, specifically, that those who grew up in Detroit themselves tend to view place as a positive partner—providing a protective racial safe space—while those who grew up elsewhere tend to view place as a detrimental partner, acting as a "false shield" and leaving their children unprepared for racism and white cultural dominance in what one mother calls "the real world" outside of Detroit.

Despite these differences, I argue that all the mothers see much of their role in their children's comprehensive racial learning as "damage control," in which they attempt to shield and protect children from societal racism, prepare children to function in a racist society, and teach children to critique and avoid internalization of racist messages. I suggest that place influences these practices as well, from mothers' decisions to raise their children in Detroit with the idea that it may delay or reduce their children's direct encounters with racism, to mothers' concerns about Detroit inhibiting their children's ability to function in predominantly white settings, to mothers struggling to refute the media-based notion that it is better to be white (more than one mother discusses driving her children outside of Detroit just to show them white people who are not rich or attractive).

Finally, I use both children's and mothers' interviews to theorize the role of gender and skin tone (the darkness or lightness of skin color) in children's comprehensive racial learning. Here I examine the mothers' emphasis on an inclusive definition of blackness, which encourages children to reject narrow conceptions of blackness that are molded by gender and skin tone in important ways—for example, the notion that lighter skin makes one less black, that lighter skin is better, or that there is a single way to manifest an authentic black masculinity. Despite the mothers' efforts, I argue, the children's interviews do reveal the sway of these ideas. I then show how gender and skin tone influence the ways children experience and deal with racism. Again I theorize that place comes into play as an overarching influence, combining with gender and skin tone to shape the children's notions of blackness as well as their experiences with racism.

This book, then, endeavors to tell the story of comprehensive racial learning, in general, and the influence of place, in particular, through the voices of African American children and mothers in Detroit. It seeks to reorient the way we look at the process by which children develop their ideas about race, centering on children and how they negotiate the conflicting and competing messages they receive, rather than exclusively on the sources of those messages. It moves to this child-centered approach by placing children's voices and experiences at the core of the inquiry and analyzing the role of parents as one of several influences on their children's developing identities and ideas. It also brings to the fore the complex and understudied power of place, positing that, while children's racial identities and experiences with racism are shaped by a national construction of race, they are also specific to each particular place, which exerts both direct and indirect influence on children's comprehensive racial learning.

2

Rhetoric versus Reality

Ambivalence about Race and Racism

Mahogany, an engaging fifteen-year-old eighth-grader, exudes both tough-ness and tenderness as she talks about her experiences growing up in Detroit. While she says the adults in her life would describe her as "loud," "having an attitude," and "greedy," she is patiently entertaining her young niece, whom she has the responsibility of babysitting during our interview. Mahogany gently shows the toddler how to pat on a keyboard quietly enough to avoid interfer-ence with the audio taping of our interview while sharing with me that her eldest sister was murdered in a drive-by shooting in Detroit less than a year prior. Mahogany reports she "hates" school and homework is low on her list of priorities. Still, she thinks her sister's murder is a sign that she needs to "change" and "do better."

When the conversation turns to a discussion of race and racism, Mahogany's responses are ambivalent, and she seems to alternately critique and internalize racism. Even though she expresses racial pride, proclaiming that her mother tells her that "black is good," she also mentions resenting her own dark skin tone. On the one hand, Mahogany articulates a sophisticated appraisal of racism in the media, denouncing the homogenous representation of African Americans, the meager value placed on African American life, and the lack of black control at all levels of media creation and production. "Sometimes it's bad," she says, "because I like MTV. They'll have black people and white people, but they'll make us look different and act different and ghetto and stuff. Or it's like, if I'm watching a movie or something, and it would be like a black movie with white people in it, but we always die first and stuff like that. We always get killed first or something. And it's really not—I mean, it's black TV shows, but they all is like ghetto and . . . there's not that many. And not a lot of people that write them. We don't have a lot of black writers and stuff like that." Mahogany's analysis is supported by scholarly literature, which finds that media images of African Americans are disproportionately based on stereotypes and show only a very narrow range of African American experiences and that African Americans are underrepresented in decision-making positions in Hollywood, such as writing, production, and creative control (Bogle 2001; Butsch 2003; Dixon et al. 2003; Gibbons et al. 2005; hooks 1992; Littlefield 2008).

On the other hand, in sharp contrast to this condemnation of negative racialized representations of African Americans in media, Mahogany at times blames black people for the racism directed toward them, seemingly embracing or internalizing the very stereotypes she heretofore condemned. Mahogany shares an example involving white, Asian, and Middle Eastern retail managers at the mall who will not hire African Americans to work in their stores and concludes that "most of the time" this is black people's fault because "we act different." She explains, "I think sometimes like if you looking for a job or something and they'll hire somebody else or something before they hire you. But most of the time it's because we act different or something. We probably come in, pants sagging, or something. So sometimes I do understand why they give, you know, a different race the jobs sometimes. Because they probably like, we come in and we be hair wild, [pants] sagging, we probably don't have our stuff to order. We probably don't know how to talk and stuff like that."

Mahogany's assertions here seem to rationalize a racialized system of hiring that excludes African Americans. Her comments take cultural expressions and norms, such as hairstyles, dress, speech and language, and place them in a racialized hierarchy. Middle-class white cultural expressions are positioned as the unstated, high-status norm, while African American cultural expressions are "different" or "wild" and inherently lower status or, as Mahogany puts it, not "to order." This presentation of the particular (white, middle-class norms) as universal (the "correct" way to dress, speak, behave) is the central tenet of colorblind racism, which normalizes and elevates whiteness while claiming race neutrality (Balibar 1990; A. Johnson 2006; A. Lewis 2003; McIntosh 1990; Tatum 2003). According to colorblind ideology, then, any "attempts to raise questions about redressing racial inequality in daily life" are met with "accusations such as 'playing the race card' or 'identity politics,' which imply that someone is trying to bring race in where it does not belong" (A. Lewis 2003, 33). This ideology—which reaches the children in this study through its ubiquity in media, curricula, political rhetoric, and various public and economic policies—encourages Mahogany and her peers to avoid a race-conscious approach and instead interpret the racialized inequities they observe as race-neutral. Colorblind rhetoric is particularly insidious in this way, creating a world in which the victims of racism are posited as the problem.

The tension between race-conscious and colorblind approaches that characterizes Mahogany's assessments of race and racism can be found throughout the interviews conducted with children in this study. Their collective narratives voice a struggle to reconcile the very real ways in which race matters in their daily lives with the national rhetoric of the United States as a colorblind meritocracy. Although some children state that the individual and not his or her race is primary, their interviews often nevertheless reveal the racialized group experience as primary. These tensions and struggles are imparted via the children's interviews as a whole in two broad ways. First, the children in this study tend to think of race and racism in historical terms. This both reflects and lends itself to a colorblind or "post-racial" ideology, which posits race and racism as things of the past (Wingfield and Feagin 2010). Second, this kind of thinking often leads to tension, confusion, ambivalence, and contradiction for children, as illustrated through their discussions of whether or not race (or, more accurately, racialization) has any impact on them, their ideas about racial pride, and the acceptability of ever taking race into account.

Children's Notions of Race: A Thing of the Past?

Most of the children in this study discuss racial identity—as well as race and racism—through a historical lens. For many, this corresponds with a tendency to think of race as something of the past, which, in turn, correlates with colorblind ideology. When asked if their parents or primary caregivers talk to them about racial identity or being black, most say their families talk to them about black history. These references include general mention of black history, African history, enslavement and emancipation, segregation and the civil rights movement, and African American inventors or African American firsts. That the children's initial responses hark immediately to the past shows either that parents and other adults focus primarily on history in their racial socialization or that these are the messages that most resonate with the children, or perhaps this is a way for the children to distance themselves from or depersonalize a difficult issue. Either way, when conceptualizing their own racial identity, nearly all of the children appear to think first of a historically based black community.

Thirteen-year-old Tanika cites African roots and pre-enslavement history when answering the question, "Does your mother talk to you at all about being black or being African American?" "Yes," Tanika responds, "She explains to me about the history and about how we came from Africa." In answering a question about a contemporary racial identity ("being black"), Tanika describes a historical identity rooted in Africa. Toussaint (eleven years old) says his parents "always" talk about racial identity, specifying that the most important thing they tell him is, "We weren't born in slavery. We once were a great people." For Toussaint, then, the most important aspect of his racial identity is that it predates enslavement and European oppression. While it is true that both Tanika and Toussaint are answering questions not about their own ideas, but about what their parents tell them, their use of the pronoun "we" indicates some identification with this historical construction of racial identity and with their African ancestors.

For Tanika and Toussaint, conceptualizing blackness means a historical identification with Africa prior to the trans-Atlantic slave trade. Most of the children, however, cite the history of people of African descent in the United States as the core of their concept of racial identity. This includes references to the struggles for emancipation and civil rights and the historical achievements of African Americans. Tyrone (thirteen) responds with a quick "Yup" when asked if his mother and stepfather talk to him about his racial identity. He explains, "They say that most black people invented stuff. And like [pause] that we used to fight in the war and stuff like that. How we got free from slavery, stuff like that." Again, although the references are historical, we see some identification with the past through the use of the pronoun "we." Also significant is Tyrone's use of active verbs, communicating black people's own agency in emancipation. Ruth (fifteen), Travis (thirteen), and Brianna (fifteen) also provide similar responses when asked what their parents tell them about being black:

RUTH: Basically, [my mom and stepdad] talk about the inventors and my grandmother basically talks about the stuff she did in the South and stuff like that.

TRAVIS: [My grandma] told us mostly about most of the black inventors made most of the things that we use today.

BRIANNA: [My mom, grandma, and granddad] talk about different people—like the first black person that did this. They generally like the pictures.

These examples illustrate the trend among the children to describe race and racial identity historically, based in the resilience of black people in the United States and passed down to them from their families.

On the other hand, a smaller group of children say their parents or primary caregivers do not talk about black identity at all. Even these children, though, move straight to African Americans' historical experiences to explain their own racial identities. When asked if her parents talk to her about being black, Terri (thirteen) responds, "You know, not really. You know, being black have its privileges because we learn in school that through slavery, African Americans stuck together, you know. And that, you know, we should stick together, the family. And that we should value our education because back then African Americans weren't allowed to read and write. So they teach us to value our education and to at least try to do our best in all classes." Although her parents do not talk to her about racial identity, Terri's teachers do, and this provides her with a historically derived concept of her racial identity.

Nina (thirteen) shares a very similar experience. Asked if her parents talk to her about what it means to be black or to have a black identity, she answers:

No. I really kind of set my own standards from what I know. . . . But, like at class, we'll talk about it. It's more of a class discussion. Like most of that stuff, we've handled that in class. Like our social studies teacher, he'll talk about it. And he'll ask why is it important . . . that some people are still fighting today or that Martin Luther King fought. And Rosa Parks. And why are we happy that it stopped? Or if it was still continuing now, how would *we* react? And like a lot of us are like, well, [*pause*] we have like, we used to have a racist that went to our school. He was white. And that was kind of hard. He got kicked out because he was so violent, and his mom and daddy, they were pure racist and did not know at first that the school was all black, and so they enrolled him. So then, that whole year was like a tragedy, because we were always afraid of what would happen.

For Nina, thinking about "what it means to be black" means thinking about the ongoing struggle against racism. When their teacher challenges them to think about how they would react to racism and segregation, she and her classmates argue that they already confront both in their daily lives. Nina's configuration of a black identity, then, makes connections between the struggles of the civil rights movement and her own experiences confronting a racist classmate in a school dealing with de facto segregation.

A few of the children not only take a historical approach to defining a black identity, but also explain the connection between their historical concept of blackness and their present-day black identity. When asked if her mother talks to her about racial identity or being black, Mahogany (fifteen) answers, "She say, she tell me black is good. Don't ever think about, like, forgetting who you are, stuff like that. She say like always know where you come from, never forget. She say we went through a lot of stuff back then, but it's all right now, just hope that we never go through it again." Unlike Nina, Mahogany believes African Americans' struggles are largely in the past but is clear that they are nevertheless relevant to her ideas about racial identity.

Trisha (fourteen), too, with the help of her mother, roots her contemporary black identity in the historical struggles of African Americans. Answering the same question as to whether her mother talks to her about racial identity or being black, Trisha responds, "Yeah. She says that—what does she say? She says a lot of things. Like, it's really rare for a black person to be on TV. She says when she was a kid, when there were black commercials, everybody would run to the TV, like, 'Oh my God, it's a black person!' And she'll say, sometimes she'll be talking about people in the neighborhood. She's like, 'Do you know how hard they worked for you to have freedom, and then they're selling drugs and stuff?'" Trisha's comments suggest her mother has taught her to interpret her racial identity with an eye toward history. Her retelling of her mother's story about excitement over the appearance of African Americans on television illustrates both a contrast with the past as well as the continuing importance of represen- tations in relation to group identity. While here Trisha punctuates the change from a time when African Americans were almost entirely omitted from popu- lar media, throughout her interview she is acutely critical of the misrepresenta- tions of African Americans in today's popular media. She says that she "feels bad for" her peers who base their racial identities on what she sees as a narrow range of misogynistic and materialistic images of African Americans on televi- sion and concludes that anyone who does so is "lost." Trisha also brings in social responsibility as a tenet of racial identity, suggesting her neighbors' participa- tion in crime dishonors a black identity rooted in the sacrifices made by those involved in the historical struggle for freedom.

At the end of each interview, the children are asked what they think is the most important thing to remember about being black. Again, a majority of chil- dren cite an aspect of black history, including heritage, pride, equality, and the struggle for freedom. A representative example of these statements comes from Josh (ten), who says the most important thing to remember about being African American is "that we were once slaves and that now we have our freedom and we're truly equal because of great people like Martin Luther King and [pause] Abraham Lincoln. They died just so everybody can have their freedom. So they could be treated equally." Like most of the children, Josh says remembering historical struggles for freedom and equality is most important, cites a famous African American historical figure (although Josh is the only interviewee to also cite a white historical figure), and uses the pronoun "we" to talk about his black ancestors. Josh is also able to identify a bridge between the sacrifices of histori- cal black communities and the lives of contemporary black communities. He moves from the past into the present, saying, "They died just so everybody can have their freedom." However, also like many of the children, he leaves the struggles of African Americans firmly in the past.

For Kenny (thirteen), the connection between history and the present is more difficult to see. Regarding whether his parents talk to him about racial identity or being black, Kenny says, "Yes, they talk to me about it. They say never take freedom for granted," but continues, saying that he does not know what to take away from that message in terms of developing his own identity because, he says, "I think all kids take freedom for granted." Although he is aware his parents want him to make a connection between historical struggles and his own racial identity, he is not certain exactly how to do so. This is true for many of the children, who immediately turn to historical references to explain how they understand blackness but rarely fully explicate their conceptualization of this link between past and present. Their evocation of history in defining race may lead to a tendency to think of it as something that is of the past—no longer relevant. Of course, this thinking pairs neatly with colorblind ideology, which suggests that we are a post-racial society and that the only remaining problems stem from those who continue to notice race at all. Because they find this ideology appealing and convincing but also confront daily realities in which race comes into play, the children's interviews as a whole show ambivalence and confusion when talking about race. This ambivalence comes through in their discussions of racial pride, whether it is ever acceptable to take race into account, and whether or not race has any impact on them as individuals.

Ambivalence, Tension, and Confusion: Does Race Matter or Not?

Social scientists today overwhelmingly argue that race is not real on an essential, biological, or genetic level (Mukhopadhyay et al. 2007; Smedley and Smedley 2005). Most of the children in this study seem to agree, saying that race does not matter to them on a fundamental level. On a social or cultural level, however, about half of the children claim that it does matter, while the others say it does not. When we look beyond the answers this latter group gives to direct questions about race, however, their descriptions of their day-to-day experiences reveal that race appears to have a significant influence on their lives in ways they do not either perceive or acknowledge.

Does Race Influence Me? Tension between Ideas and Experiences

As described in chapter 1, roughly the first third of the children's interviews was spent on questions about themselves and their daily lives, while the second third of each interview asked about their favorite things. It was not until the final third of the interview that the children were asked directly about racial identity and racism. While the children's answers to direct questions about the importance of race vary a great deal, their answers in the first and second sections of the interview, especially their discussions of their "favorite things," suggest racialization plays a prominent, albeit perhaps unconscious, role in their everyday lives, even for those children who insist it does not. For example, Ruth (fifteen) clearly states that race is not an important part of her own identity:

ERIN: I'm just curious if you feel like [being African American is] part of your identity? Just in the same way being Christian is, or being a woman is, or any of those things—being from Detroit? Do you feel like it's something that makes up who you are? Or not really?

RUTH: It really, it really doesn't.

ERIN: No? OK. You're saying it's not part of your identity. Do you feel like other people impose it on you? Do you have people tell you, "This is what it means to be black"?

RUTH: No.

At the same time, every single one of Ruth's "favorite things" is African American–themed or "culturally specific" (Bishop 1992). Rudine Sims Bishop (1992) introduces the term *culturally specific literature* to distinguish children's literature that includes people of color as main characters as well as significant cultural details from literature that includes only "token" representations of people of color. Applied to media more broadly here, all of Ruth's favorite media are culturally specific, including the television show *One on One*, the musical group B2K (one of whose members was her choice for "most attractive"), the magazine *Word Up!*, and the book *Their Eyes Were Watching God*. It appears, then, that Ruth's stated belief that race is unimportant in her own identity and life is somewhat belied by her choices. It is possible that Ruth's answers about race were shaped by what she believed I wanted to hear but that she was less inhibited in her responses about her favorite things. It is equally possible, however, that Ruth does not see race as a critical or salient part of her identity. Psychologists argue that "the parts of our identity that . . . capture our attention are those that other people notice, and reflect back to us" (Tatum 2003, 21). If this is true, it is possible race may become a less salient aspect of identity for black children growing up in Detroit and functioning within predominantly black realms of daily interaction. However, Detroit is still "of the United States" and, as we will see throughout this book, children there cannot escape the broader racialization present within US society (J. Brown 2005, 8). Although we cannot be sure here, it is possible Ruth truly does not see race as an important aspect of her identity. In this case, I argue, her answers about her favorite things do not reveal dishonesty, but rather that she simply sees her preferences as natural and not part of a racialized process.

In relationship to music, in fact, studies have shown that among elementary, middle school, and college students, black students show more same-race preferences in musical performers than white students, although the authors speculate this may simply be due to the overwhelming popularity of hip-hop and R&B music in US popular culture overall (McCrary 1993; O'Connor et al. 2000). Only two children in this study say they do not have a favorite musical artist, and the remaining twenty-five children cite hip-hop and R&B artists, with twenty-three of them citing African American artists (see table 2.1). Moreover, all of the children who named a favorite music video cited videos by African American artists. The two children who do not cite African American artists as their favorites instead cite Eminem, who is a white rapper who grew up in and around Detroit. Eminem is also associated with African American rap artists, including Dr. Dre and 50 Cent. Thus, while Eminem is white, he was one of the few famous contemporary artists out of Detroit at the time of this study, and his art form—rap music—is certainly an African American art form. In other words, the children who cited a white artist as their favorite were not choosing an artist associated with a style of music that is considered "white" (O'Connor et al.

		TABLE 2.1	

Children's favorite musical artists—first choice

Artist	Genre	Number and gender of children
B2K	R&B	5 females
50 Cent	Rap/hip-hop	3 females, 1 male
Alicia Keys	R&B	2 females, 1 male
Aaliyah	R&B	2 females, 1 male
Eminem	Rap/hip-hop	2 males
Nelly	Rap/hip-hop	1 female, 1 male
Beyonce	R&B	1 female, 1 male
Ashanti	R&B	1 female
Bow Wow	Rap/hip-hop	1 female
Jay Z	Rap/hip-hop	1 male
Notorious BIG	Rap/hip-hop	1 male
No favorite		2 females
Data not available		1 female

2000) but an artist who uses a medium that is recognized as African American in origin. It is possible, however, that the choice of Eminem could be read as a "colorblind" statement, although of the two boys who named him, only Carlos (ten) displays colorblind ideas throughout his interview, while Kenny (thirteen) is more race-conscious.

In contrast to the ubiquitous popularity of black musical artists in the United States, the number of television shows with predominantly black casts was on a steady decline at the time of these interviews (Freeman 2002), a trend that has continued such that, in 2010, "the number of scripted, live-action shows on broadcast television with all-black (or predominantly minority, for that matter) casts is exactly zero" (Consoli 2010). Even so, a full half of the children in this study cite culturally specific television shows with predominantly black casts as their favorites (see table 2.2). Of those fourteen children who did *not* choose African American television shows, one said he only watched his favorite television show (*WWF Wrestling*) because of the biracial (black and Samoan) personality (Dwayne "The Rock" Johnson) on the show, and nine picked cartoons, including a majority of the ten- and eleven-year-olds who

TABLE 2.2

Children's favorite television shows

Television show	African American themed?	First run or syndicated	Cartoon or live action	Number and gender of children
One on One	Yes	First run	Live action	5 females, 1 male
106 & Park	Yes	First run	Live action	1 female, 2 males
The Simpsons	No	First run	Cartoon	2 females, 1 male
Sponge Bob	No	First run	Cartoon	1 female, 1 male
Rugrats	No	First run	Cartoon	1 female, 1 male
Romeo!	Yes	First run	Live action	1 male
Like Family	Yes	First run	Live action	1 female
Cosby Show	Yes	Syndicated	Live action	1 female
Steve Harvey Show	Yes	Syndicated	Live action	1 female
Anything on BET	Yes	Both	Live action	1 female
WWF Wrestling	No	First run	Live action	1 male
Inuyasha	No	First run	Cartoon	1 male
Yu-Gi-Oh	No	Syndicated	Cartoon	1 male
Charmed	No	First run	Live action	1 female
Dharma & Greg	No	Syndicated	Live action	1 female
Fear Factor	No	First run	Live action/ reality	1 male
Degrassi	No	First run	Live action	1 female

participated in this study. Thus, fourteen of the nineteen children who chose non-animated favorite television shows named shows with predominantly black casts. Similarly, half of the children who named a favorite magazine chose African American magazines. In the case of television and magazines, unlike in that of music and music videos, explaining these preferences via the overall popularity or ubiquity of African American–themed media in US popular culture would not apply. Indeed, the children's choices are especially noteworthy in light of the dearth of African American television shows and magazines in the market overall. Of course, the local media market must also be taken into account. It is likely that local newsstands and corner stores carry a higher proportion of black periodicals and that local Detroit television stations pick up black television shows in syndication. However, of the fourteen children who chose an African American television show, twelve chose a show that was a first-run, prime-time television show, either on network television (ABC, UPN, WB) or cable (BET, Nickelodeon), and only two chose shows in syndication. It appears, then, that the children really were seeking out the few prime-time shows featuring predominantly African American casts.

Finally, although only one quarter of the children cited African American–themed books as their favorites, this included children who said that blackness was not at all important to them. Of course, there are many possible explanations for this, including availability of culturally specific literature, visibility of characters therein, and children's exposure to such literature (E. Gray 2009). Interestingly, the only three adult reading-level books cited were African American–themed. This may indicate that books discussing issues of race and racism are sometimes aimed toward more mature readers or that advanced readers are more likely to seek out books that deal with challenging topics such as struggles with racial identity and racism. Some children explicitly say the reason they like a book is because they can relate to characters or situations therein. Sometimes this is an African American–themed text, as when Trisha (fourteen) explains her favorite book is the novel *B-More Careful*, described on its book jacket as being about "growing up on the cold, mean, inner-city streets of Baltimore . . . with no father and a dope fiend for a mother . . . chasing the almighty dollar" (S. Holmes 2001). Trisha says it is her favorite "because [she] can relate to what the narrator's talking about, like how people talk about people, and her neighborhood." Although this could be read as Trisha relating to the text based on socioeconomic status or circumstance, Trisha's family is among the higher-income families in this study, solidly middle class in the $45,000–$55,000 annual income range, well above the median for Detroit. Her mother is employed as an executive director, and while Trisha does not live with her father, she does see him. However, both Trisha and her mother do describe the neighborhood in which they live as "ghetto . . . [but] not *that* bad" and "the hood," respectively, which may be part of the reason Trish says she can relate to "the narrator's . . . neighborhood." Sometimes, however, the characters the children say they can relate to are white. For example, Travis (thirteen) says *Harry Potter* is his favorite book: "because I can really relate to Harry, how he was, like, a typical eleven- or twelve-year-old, just sent away because his parents was killed, and he's stuck with his aunt and uncle that don't like him, and he's got an annoying cousin. And my life is kind of like that, except my mom and my dad and my brother are annoying!" And Terri (thirteen) identifies *Little Women* as her favorite book because she can relate to "the way even though they're poor, they stick together as a family, and . . . one of their daughters cut off her hair just so they could have a Christmas. That's like, that is like the most beautiful book I have ever read."

Interestingly, this did not happen in relation to television shows—none of the children said they chose their favorite television show based on relating to a white character, even though a few picked television shows with predominantly white casts. Since connecting to characters is the primary criterion for children in selecting books (E. Gray 2009), this may mean that the children are better able to relate to non-black characters when relying on written descriptions as opposed to visual and aural representations. Again, these choices are noteworthy in light of the relatively low availability of culturally relevant literature for black children. As Erika Gray points out, despite gains in this area, only about 3 percent of new children's books published in 2006 "included significant African American content or characters" (2009, 472). In this context, the fact that 25 percent of the children in this study cite an African American–themed book as their favorite indicates that cultural relevancy may be playing a role in their choices.

The topic of attractiveness was also broached with children, who were asked for the best-looking person they could name. Only two children declined to name anyone at all (one said she could not think of anyone, and the other said that she preferred not to answer). All of the remaining twenty-six children named an African American person, except Corey (thirteen), who chose Puerto Rican–American singer and actress Jennifer Lopez. But do these choices have anything to do with race? Some studies have shown same-race preferences in attractiveness (Allen 1976), but evidence is mixed, with some studies showing preferences varying by gender (M. Lewis 2010) or preferences for mixed-race faces (Rhodes et al. 2005). For the eleven children who named someone they actually know personally—a family member or someone at school—this may simply be shaped by their daily realms of interaction and who they encounter, know, and love. For the seventeen children who mentioned celebrities, most were musical artists, although actors like Morris Chestnut and Will Smith (who is also a rapper, but has not been as well known for that in these children's lifetimes) were also mentioned. In these celebrity cases, it could again be the popularity of hip-hop and R&B music coming into play in their choices as opposed to race. Interestingly, for the two girls who also each name a white male musical celebrity (Justin Timberlake and Eminem), they do so only after first citing a black male musical celebrity (Omarion and 50 Cent). In each case, in addition to mentioning the African American men first, the girls both list *physical* traits for why the black men are attractive, but *personality* or *skill* for why the white men are attractive. Regarding Omarion, who is African American, Mahogany (fifteen) says, "He got a big smile, he handsome, and he got long hair." Regarding Justin Timberlake, Mahogany explains, "I love his moves and the way he sound." Similarly, Cara (thirteen) cites 50 Cent's physique ("His chest. Oh my God! When he take off his shirt!") but cannot think of anything specific about Eminem.

Experiences with friendships reveal another kind of disconnect between ideologies and real-world experiences. Although they were not asked, several children volunteered that race was not a factor in choosing their friends. However, because of structural racism and the racialization of space, many of the children do not have the chance to put their values about racially diverse friendships into practice. For example, Nina (thirteen) compares her group of friends in Detroit with the groups of friends she has when she visits family in Atlanta and California. "I have many friends," she declares, "and here [in Detroit], I have mostly African American friends. But in Atlanta, they're Asian, some Caucasian, and then two black, maybe. . . . My old grandma lives there, and I go down there every summer and during winter and Christmas. So it's like I live there. But in California there's a lot of Mexican friends I have. Lots of Mexicans. And I like variety. I just can't stick—because it's like, everybody, everybody's different. I like different environments and different cultures and ethnicities." Nina is clearly fond of her "mostly African American" Detroit friends but seems frustrated she is not able to maintain her ideal group of friends from "different cultures and ethnicities." It is not clear exactly why Nina sees a multiracial group of friends as ideal—the idea could come from media or from a colorblind ideology. However, as we will see in chapter 4, it is clear that her mother, Sharon, sees living in a predominantly black city as negative and shares this idea frequently with her children, telling them it is "not normal" and even "crippling" for them. In this case, then, Nina's ideology may in some ways reflect her mother's.

Rebecca (eleven) also expresses the idea that a racially mixed group of peers is ideal because she "like[s] both" black and white people.

ERIN: Which class [in school] do you like the best?

REBECCA: Art, until my teacher moved. I had a black teacher. Her name was Miss Morehouse. Now I have a white teacher named Miss Namouth.

ERIN: OK.

REBECCA: My favorite class is art.

ERIN: Are most of the teachers at the school black or white? Or is it mixed?

REBECCA: Mixed.

ERIN: It's mixed? What about the other students?

REBECCA: Mixed.

ERIN: It's mixed? Is that good or bad? Or it doesn't really matter?

REBECCA: It's good.

ERIN: It's good? Why is it good?

REBECCA: Because it's not like all black people. I like white people too because our mother didn't teach me to be prejudiced. So it's, it really don't matter. I like both.

It is conceivable here that Rebecca is simply trying to placate me, especially because her teacher is also a white woman, and she may want to give the "right answer" (Eder and Fingerson 2001, 184). Even if we question her statement idealizing racially mixed environments, though, her reality is nevertheless such that she does not have many opportunities to be a part of such environments. While declaring that the student body of her school is racially "mixed," Rebecca goes on to share: "I don't have no white students in my classroom. I have all black students." Indeed, a check of the statistics on race for Rebecca's school reveals that, out of 853 total students enrolled, 851 were African American and 2 were white.[1] Moreover, although Rebecca also indicates it is positive to have a mixed group of teachers, she answers the question about her favorite class by stating that art class used to be her favorite when she had a black teacher. Rebecca suggests that, while a mixed group of teachers may be theoretically ideal, in practice race may have an impact on her experiences with her teachers (Ladson-Billings 1995; Valenzuela 1999).

In the few interviews in which children report having white friends in Detroit, it is always revealed that they are actually talking about biracial friends or, sometimes, light-skinned black friends. One example comes from Elina (thirteen), who talks about her white friend Janelle, before revealing that Janelle has one white parent and one black parent. "I'm learning about [racism]. And people would start making fun of other people, like my friend, she was white—Janelle. . . . So she was white, and everybody would make fun of her. And they used to think I was white because when I was little I used to be really light. So I would hang around Janelle, and they would be like, 'Oh, look at the two white couples.' I would be like, 'First of all, I'm not white. I'm black and Puerto Rican. First of all, she's not all white; she's black *and* white.'" The first two times Elina refers to Janelle, she calls her white. It is not until Elina is defending herself and Janelle against taunts from other children that she reveals that Janelle is "not all white; she's black *and* white." Ironically, although Elina resents having been called white when she was younger and sees this as an example of racism, she nevertheless slips into the same practice she is criticizing, referring to Janelle repeatedly as white (although Janelle does have one white parent). I argue that here (and with other similar examples) we see at work the combination of both acute hyper-segregation and the notion, deeply embedded in US society, of race as a black/white dichotomy (Celious and Oyserman 2001; Charles 2003; Denton and Massey 1989; Spickard and Daniel 2004). If children are functioning primarily in spaces in which they encounter very few non-black children or people, their notions of race are likely shaped by that. This, combined with the historical construction of race as a black/white dichotomy, may lead some children in this study to think of whiteness as including the lightest-skinned people they know, even if those people are known to have one or two black parents.

None of the children expresses the idea that race should impact their friendships, and several children make the explicit argument that it should not. However, it is clear that in their lived experiences they are mostly only able to have racially mixed groups of friends when they travel or otherwise move outside of their daily realms of interaction. This may be less true for those who attend more diverse schools, but only four children in this study attend schools that have African American enrollments under 95 percent.[2]

My intent in this section has been to show that, although many of the children express the idea that race does not hold influence over their interpersonal lives, ultimately, racialized identities, structures, and spaces do so in many ways, albeit perhaps in ways that are not obvious to the children. In the case of friendships, racialization of space and structures of segregation thwart the children's ability to implement their value systems about racially diverse groups of friends (Lipsitz 2011). In the case of favorite things and ideas about attractiveness, racialized patterns emerge despite the structural constraints of underrepresentation and misrepresentation of black people in media and popular culture.

"That Don't Sound Right": Ambivalence about Racial Pride

As we moved into the third and final section of the interview, I began asking each child directly about his or her ideas about and experiences with racial identity and racism. In their responses to these questions, the children's collective voices exhibit a tension between embracing racial identity and denying its importance. Some children affirm a strong, positive, black racial identity. For example, Matthew (thirteen) conceives of racial identity as a gift from God. "It's important to know that you're black," he says. "God made us that way. We gotta thank him for that." Moreover, he adds that dissociating oneself from blackness—as he jokingly says Michael Jackson had done—would be "a sin, for not wanting to be who you are." Toussaint (eleven) echoes this sentiment, stating that "being black is not a curse. It's a blessing." Similarly, Travis (thirteen) asserts that the most important thing about being African American is "having our pride." Other children, however, are not as comfortable embracing racial pride. They worry aloud that acknowledging race at all is problematic and possibly indicative of racism and hypocrisy. While some might argue these children are saying this for my benefit, black researchers conducting interviews with black children have also found a reliance on the colorblind script (R. Lewis 2010). Furthermore, the fact that many children give colorblind responses, regardless of their motivations for doing so, indicates the extent to which that ideology permeates even black-dominated cultural and social spaces such as Detroit. This shows, I argue, that for all its uniqueness, Detroit is still very much a "production of the United States" (J. Brown 2005, 8), subject to the permeating power of white privilege, which reaches children via mainstream media, state-mandated curricula and course materials, and various political and economic policies. If those children invoking the colorblind script do so for my benefit, this illustrates what psychologists call "outcome dependency," or the idea that "people pay extra attention to those who control their outcomes" and "adjust their behavior to comply with top-down standards or norms" (Operario and Fiske 1998, 50–51). In other words, taking on a colorblind ideology may be a coping strategy adopted well beyond the confines of these interviews.

Let me not overstate, though, the extent to which the children in this study embrace a colorblind ideology: only about half of the children adamantly do, while others are openly race-conscious and still others go back and forth. All of the children are still in the process of comprehensive racial learning, as yet developing their ideas. Yet their responses at this moment in their development do show the tension and ambivalence that arose on this count in the children's interviews as a whole. To illustrate this, I turn here to two examples: thirteen-year-old twins, brother and sister Corey and Cara (who, surprisingly, were not the only set of thirteen-year-old fraternal twins in this study). Cara and Corey live in a zip code with a higher-than-average median income for the city of Detroit, although their household income falls right around the median income for the city. They attend different middle schools—she attends a school of choice (a public school which requires an application and entrance exam), while he attends a neighborhood school (a regular public school).

Corey is an engaging, soft-spoken eighth grader with a big, endearing smile. His friends and teachers, he says, would describe him as "a nice person . . . the type of person that respect people," but his family would be more likely to focus on his silly side because, he says, "I'm different at home—just playful." Corey describes a daily life busy with school, homework, chores, helping care for his younger siblings, and participating in after-school activities. He complains that his middle school does not challenge him enough and worries that this will prevent him from getting into one of Detroit's "Gifted and Talented" high schools, which require an examination for admittance. He also displays a healthy dose of sibling rivalry, claiming that, although Cara attends a more highly ranked school than he does, he is actually "past her level" because he has "been taught so much from [his] life."

Corey conceives of race as unimportant, asserting that even discussing or acknowledging race is problematic. Having black pride, he therefore posits, would be racist. When asked if his mother ever talks to him about "anything special or good about being black," Corey replies, "I mean, no, because we not racist. So, to me, that would be like racism, because it seem like it's talking about different races differently. . . . I mean, that's like saying, 'I'm just happy I'm black.' That don't sound right." Too much acknowledgment of racial difference, then, is what Corey sees as the problem. His discomfort with the idea of black pride stems from his belief that it condones a racialized hierarchy, equating black pride with white supremacy. Psychologists, however, argue that racial pride amongst racially subordinated groups arose as a form of resistance to racialized oppression and is a healthy part of identity (Cross 1971, 1991; Hughes et al. 2006).

Corey's twin sister, Cara, is a bubbly, extroverted eighth grader. She describes a very full life of extracurricular activities, including cheerleading, a number of social, academic, and service clubs, and a preparatory course for her upcoming high school entrance exam, which determines whether or not a student is eligible to attend one of Detroit's "Gifted and Talented" high schools. Cara also has cheerleading on the weekends, but she says she does not mind the time commitment, adding, "I just can't explain it to you how much I love to cheer." After her busy day, she usually arrives home around six o'clock and does not have time to talk on the phone or watch television. Like Corey, Cara indicates that she is often responsible for caring for her younger siblings but would often rather have the freedom to go out with her friends. Cara says her friends would describe her as "silly and jolly and always happy," while her teachers and family would describe her as nice, smart, and someone who "stays on task."

Cara, too, is confused about whether or not she should take pride in her racial identity. On the one hand, Cara has overheard her grandmother telling some light-skinned children in the family that they should attempt to pass as white if they are able. On the other hand, Cara says that her grandmother tells her she "should be proud to be black." When asked whether or not anyone in her household talks to her about racial identity, Cara says:

> In a way, they do. Because my grandma had adopted some foster kids, and they was white, but they wanted to be black, and my grandma was telling them how if you want to be a black man then some black mens don't get everything that a white man gets. I mean, they actually looked like they was white, but I think they was mixed. But my grandma said if you have a chance to pick if you was white or black, to go white because white people have special, just . . . [*pause*] access to stuff. But I really didn't understand what she was saying. But I do. I do, but I don't. [Because to me] she will say stuff like . . ."You should be proud to be black." . . . So I'm like [*sounding uncertain*], "Okaaaaaay."

Receiving what she sees as conflicting messages from her maternal grandmother, who lives in the home with her, has Cara confused. Should she be proud to be black or not? Is blackness something to be embraced or rejected? The mixed signals Cara receives from her grandmother mirror those received by the children in this study from a wide range of sources, both familial and societal. Her confusion exemplifies the tension and uncertainty the children in this study express about this issue. Their ambivalence about the morality of racial pride reveals the children's collective struggle to reconcile the very real ways in which racialization impacts their daily lives with the alluring rhetoric of colorblindness.

Colorblind versus Race-Conscious Ideas:
Is It Ever OK to Take Race into Account?

At the opening of this chapter, we heard from Mahogany, whose story revealed her ambivalence about colorblind versus race-conscious ideas and practices. Mahogany is not alone in this; many of the children express some uncertainty about whether or not race should be "noticed," not just in relationship to their own identities, but in society in general. As we have read, Corey is clear that race should not be invoked at home, and he believes this is just as true at school. When asked if his teachers talk about race or racism at all at school, Corey replies, "Nope. Unless somebody mention it. But nobody mention it because it really don't matter. I mean, I don't know why slavery was started in the first place." Here, the school's omission of any discussion of race or racism as part of the curriculum serves to confirm Corey's notion that race should not be noticed. Interestingly, up to this point in the interview, there had only been discussion of *contemporary* Detroit and Corey's ideas about race and racism in that context. That Corey evokes the *historical* legacy of racism when he denies the need for any consideration of race or racism in the academic curriculum serves to posit race and racism as things of the past (Urrieta 2006). Ironically, in the same moment in which Corey says that the study of race and racism is not necessary, he admits that he has no idea why racial slavery, which scholars point to as the genesis of contemporary ideologies of racism (Fredrickson 2002), even began. Thus, Corey's lack of understanding of the historical invention of the social category of race and how and why the ultimate expression of racism—racialized slavery—began would seem to disprove his point that this is not a topic worthy of academic attention. Where they exist, however, multicultural curricula tend to focus only on the celebration of culture and individual heroes, while leaving out any dis-cussion of continuing structural inequalities (Hirschfield 2008; A. Lewis 2003; Van Ausdale and Feagin 2001). Educational resources of this kind often present the issue of racial discrimination as something that happened in the past, has been entirely overcome, and is today only perpetrated by a few bad individuals. This can actually reinforce racial prejudice in children (Hirschfield 2008) because the take-away message is that any remaining inequities are either natu-ral or the fault of people who suffer from them. Understandably, this is confusing for many of the children in this study, who see racial inequity impacting them and the people around them every day. Corey's response speaks to the greater tension within many of the children's conceptualizations of race as irrelevant and therefore something that should be ignored: when race and racism can only be acknowledged as something relegated to the past, then the children's lived experiences of race and racism today cannot be validated or explored.

Corey's belief that race should not be acknowledged extends beyond school walls. In fact, he argues that anyone who dwells on race is unenlightened or racist. He even applies this criticism to his twin sister, who he thinks makes too much of a fuss about race in the entertainment industry.

COREY: When movies come on, she's like, "Aw, that's produced by a white person" or "Why's there too many—there's too many white people seeing this movie" or something. Stuff like that.

ERIN: OK. Do you think it's important for there to be movies produced by black people too?

COREY: It really don't matter to me. I really don't care. I'm not making a movie.

ERIN: OK. So do you think it's important for there to be like, equal representation in different—

COREY: I mean, I think *that's* important.

Corey begins by asserting a colorblind ideology, saying that race is completely irrelevant in relationship to Hollywood. The race of people involved in producing movies is unimportant, he says. However, when the same question is phrased differently—as an issue of "equality," which fits more closely with the colorblind rhetoric of race-neutral meritocracy—Corey says that is indeed important. Cara, however, is clearly comfortable expressing a race-conscious point of view in our interview. A clue as to the reason behind the difference in their approaches can be found in their mother's interview. Their mother, Desarae, points out that Corey finds himself "in more white settings" more frequently than his sister because of his job as "a caddy at a white golf course." There, according to Desarae, he comes into contact with whites who tell him he is "not like the rest of them [black people]." Dealing with this kind of racism— in which whites maintain racist notions about black people in general but posit those who disrupt these ideas as "exceptions and not necessarily typical of their group as a whole" (Gaertner and Dovidio 2005, 79)—may have primed Corey to either internalize these ideas in a way his sister has not, or finesse his interactions with whites in particular ways (Operario and Fiske 1998). It is impossible here to determine whether Corey would give entirely different answers to an African American interviewer; but, again, other researchers have found the colorblind script to be prevalent among black children even in same-race interview dyads (R. Lewis 2010).

Despite her greater willingness to engage in race-conscious thinking, Cara, too, shows some ambivalence about whether it is morally acceptable to do so. She shares a story in which she began firmly in the camp of race-conscious thinking and then wavered a bit after her teacher challenged her thinking:

I remember my teacher was talking about that one day. . . . She was like, "If it was someone about to employ someone, and there was a white person and a black person there, and it was a black person about to employ the people, would you rather for that black person to pick the black person instead of the white person?" We was like, "The black person!" But then she was like, "Well, that wouldn't be fair for the white person. If it was a white person employee, it wouldn't be fair for the white person to pick the white person." So she was like, "So why should you all think that?" So she was saying if you, like, think about it, if we do it, then of course they're going to do it. If they do it, then we going to do it. So why encourage what they do? So that's what she was saying.

While many of the children in this study argue that the individual and not his or her race is primary, in practice, the group experience often emerges as primary. This is displayed in Cara's testimony that she and her classmates initially responded unequivocally that black employers should hire black candidates if given a chance.[3] Perhaps Cara and her classmates saw either affirmative action or racial solidarity as strategies to redress racial inequities in contemporary society. After prompting by her teacher, however, Cara is bothered that this might exacerbate the problem of racism or "encourage what they [white people] do." Here we see her shift from race-conscious to colorblind thinking, worrying that taking race into account at all is equivalent to racism. Social scientists generally argue that racism is structural and involves group social power (Omi and Winant 1994; Operario and Fiske 1998; Small 2002). Therefore, according to the scholarly definition of racism as a practice that "*creates or reproduces structures of domination based on essentialist categories of race*" (Omi and Winant 1994, 71, emphasis in original), affirmative action in hiring would not constitute racism but rather a partial attempt to redress racism in employment (Tatum 2003).

Still, to some of the children in this study, it is racist to even respond to or deal with racism because it is impossible to do so in a colorblind way. Corey illustrates this idea, explaining an event that took place at his former school. "One day I was in school," he says, "and it was . . . a lot of racists in that school. It was like a mixed school. And so then, it was a white person who walked up to me, and he was like 'Move over, you black person!' or something like that. He said something. And I didn't really say nothing to him because I didn't want to— I wasn't racist!" How can racism be addressed if one is not allowed to notice or acknowledge race? As Supreme Court justice Harry Blackmun wrote in his separate, dissenting opinion to the 1978 *Regents of the University of California v. Bakke* decision, "In order to get beyond racism we must first take account of race. There is no other way" (Blackmun 1978). Nevertheless, while the children in this study are absolutely clear that racism is wrong, they are ambivalent, as a group, about whether or not the road to addressing it can or should involve any consideration of race at all.

Bridging the Tension: Race Matters and It Does Not

While the tension regarding whether or not race matters can be found across the children's narratives, some children are closer to finding balance in this struggle. These children recognize their racial identity and the significance of race on a more systemic level but argue that race does not matter in their interpersonal relationships and abilities. Elijah (twelve), whose family encourages a strong black identity, says that race used to matter to him in forming his relationships but that he no longer feels that way. "Back when I was little," he explains, "I used to always have a little grudge against, uh, Caucasians, white people. . . . And then [my grandmother] had taught me; she had said, 'As long as they don't do anything to me, I don't have a problem with them. They're just like us; they're just light-skinned.' And then from there on out, when I grew up, I really realized that my sister was light-skinned. I was like, 'You're white, too!' And so, ever since, like I've been hanging around more and more white people since I went to Las Vegas." Elijah's quotation is interesting on multiple levels, including his definition of race as based on skin tone, which will be discussed in detail in chapter 6 (Elijah's sister, Trisha, has two black parents and describes her skin color as "caramel"). For our purposes here, however, it is important to look at Elijah's changing perception of race and interpersonal relationships over time. At first, he says, his experiences and racial identity caused him to "have a little grudge" that made him wary of white people. Over time, and with racial socialization from his grandmother, Elijah decided that it would be acceptable for him to engage in some cross-racial friendships with white people as long as they were respectful and did not do anything negative to him. This kind of thinking is associated with one of the more advanced stages of William E. Cross's (1991) racial identity development model for African Americans. In terms of putting this attitude into practice, however, segregation appears to create obstacles to interracial friendships. Perhaps because he lives in a zip code that is 96.0 percent African American and attends a school that is 99.5 percent African American, Elijah specifies he was able to make white friends when he went on a trip to Las Vegas the previous summer. In other words, leaving Detroit seemed to facilitate his making cross-racial friendships. As chapter 3 will explore in more detail, however, Elijah also experienced some blatant racism on this same trip to Las Vegas when a shop clerk presumed he did not have enough money to purchase souvenirs. Thus, he demonstrates the mature ability to recognize and reconcile the ways in which race matters (structurally and in relationship to systems of power) and does not (in an inherent or essential way).

Conclusion

For evidence of the power of the colorblind ideology in the United States, one need look no further than Detroit. As mentioned, Detroit has the highest percentage African American population of any large city (over 105,000) in the United States, with a population of just under a million and around 83 percent African American (US Census Bureau 2001). As we will hear in chapter 4, many of the mothers cite Detroit's unique demographics and the civic, cultural, and social empowerment of black people in Detroit as reasons to raise their children here. The young people in this study have grown up in predominantly black neighborhoods and schools and with black mayors, police chiefs, school board presidents, school superintendents, and city council presidents, and many black teachers and doctors. Yet even here, the dominant narrative of colorblindness creeps into the children's consciousness due to its sheer ubiquity in US society. By subtly normalizing and privileging whiteness, this ideology reinforces existing systems of power. It is therefore reproduced in arenas controlled by those who stand to benefit from it, including arenas that reach the children in this study, such as textbooks, curricula, mainstream media, and public policy. As a result, while these children's individual understandings of race vary, overall they reflect some ambivalence about whether or not race matters. I suggest this ambivalence reflects a tension that emerges from the contrast between the social script of colorblindness and the myriad ways in which race impacts their daily lives. It also reflects their ongoing struggles within their own comprehensive racial learning to balance the conflicting messages they receive about race. Societal sources, such as mainstream curriculum and media, are steeped in the rhetoric of the United States as a colorblind meritocracy in which everyone has an equal chance of success or failure. Research shows parents sometimes also send "egalitarian" (Hughes and Chen 1999) or "individualistic" (Demo and Hughes 1990) messages as part of racial socialization (Hughes et al. 2006; Winkler 2008). On the other hand, the children discuss experiences with peers, teachers, family members, media, store clerks, material surroundings, and travel, which communicate to them that race has a strong influence on daily experiences and life outcomes.

Despite their real-life experiences, the strength of the colorblind social script is evidenced in the children's ambivalence about whether or not race matters and whether it is racist to take race into account, have racial pride, or even notice race. R. L'Heureux Lewis finds a similar pattern in his study of black and white fourth graders, who, when asked directly about race, begin with reliance on "public scripts" of colorblindness but later often state that race does matter, at least to *other* people (2010, 401). Lewis's findings, like those discussed in this chapter, illustrate the power of the colorblind social script, even for children. Lewis concludes that children's "employment of colorblind narratives suggests that children are not only products of the Civil Rights era but also producers of racial discourse" (416). While parents and other adults do socialize children about race, "children are not merely passive receptors of information but are themselves active in the interpretation and construction of their own understanding of matters of race" (Thornton et al. 1990, 408). Indeed, the ambivalence expressed by the children in this chapter reflects their endeavors to sort through, interpret, resolve, and make meaning out of the various and conflicting messages they receive about race.

3

Racialized Place

Comprehensive Racial Learning through Travel

This chapter begins to reveal the ways place emerges as influential in children's comprehensive racial learning. Remember that by place, I mean not only the location and geography, but the material environment (buildings, vacant spaces, public spaces, and so on), the social character and cultural milieu, the history, the racial demographics, the economic identity, and the civic leadership, character, and control (Gieryn, 2000; Paulsen 2004). People, then, are both creators and products of place (Wilkins 2007, 106); they "are both shaped by [it], and challenge [it]" (McKittrick 2006, xvi). Here I am considering place, as Thomas Gieryn suggests, as "not merely a setting or backdrop, but an agentic player in the game—a force with detectable and independent effects on social life" (2000, 466). In this chapter, place's active role is made plain through the interviewee's use of travel as a point of reference in explaining children's understandings of race and racism. Some told stories about travel to places as far away as Florida and California, while others referenced experiences in cities just outside of Detroit. They talked about traveling to visit family, to participate in scouting activities, to compete in state-wide sports or band competitions, or simply to run errands or go bowling, swimming, or roller skating. The travel did not need to be extravagant—the keys were simply seeing the contrast between places and being forced to negotiate the color line.

Through their discussion of travel, the interviewees reveal that place impacts the children's developing understandings of race in four ways. First, children and their mothers raise place, especially as experienced through travel outside of Detroit, to explain children's understandings of racism, particularly racialized hostility, exclusion, and expectations. Travel influences their developing understandings of place as raced and race as placed, especially in relationship to who belongs in which kinds of spaces. Second, some of the children use place, as understood through travel, to articulate an understanding of the structural racism impacting Detroit. Third, narratives of travel bring to light some children's ideas about race as prescriptive of behavior. In these cases, the children use travel stories to illustrate these understandings, tying the behaviors they have seen in various locations explicitly to race. Finally, mothers especially see place as restrictive of children's ideas about race, and both they and their children speak of travel as pivotal in expanding those ideas.

Delving into how children sift through and navigate the various and often conflicting messages they receive on a daily basis, I wondered how, if at all, their processes were influenced by demographic factors like socioeconomic status, household structure, gender, and skin tone. I was not initially considering how place might come into play. Nevertheless, place emerged so frequently in the interviews that it could not be ignored. In fact, although none of the interviewees were asked about the role of place, a pattern emerged whereby approximately one-third of the children and two-thirds of the mothers raised place, unsolicited, as a point of reference to explain the children's understandings of race and racism. Because the interviewees were not asked directly about the role of place or travel in comprehensive racial learning, the stories in this chapter come only from those who raised it. It's important to note that the voices absent from this chapter do not contradict the analysis presented here; they are only left out because they do not speak directly to this issue.

Understanding Racism through Travel and Place: "Why Can't We Do What They Do?"

While twenty-two of the twenty-eight children interviewed report already having experienced racism, almost all say these experiences took place beyond Detroit's city limits. This is not surprising in light of the finding, presented in chapter 4, that virtually all the mothers believe Detroit provides a "racial safe space" of sorts, largely shielding their children from daily, direct encounters with blatant racism. Although not of one mind as to whether this has a beneficial or detrimental effect on their children in the long run (again, see chapter 4), they acknowledge that their children, like themselves, are much more likely to encounter racism outside of Detroit. "I left [Detroit] for about a year and a half," a mother named Desarae says when recalling her own first experiences with racism as a teenager. "That's when I realized what racism was. . . . Because living here in Detroit, I didn't know what it was." Her experience is echoed in the memories of the other mothers who grew up in Detroit, as well as by the children in this study, who report encountering racism throughout their travels, at retail stores, restaurants, hotels, airports, amusement parks, and other attractions. Several children also relate experiences with racism in their travels closer to home, throughout Michigan and in the Detroit suburbs.

Terri (thirteen) is an eighth grader with a sharp wit. She says that she is "a nice person, cool to hang out with, a good listener" but that her brothers can bring out her "mean side." "I'm the only girl," she says, "and they just always aggravate me!" Terri is an excellent student and talks about applying to local and out-of-state prep schools for high school. She says she does not waste a lot of time watching television because it perpetuates racist stereotypes. "They make like black people always like they the crackheads, or they're the drug dealers, or they always doing the bad stuff," she says, "and the white person's just like the rich, laid-back guy who doesn't have anything wrong." Instead of wasting her time watching such images, Terri says, she prefers to spend her time doing homework ("I do all my homework, *all* my homework"), hanging out with friends ("I have a lot of friends"), listening to music ("Right now it's 50 Cent and Lil' John because I like their raps"), and reading novels ("People call me a bookworm. I know I'm a bookworm because I read all the time").

When asked if she has had any experiences with racism, Terri shares an incident that occurred when she traveled to a bowling alley in a Detroit suburb. "Me and my friends," she begins, "we went to this one bowling alley and it was us and some white kids and we were all sitting there, and . . . we didn't know we couldn't drink at the [scoring table]. He told us we couldn't have drinks there or food, but they were doing the same thing and he didn't say anything to them. I just felt that was wrong because, you know, they were doing the same thing. Why can't we do what they do? . . . I felt that just because their skin was lighter than ours doesn't mean that they had the right to put drinks on stuff that we don't have the right to, that we can't." Terri's story illustrates the trend among the young interviewees of using travel (even a short way outside of Detroit's city limits) to discuss experiences of racism. Again, this exemplifies the finding that, of the twenty-two children who say they have had direct experiences with racism, almost all say this took place outside Detroit proper. The conundrum that Terri and the other adolescents in this study face is that if they want to engage in leisure activities like bowling, roller skating, swimming indoors in the winter, going to the movies, or hanging out at the mall, they are often forced to leave the city limits and go to the predominantly white suburbs. For example, Nina (thirteen) says, "There's not a lot of things for us to do here. . . . In California you have a few teen clubs. Here you have nothing. Go to the movies. When the movies is out, people are tired of going to movies. Bowling is like so far away. . . . It's just, where do you want to go? We don't have any Disney inter- actions or anything like that. We don't have a Six Flags; we don't have a—the water park we do have is closed. It's not indoors. The places we do have are all the way out somewhere in West Bloomfield Hills or somewhere near Canada's border, the Canada borderline." The locations Nina mentions where teens can go are each at least a thirty-minute drive from Nina's home in Detroit; and, of course, going to Windsor, Canada, also requires passing through US Customs and Border Protection and the Canada Border Services Agency. Detroit is notorious for its lack of effective public transportation, especially between the city and suburbs (Crowell 2005; Farley et al. 2000), which means middle-school students like Terri and Nina need rides from adults to access these far-away activities. Nina's mother, Sharon, agrees with her daughter's assessment. "If [they] want to go to the movies, you know, [a] parent's got to drive them. You know, you've got to drive a ways. . . . There's not local stuff for them to do."

Furthermore, Nina's description of these places as "way out" may have a double meaning, referring not only to physical distance but also to spatialized difference (McKittrick 2006). Although there is not actually a "West Bloomfield Hills," as Nina says, there is a Bloomfield Hills as well as a West Bloomfield Township, one next to the other, northwest of Detroit. While Detroit is 83 percent black (US Census Bureau 2001), Bloomfield Hills is over 90 percent white and West Bloomfield Township is over 84 percent white (US Census Bureau 2000b, 2000i). For places of comparable size, West Bloomfield Township is ranked in the top ten in the nation in terms of income—a fact made more notable because it is one of only two places on that list located in states with median incomes below the US median (US Census Bureau 2008a, 8–9). Even more exceptional, Bloomfield Hills ranked very first in the nation in household income for places of its size (US Census Bureau 1990). In sharp contrast, Detroit was ranked the fourth lowest nationally in household income among places of its size (US Census Bureau 2006, 6). While only 1.4 percent of families in West Bloomfield Township and 1.8 percent of families in Bloomfield Hills fell below the poverty line in 2000, a full 21.7 percent of families in Detroit did (US Census Bureau 2000i, 2000b, 2000d). Moreover, in 2005 Detroit had the second highest rate of households in poverty nationally among cities its size (US Census Bureau 2006, 18). Alongside these demographic differences come stark differences in material space, cultural and social capital, and access to certain types of resources. This "spatializing [of] 'difference'" leads to the false "naturalization of 'difference'" (McKittrick 2006, xv), making this space seem not just literally but also symbolically "way out" for the children of Detroit. Both Terri and Nina would rather have access to entertainment within the city but say it either does not exist in Detroit or exists but is substandard. So there are two clear messages communicated here through place and travel. The first message is that white spaces are more desirable and white people get the nicer stuff and better facilities (Lipsitz 2011; Wilkins 2007). The second message is that the borders (both literal and figurative) between the black-controlled spaces and the white-controlled spaces are strictly enforced and movement, particularly from the black-controlled places into the white-controlled places, is not welcomed. In other words, the racialization of space works "to keep the Black body in its *place*" (Wilkins 2007, 21, emphasis in original). When these children do breach these borders, they report finding unfair treatment and racialized hostility.

Place is often so elided with race in a way that is falsely naturalized that it gets used as a colorblind excuse for racialized exclusion (Kobayashi and Peake 2000; Lipsitz 2011; McKittrick 2006; Wilkins 2007). When her eleven-year-old daughter, Kaiya, was left off of a dance team, a mother named Cora says it was ostensibly due to residency; but really, Cora believes, it was racism. "Did [Kaiya] tell you," she asks, "the reason why she couldn't join the dance team that was at this center in Redford was because she was black? . . . Yeah. . . . But they just told her [it was] because she don't live in this area. But—and still—the [white] little girl that stays on the block behind us, who I heard about [the team] from her mom, is on [the team]." The city of Redford runs along Detroit's western edge, and Kaiya and her family live only a few blocks from its border. Cora's suspicion that the municipal borders were being used—as we heard Terri (thirteen) and Nina (thirteen) also observe—to keep African Americans out of white spaces is bolstered by the fact that a close neighbor, also living within the Detroit city limits but who is white, is allowed to participate. The little girl is still allowed to stay on the team, even after the team leaders cited the residency issue in Kaiya's case. Cora is certain Kaiya "knows what is going on" and is able to recognize the racism at play, especially since this white neighbor was the person who encouraged Kaiya to join the dance team.

Michelle, mother of Carlos (ten) and Elina (thirteen), says this racialization of space and the racialized hostility, expectations, and exclusion that go along with it are just things her children see as facts of life. "I told them that's just something that's just going to happen," She says. "You can't get by it." She continues, "When we've driven through suburbs, I'm like, 'OK, can you please put on your seatbelts; can you please act right?' And I will actually say, 'We are riding through white country. OK, kids, let's not bring any attention to ourselves so we do not get pulled over by the police.'" Already by the ages of ten and thirteen, Michelle's children are keenly aware of the racialization of space, of who supposedly belongs where and lays claim to what. These ideas, Katherine McKittrick argues, derive from "practices of domination . . . [that] naturalize both identity and place, repetitively spatializing where nondominant groups 'naturally' belong. This is, for the most part, accomplished through economic, ideological, social, and political processes that see and position the racial-sexual body within what seem like predetermined, or appropriate, places and assume that this arrangement is commonsensical" (2006, xv). Framing the suburbs as "white country" and simply being there as potentially outlaw behavior and understanding "acting right" as essentially acting according to white middle-class or upper-middle-class norms, all originate in these "geographies of domination." As a result, the children know they face racialized hostility and suspicion if they cross the city limits into the suburbs. The heightened sense of stress and vigilance this evokes is a regular part of their lives. Michelle works as an information technology (IT) consultant, and in recent decades such white-collar jobs have left the city proper in droves, so Michelle must drive to suburbs each day for work (Darden et al. 1987; Farley et al. 2000; Thompson 2001). Moreover, Detroit, despite being one of the nation's largest cities, has no major grocery stores, nor any super-stores such as Target or Walmart (Smith and Hearst 2007). Unless they want to shop at convenience, liquor, or small neighborhood stores, where selection is slimmer and prices are much higher, Detroiters must drive to the suburbs. Again, as Terri and Nina expressed, Detroiters are faced with the impossible situation of being unwelcome in the suburbs but essentially forced to go there for access to basic needs, work, and entertainment.

Even traveling for vacation raises the same types of experiences. Cara (thirteen) recalls her only direct experience with blatant interpersonal racism, which happened at a hotel between Detroit and Lansing, Michigan. "We had went to a hotel," she says, "and we was in the pool and there was this girl. She was like, 'Move, you nigger!'" In a separate interview, Cara's mother, Desarae, told the same story, prefacing it by assessing the racial atmosphere of the place. "[We were] on the other side of Howell . . . in Fowlerville. You know, it's very KKK up there." Howell, Michigan, is located in Livingston County, about sixty miles northwest of Detroit. It is a small city of just over nine thousand residents, less than one-half of one percent of whom reported as black or African American at the time of the 2000 census (US Census Bureau 2000e). According to a May 23, 2005, *Detroit Free Press* article, "Livingston County, located between Detroit and Lansing, has struggled to overcome a reputation for racism, earned in part because of [Robert] Miles, a Klan grand dragon who used to draw white supremacists from a wide area and who held rallies that included cross burnings." Desarae took her family to the Howell area to attend a carnival and do some shopping. She recounts the story of the children in the pool and says, with some consternation, "And [my kids] couldn't understand it. And at that time, I realized that they don't understand racism, but at some point it's going to come up." Not only a key moment in her children's comprehensive racial learning, this event was also critical to her own thinking about racial socialization. Cara reports that her mother told her, "Don't let that get to you," but Desarae says she did not follow her own advice. "I really, you know, wanted to go to the parent and say, 'You know, they're kids. If they want to play in the pool, what do you think? Do you think, what, the black's going to rub off?!'"

Like her daughter, though, Desarae says "that was really the only time" she had to deal with direct racism in relation to her kids, but she anticipates it will happen more now that Cara is joining school activities requiring travel. "Cara's going to find out," Desarae acquiesces, "because now she's on the cheer team and they're going to be going to different states. So . . . I'm going to have to let her know, 'Well, you know, sometimes you're going to go places and people are going to judge you, but that doesn't mean that you're a bad person. I don't want you to feel bad about yourself. It's just some people are ignorant.'" Here again Desarae anticipates racism in direct relation to place, specifically, spaces outside of Detroit. In fact, she says Cara's twin brother, Corey, is already dealing with more direct racism than his sister because "he's in more white settings and she's in more black settings." She continues, "Because of him being a caddy at a white golf course, they look at him like, 'You're not like the rest of them.' And he came home and he said, 'What do they mean, the rest of them?' And I was like, 'You know, they've got two classes.' I say, 'Well, we've got the ones they think that are ghetto and then you've got ones they think you have some education, you have some morals, values, and have been taught right from wrong.' So I do see that, with Corey, I'm having to explain things." The specific form of racism Corey is experiencing here is referred to by psychologists who study prejudice as "failing to generalize." Members of one group (in this case, whites) "fail to generalize" their positive experiences with a specific member of another group (in this case, African Americans) to the entire group and instead think of that person (here, Corey) as an *exception* and atypical of their group (Gaertner and Dovidio 2005, 79). Studies have shown that whites are more likely to generalize negative traits and experiences to the category "black" and black people as a group while viewing positive traits and experiences as exceptions to the rule (Richeson and Trawalter 2005). Corey's work and other activities take him out of Detroit and into "more white settings," which expose him to these kinds of direct experiences with racism that his twin sister, Cara, has not yet faced, their mother believes, because Detroit provides a sort of racial safe space. In her own experience as a young person, Desarae says, she did not really know what racism was until she left Detroit, although she had read about it. "Reading about it didn't mean anything because I wasn't affected by it," she says. "I was only affected by it when I left."

Similarly, the only experiences with racism Elijah (twelve) and his sister Trisha (fourteen) discuss in their interviews involve racist expectations and hostilities they faced during a family vacation to Nevada. When he paid for a souvenir with a large bill, Elijah said, the cashier "looked at me like I was crazy. And he was like, he threw my money at me like I'm not supposed to have a lot of money." In a separate interview, Trisha incredulously explains the racist treatment she and Elijah faced. "I experienced racism when I went to Las Vegas. They were just *staring* at us! They didn't even like us! . . . We were at [an attraction], and my cousin and my brother, we were just sitting there in line. And we said hi to these kids, and they just stood, looked at us, and rolled their eyes. We said, 'What did we do?! We were just nice!' Then we told my mom, and she was like, 'Some of them really are not going to like you, maybe because of their parents. They're sick.' [*Laughs.*]" In this response to the question, "Does your mom ever talk to you about racism?" Trisha does not specify to whom "they" and "them" refer. However, she clearly uses the terms to identify people who were racist toward her; and at the time of her visit, Las Vegas's population was approximately 70 percent white and 10 percent black (US Census Bureau 2000f). For many of the children in this study, travel to predominantly white spaces creates lasting ideas about racism. In a separate interview, Trisha and Elijah's mother, Sarah, recalls this same incident, saying that she tried to prepare her children for the racism she expected they would encounter, emphasizing the predominantly white space and culture and its contrast to their everyday space.

> Before we left [Detroit for Las Vegas], I did sort of try to prepare them—this is a different culture and this is a different place. And I didn't want to tell them that it was going to be a lot of white folks there and you were going to experience racism. My preparing them was telling them, "It's a different place; it's a different world than where you live. OK?" And so, I felt like if I said anything else to them, I would just be putting certain things—and I just wanted them to experience it for what it was. And so, they did come back and tell me, "Mommy, you know, why were people just staring at me? You know, they looked like I didn't belong there!" And I said, "There's nothing too good for you. You *were* there; you *do* belong there. Were *you* comfortable?" "Yeah, but why did people try to make us feel uncomfortable?" I said, "Because they probably don't like you. Next?"

Place is central to Sarah's wariness. While Sarah is certainly concerned about her children having to deal with racism under any circumstances, her heightened vigilance is directly related to place. She is clear that her children will likely face racism in this place, and mentions not only the racial demographics ("It was going to be a lot of white folks there") and different physical space ("It's a different place"), but also a culture and environment so different that it qualifies as a "different world" from Detroit. This description, which recalls Nina's talk of "way out" spaces, shows the importance of place in the children's developing ideas about racism. As Sarah predicted, her children did encounter instances of direct, individual racism that were unlike their experiences in Detroit. Moreover, her children experienced the independent power of "place [as] matter that acts" (J. Brown 2005, 10), impacting constructions of race (J. Brown 2005, 9) and "spatializing where nondominant groups 'naturally' belong" (McKittrick 2006, xv).

The salience of travel as a point of reference for the interviewees again highlights the role of place in the comprehensive racial learning process and may reflect Corey's observation that "there is not a lot of racism in Detroit" because "it's not that many Caucasians in Detroit." In other words, as I will explore in more depth in chapter 4, Detroit serves in some ways as a type of racial safe space, shielding children from direct, daily encounters with individual racism. By the same token, it seems this may cause them to be even more affected by the overt, individual racism with which they are confronted when

they travel to places outside Detroit; and such travel often defines their thinking about racism and (as shown later in this chapter) racialized behaviors.
In other ways, the material environment of Detroit exposes children to institutional racism, which often comes into stark relief when they travel.

"It's like a Ghetto City": Gleaning Structural Racism through Travel

Metropolitan Detroit's hyper-segregation concentrates the burden of systemic
racism, making Detroiters especially "vulnerable to the fatal couplings of power
and difference signified by *racism*" (Gilmore 2002, 22, emphasis in original) and
translating into lived experiences with poverty, crime, incarceration, urban
blight, excess mortality, racialized glass ceilings, and lack of accessible and safe
activities for young people (Farley et al. 2000; Geronimus 1998; Geronimus et al.
2011; Welch et al. 2001). Of course, these realities are experienced and interpreted in different ways by different children. As we will see in the next section,
some view them as proof that behaviors are racialized in some essential way.
Others, however, view them as manifestations of systemic racism, and it is these
latter interpretations I want to examine here.

One such example comes from Nina, a thirteen-year-old eighth grader.
Nina is an earnest, loquacious young woman who freely shares her experiences
growing up in Detroit. She has extended family in California and Georgia and
regularly travels to visit those family members. Through her travels, Nina says,
she has determined that Detroit is "not a healthy environment" and that she
would not want to raise her own children there. Nina makes connections
between Detroit's lack of economic development and its status as a black city.

> I don't really like Detroit because it's—it doesn't seem like a healthy
> environment. I wouldn't want to raise my kids here. It's not [*pause*], it's
> like, it's not diverse. . . . We're a kind of poor city because we're still—we
> still need money and stuff. . . . The parts that are not well developed need
> funding, like all these buildings we have that's empty and should be
> knocked down. . . . And we do need money to knock down the buildings,
> the buildings that are just tore up, have been burned down, are half-way
> burnt and still stand with the bricks on the bottom. That's just crazy.
> I don't want my child to go through that.

Nina mentions Detroit's lack of racial diversity as well as its status as a
"poor city." However, she also refers to the affluence of certain Detroit suburbs
but fails to comment on their similar lack of racial diversity. In fact, African
Americans make up only 5 percent of the population of Detroit's suburban ring,
which is overwhelmingly white (Farley et al. 2000). Thus, in this case, Nina's
discussion of Detroit's lack of racial diversity seems to be a euphemism for its
blackness, and she is tying its lack of development to its status as a black city.

Indeed, according to John Logan and Harvey Molotch, "Financial institutions take more money out of black neighborhoods (as deposits) than they put back in (as home mortgages)" (1987, 129); and this, along with absentee landlords and business owners who "cut back property maintenance . . . for short-term gain" (130), results in conditions that make it "difficult for a critical mass of respectability to develop and take spatial form" (133). As we have heard, for Nina this often means that she and her friends are forced to go to affluent white suburbs in order to engage in leisure activities, even though they would rather have access to those activities in their own neighborhoods or at least within their own city. When Nina discusses having to go to "way out" places in order to have fun, she is pointing out Detroit's lack of a particular kind of resource. Her mother, Sharon, reinforces this point, noting, "There's not local stuff for them to do. You know, they can't go to the rec center or go hang out, you know, so. That's kind of—not a good thing." The implication is that predominantly black Detroit is underdeveloped and underfunded, while the predominantly white suburbs are places of abundance. George Lipsitz points out that this racialized system provides whites with "advantages and amenities" far beyond recreational resources for teens, including "access to superior schools, protection from environmental hazards, proximity to sources of employment, inclusion in word-of-mouth networks about jobs and business opportunities, and the use of better services than those that can be secured from the underfunded public sphere after three decades of suburban tax rebellions" (2011, 30–31). African American Detroiters often face the no-win situation of either dealing with this systemic racism in Detroit or attempting to cross borders into the suburbs and being met with both systemic and individual racism.

Matthew (thirteen) is an eighth grader who lives with his mother and father and attends a public school of choice. Matthew agrees with Nina (thirteen), Terri (thirteen), and others that "there's nothing downtown for people to do" and not a lot for young people to do in Detroit, period. Although he thinks Detroit needs to "build up the downtown" in order for it to be "a better place to grow up," still he would not move somewhere else if given the chance. "[My] parents want to move. I don't want to move," he says. Also, like Nina, Matthew uses his travel experiences to tie some negative aspects of Detroit's physical space to race. He uses the racialized term *ghetto* to describe Detroit and contrasts it directly to other places he has traveled. When asked about the good and bad things about growing up in Detroit, Matthew responds, "The good thing [*pause*], there are many schools that can take you to a good college. And the bad thing [*pause*], the city, it's not that great of a—it's like a, I could say, a ghetto city. I don't know. Because I think of, like, Florida, how nice it looks. And you come to Detroit; it just looks like a messy city and lots of bad areas." Certainly, Florida has its "messy cities" or "bad areas" as well. However, Matthew's travel took him to an area of Florida he deemed "nice," which he then saw as directly contrasting with Detroit. While he uses the racialized term *ghetto* to talk about Detroit's physical space, he does not necessarily put the blame for this space on black people themselves. What is clear, however, is that Matthew, like Nina, makes connections between race and material condition and uses his travel experiences to do so.

Audrey and her husband, Dumay, have disagreements about how to handle these issues with Toussaint (eleven) and their two younger sons. Like some of the children from whom we have heard, Audrey wants to have access to high-quality resources, particularly in terms of the food she feeds her family. For this reason, she often wants to go to the suburbs—which she, like Nina (thirteen) did, describes as "way out"—for groceries and restaurants. Her husband, however, wants to patronize businesses inside the city so that their children see positive examples of African American entrepreneurship and see their parents supporting black-owned businesses. In the following passage, when Audrey mentions the intersection at Outer Drive and Seven Mile Road, she is referencing a site within the city, and when she mentions the intersection at Gratiot Avenue and Ten Mile Road, she is referencing a site in the suburbs.

> Don't think of me as racist, but my friends all tease me because I've been going further out on Gratiot [Avenue] now to do my grocery shopping and not within the city and not within this neighborhood because the quality isn't there. You know, it just rots quicker. So I have gone to what I call *el mundo blanco*. You know. So, I drive out there to the [grocery store] at Ten Mile and Gratiot now, and not just here at Seven Mile and Outer Drive. Because, you know, I still want to buy stuff for my family that's, you know, better for them. . . . But that's something that I struggle with my husband on because he's like, "No, I want to eat at the Pizza Hut *in* the city." And I'm like, "But honey!" You know? And he's just, he's—and so we end up, I give in to him. Because I'm just, you know, I'm tired of fighting him. And we do that instead of going way out and wherever, where the food is better and it's just cleaner and all the rest of it. He just want his kids to look at his people moving around and doing it.

Audrey understandably wants the best for her family but struggles with the fact that she has to travel "way out" to what she calls "*el mundo blanco*"—the white world—in order to get it. Still, she believes the trade-off of healthier food is worth it. Her husband, however, wants to support black-owned businesses within the city precisely so that his children can see black people "moving around and doing it" or running things, taking charge. This suggests his motivations are related to the racial socialization of his children. Because Audrey and Dumay's children are relatively young at ages one, six, and eleven, perhaps Dumay is hoping to avoid the at least partial internalization many older children in this study have made between race and "good" or "bad" neighborhoods, stores, and other facilities. Audrey mentions this as one of many reasons why they have decided to move to a Caribbean island in the near future. "Everybody down there's black, first of all," she says, "either the good, bad, or indifferent." In her opinion, this may remedy the children's potential association of race with good or bad. Furthermore, she says, there is not the same feeling of racialized rights to space as her children experience in Detroit. "All the beaches are public," Audrey explains:

> However, some of the hotels are situated in a way that are right in front of there. You've got to go through the hotel to get to the beach. But that doesn't stop [the residents of the island] from going through the hotel to get to the beach. It doesn't stop them from going to the party that [the resort] is having on [the beach] and getting in line with the rest of the people that are coming out from [the resort] to get them a piece of chicken or to dance to the music. They do not feel excluded. They will walk on any part of the beach and not feel that, uh, you know, "Oh, the tourists are down there. We shouldn't go there. Oh, they're white people down there. Maybe we should just stay right here." . . . So, that's another thing that intrigued me [about moving there].

Audrey expresses admiration—and, she admits, possibly romanticization—of the relative lack of racialization and spatialization of belongingness, or at least the relative lack of internalization of it, on this Caribbean island. Whether or not Audrey's perception of life on the island is correct, her comments still show the centrality of systemic racism, here played out through physical and material space, to her children's comprehensive racial learning. While she and her husband struggle with this issue in Detroit, frustrated by the impossible choice between better resources or black spaces, they hope moving to the Caribbean will eliminate this false dichotomy for their children. Until their move, Audrey's husband insists on keeping his children primarily within black spaces in order to avoid the internalization of the idea that white is better.

"They Don't Act Right": Travel, Place, and Interpreting Behaviors as Racially Ascribed

In their interviews, the young people mentioned several positive aspects of childhood in Detroit, including nice, laid-back, friendly people, good neighbors who always speak to one another, good schools, and a multitude of museums and cultural events. They also discussed negative things, such as poverty, crime, drugs, "bad neighborhoods" or rough areas, physical neglect of property, and there not being a lot of things for young people to do. In responding to interview questions, some of the children used travel to frame their answers in ways that ascribe the named traits of the city and its people to their blackness.

For example, Corey (thirteen) shares that he is not glad to be growing up in Detroit and would rather live in Las Vegas. He has visited his cousins in Las Vegas and left with the impression that Las Vegas is in better condition than Detroit because Detroit is, in his words, "a black city," while Las Vegas is not.

ERIN: So why would you like [Las Vegas] better than Detroit? What—

COREY: I mean, the black people, they don't act right. . . . I mean, they litter and sell drugs, a lot of stuff like that. In Las Vegas, they don't do a lot of that.

ERIN: Do you think white people litter and sell drugs?

COREY: On TV, but not for real. This far I've never seen it.

When asked *again* why he thinks Las Vegas is different from Detroit in these ways, he responds that the differences are attributable to race, saying, "I mean, Detroit seem like a black neighborhood, black city, I mean. And just Las Vegas seem like, just for everybody."

Corey's interpretation of the differences between Las Vegas and Detroit illustrates the impact of travel and place on the formation of understandings of race on several levels. First, the physical and material setting of Detroit comes into play. Corey talks about what are essentially the symptoms of economic decline and urban decay in Detroit. That is, as the formal economy of the auto industry moved out of Detroit, an informal economy, including the sale of drugs, moved in. Thomas Sugrue writes, "In the 1940s, Detroit was America's 'arsenal of democracy,' one of the nation's fastest growing boomtowns and home of the highest-paid blue-collar workers in the United States. Today, the city is plagued by joblessness, concentrated poverty, physical decay, and racial isolation. Since 1950, Detroit has lost nearly a million people and hundreds of thousands of jobs" (1996, 3). Nevertheless, as explained in chapter 1, alongside this urban decay occurred a black political renaissance. Over the last four decades, Detroit became the United States' "blackest city" (Hartigan 1999, 4) and has seen a clear empowerment of the black middle class, with an increase in African American political and social power (Thompson 2001; Welch et al. 2001; Widick 1989). Heather Thompson notes that this time period presents an "odd juxtaposition of historically unprecedented African American middle-class presence and civic power amid extreme urban decay and economic decline" (2001, 217). While several historians note these concurrent trends (Thompson 2001; Welch et al. 2001; Widick 1989), they caution that "increased black presence and power" and "urban decline" should not be "associate[d] . . . in some linear or causal way" (Thompson 2001, 217). However, when Corey notices the consequences of urban decline in Detroit, he *does* make a causal connection, attributing it to black people themselves. The only solution he sees is to move to a city that, in his words, is "not a black city."

Corey was born in the 1990s, after the aforementioned changes had already come to Detroit, and lives in a contemporary Detroit in which a significant majority of the census tracts are at least three-quarters African American. In this way, it is only logical that most of the behaviors of any kind Corey has observed would have been enacted by African Americans. However, from Corey's narrative it appears that it is only when he travels to Las Vegas, which is 70 percent white and only 10 percent black (US Census Bureau 2000f), and observes physical, material, and behavioral differences, that he decides to ascribe Detroit's characteristics to race. Through his statement, "Black people, they don't act right," Corey makes it clear that he is not blaming Detroit's problems on racism or structural inequities tied to race, but rather on behaviors he sees as racially ascribed. Corey even dismisses television images of white people engaging in the same behaviors he has described as being exclusive to black people because, he says, he has never seen such things with his own eyes. In these ways, travel and place have a clear impact on how Corey is thinking about race and ascribing racial meaning to behaviors, physical spaces, and material circumstances.

It is important to note that the connections the children in this study make between race and behavior are not always negative toward African Americans. In similar examples, other children also use their travel experiences to describe ideas about ascribed racial behaviors; but, unlike Corey, they assign positive attributes to African Americans and less flattering attributes to whites. For example, Corey's sister Cara (thirteen) defines Detroiters as more "laid back" and friendly than people in the predominantly white cities she has visited both in and outside of Michigan. Cara derides the behavior she encountered when she traveled to an amusement park in Sandusky, Ohio, a city approximately 75 percent white (US Census Bureau, 2000h). When asked to give specific examples of why she says it is nice to live in Detroit, Cara answers, "When I went to that carnival at [a middle school in Detroit], it was real fun or whatever. But then when I went to Cedar Point [Amusement Park in Sandusky, Ohio], it was like, 'Oh God!' It was a *whole different people that act so different*" (emphasis added). She goes on to explain that the "whole different people" in Sandusky act more "uptight," while Detroiters are more "laid back." Other scholars have also found evidence of black adolescents identifying "laid back" as a racial trait, or "just the way we are" (Blyth and Milner 1996, 67), and equating whiteness with being "more inhibited" or "more formal" (Tyson 2011, 11). Another interviewee, eleven-year-old Rayna, agrees with Cara's assessment, stating, "I don't want to live no place else" because, she says, people in Detroit do not focus on race the way white people do. "The thing that I'm most proud of [about] being black," she says, "is that black people don't really think about your color."

Looking at this same issue from a parent's perspective, Michelle, mother of Elina (thirteen) and Carlos (ten), finds herself fighting against the ideas her children have formed through their experiences in Detroit's overwhelmingly white suburban ring. "You know, they'll even say, if we're in the suburbs, they're like, 'OK.' Elina will be like, 'We're in white country. OK, what does that mean? Everybody act right!' [*Laughs.*] . . . Or we're in the suburbs and we see these really nice houses, and Elina is like, 'White people live there.'" Elina's comments, connecting "acting right" to acting in a manner acceptable to whites and nice houses with white occupancy, both show how place facilitates children's comprehensive racial learning. Worrying that Elina is not thinking critically about these elisions, Michelle responds incredulously to her daughter's comments: "'So, only white people live in nice houses?' I've actually found myself having to counteract [this way of thinking] now that they're getting older." Indeed, as James Duncan and Nancy Duncan argue, "landscapes . . . can act as subtle but highly effective excluding mechanisms for reaffirming class and race identities" (2006, 160). Michelle feels she is essentially fighting against place for influence over her children's understandings of race. The ideas they garner from place, she says, are simply "what they know . . . what they see just in everyday interactions. Like little stuff we don't even think about. Like when we go to the store, or out in the 'burbs. Or, you know, we'll go down the street [in Detroit] and see someone and they're like, 'Oh, what's a white person doing in this neighborhood?!' [*Laughs.*]" These insidious ideas about who belongs where or who gets what types of homes or stores or facilities are reminiscent of those shared by many children and mothers in this study and seem to be some of the most difficult for parents to counteract since they are, as Michelle says, what the children "see just in everyday interactions." Again here, as with Corey, Cara, and Rayna above, the issue comes into relief for the children when they travel outside of Detroit and compare what they see and experience there to that at home.

Such striking examples evidence the power of place and travel in shaping racial attitudes since the interviewees label behaviors and characteristics as "black" or "white" only after they have traveled to places outside of Detroit. All of the children in this study operate primarily within predominantly black realms of daily interaction (family, school, neighborhood, church); and, as we will see in chapter 4, many (although not all) of their mothers view this as a kind of racial safe space in which they can shield their children from direct encounters with racism or racial denigration (Winkler 2008). From the adolescent interviews, it appears that this space also influences children's ideas about behavior—or how black and white people "act" or "are"—when they travel into white-dominated realms and observe differences. Here again, as we saw in chapter 2, although the children may articulate a conceptualization of race as insignificant, their lived experiences suggest the contrary.

"You Will Find Out . . . When You Go to Different Places": Place, Travel, and Expanding Racial Thinking

Believing that ideas about race in Detroit are too restrictive, some mothers are invested in travel as a way to expand their children's perspectives. Indeed, as we will see, the children (and some of the mothers) do evidence a heavy reliance on a strict black/white binary in understanding race. However, the construction of race as a black/white dichotomy is not a local issue, but rather is deeply rooted at the national level (Celious and Oyserman 2001; Denton and Massey 1989; Spickard and Daniel 2004). Still, while this ideology is being challenged and perhaps slowly broken down in parts of the United States, it remains relatively strong in Detroit (Fernandez 2008). Part of the reason for this may be the hyper-segregation of the area (Charles 2003) and the vastly disproportionate distribution of resources along those lines (Farley et al. 2000; Fernandez 2008; Lipsitz 2011; Shyrock and Lin 2009). Whatever the reason, the reliance on an absolute black/white construction of race among several children is striking. For example, as discussed in chapter 2, in the few cases in which the children report having white friends, it is always revealed that they are actually talking about biracial friends or light-skinned black friends. This may reflect the ideology, as expressed by a mother named Gina and explored in more detail in chapter 6, that "it ain't nothing but two true races, black and white," and if someone is not black, then they are white, and vice versa. We heard some examples of this in chapter 2, where Elina (thirteen) describes her friend Janelle as white before clarifying that Janelle is "not all white, she's black *and* white." We also saw similar slippage with Cara (thirteen), who described her grandmother's foster children first as "white" and then later as "mixed." Elijah (twelve) uses the term *white* to refer to light-skinned African Americans, including his older sister, Trisha. In talking about his changing perception of race over time, Elijah says that his grandmother taught him that white people are "just like us, they're just light-skinned." Immediately after sharing this, Elijah says that he has recently been making more "white" friends. However, this statement follows one in which he explains that he thinks of his sister, Trisha, as "white." (Trisha, who was also interviewed, identifies black and describes her skin color as "caramel.") Thus, it is not entirely clear whether Elijah's "white" friends are white or black. Kaneka (thirteen) describes classmates with one black parent and one white parent as "white." She says her school is "mostly black. It's only one—like a few white people. And they act like black because their mom is black and their daddy's white." Again, it may well be the combination of acute hyper-segregation and the deeply embedded national black-white dichotomy of race at work here. If these children are operating in multiple realms of daily interaction in which they encounter very few non-black children or people, their notions of whiteness may include the lightest-skinned people they know, even if those people are known to have one or two black parents. Indeed, Josh (ten), the only interviewee in this study who has one white parent, reports having been teased about being black when he used to live in a predominantly white city but says that in Detroit the children tease him by calling him "white," "white snowflake," "Chinese," and "Asian." With the latter two monikers, the reliance on a black-white dichotomy is clearly not in play, but the contrast with his earlier experience is clear—in the all-white city, he was seen as black, in Detroit, he is seen as not black. Again, this highlights that race is spacialized, much as space is racialized (J. Brown 2005; Kobayashi and Peake 2000; McKittrick 2006; Wilkins 2007).

Moreover, as I have discussed, the interviews at times evidence a narrow delineation of what it means to be a member of a particular racial group. Again, this is not a phenomenon specific to Detroit, but it is intertwined with and shaped by place in particular ways. In her study of "geographies of race in black Liverpool," Jacqueline Nassy Brown points out that she "often use[s] the term *Liverpool/Britain* in order to . . . keep Britain in view at precisely those moments when one might be tempted to view Liverpool as 'specific,' 'particular,' and hence a place apart" (2005, 8). While I am not using the term *Detroit/United States* in this book, it is important to remember that constructions of race, the racialization of space, and manifestations of racism in Detroit intersect with and are part of those same processes in the United States as a whole. As such, because place is racialized in the United States, constructions of race on the part of young Detroiters are necessarily impacted by place.

We have already heard Corey's notion that black people litter and sell drugs, Cara's idea that black people are laid back and whites are uptight, Elina's idea that white people have nice houses, and so on. Lena, mother of Tanika (thirteen) and Lanáe (ten), is not originally from Detroit and blames these ways of thinking on the racialization of space as manifested in Metropolitan Detroit.

> Racially speaking, I think Detroit is very, uh, I can't even describe it. And I don't know that if you're from this area you even notice, but when I talk to other non-Michiganders, then we talk about it all the time, about how everything is so separate and people are so closed-minded; And they don't want to expand. . . . I was just thinking about this [*laughs*] probably within this week. How it would be nice if there was someplace that I could take my children where there was more of a mix. . . . Because, I mean, we're all essentially the same people. And when you're separated so much, then you don't realize that, if you never have to interact. . . . If you're not in that situation, I mean, you won't know how to coexist. So, it would be nice if I could [have my children in racially mixed situations], but in this city it's difficult. There is not a place that I'm aware of.

From Lena's point of view, this is a problem caused by the racial geography of southeast Michigan. The racialization of place implicitly teaches her children there are inherent or insurmountable differences between people based on race; place does the work of "naturalizing" difference (Kobayashi and Peake 2000; McKittrick 2006). Moreover, she worries the lack of actual cross-racial contact leaves her children without the requisite skills when they do eventually find themselves in multiracial environments (Boykin and Ellison 1995; Hamm 2001). Despite the possible advantages of living in a place where black culture is locally dominant, Lena concludes it is "not necessarily a good thing" for her children. She sees herself as having a different racial attitude than other Detroiters precisely because of place and travel; she moved frequently as a "military brat" and later as a member of the military herself. "I think a lot of [my openness] does have to do with the fact that I've been different places. And I'm a little concerned with the girls being here, where all they're getting, for the most part, is just one perspective, instead of a wide perspective." Of course, with several hundred thousand African Americans living in Detroit, Lena's notion that they represent "just one perspective" is impossible to support. But as we will see in chapter 6, at other points in her interview Lena focuses a great deal on the diversity of perspectives within the African American community. Her point here, then, revolves around her concerns that her children's comprehensive racial learning is being molded by the relative lack of *racial* diversity in Detroit.

Roughly a third of the mothers worry about these same issues and prescribe travel as the solution. Although they try to get their children to challenge rigid ideas about race—including those about how people of particular races are or act as well as the reliance on a black-white binary—some believe that travel outside of Detroit is the only thing that truly disrupts this way of thinking, that children learn best through experience (Kolb 1984). One example comes from Desarae, who worries that her twins, Corey and Cara, and their younger siblings are close-minded toward other cultures due to lack of exposure. For this reason, she says, "I take them a lot of different places around different cultures because I don't want them to just see black cultures. You know. I have a friend that's Arab. And we go visit her and they look at the food and they go, 'I don't want none of that.' And I'm like, 'Why?' . . . I don't want them to just think in the black culture because *once you go somewhere else*, you're going to find out that this is our culture, but then every race has their own culture, their own way of doing things" (emphasis added). That Desarare has to take her children "somewhere else" to give them exposure to other cultures highlights the connection between race and place. Despite the fact that suburban Detroit has the largest Arab population in North America, and some experts say the largest Arab population outside of the Middle East (Schopmeyer 2000; Shyrock and Abraham 2000), Desarae says her children are reticent to try Middle Eastern food. Lena reinforces this point, noting, "So here we are, we have the Middle East in our back yard, but I bet you 80 percent of the African American population has never eaten Middle Eastern food, whereas, in New York, people eat anything and everything. So why is it so different in New York or Chicago than it is in Detroit? I haven't figured that out, but people tend to stay to themselves, and they look at other things as being foreign." Part of the reason could be that, in New York and Chicago, while both are segregated by neighborhood, significant racial diversity exists within the cities themselves. In Detroit, the racial and ethnic diversity and segregation fall more clearly along a city-suburb divide, although there are small predominantly white and predominantly Latino neighborhoods within the city (see map 3.1; US Census Bureau 2000g, 2000c, 2000d). Thus, of the significantly large Arab population in Metropolitan Detroit, more than 90 percent live in the suburbs, and only 1.6 percent of the city of Detroit's population is Arab (Schopmeyer 2000; Shyrock and Abraham 2000).

Travel allows exposure not only to people of other races, but to examples of those people interacting and sharing spaces and friendships. Lena worries that, in Detroit, meaningful interracial interaction is not something her daughters see frequently. Lena and her family live in a zip code with an almost 99 percent black population, and her girls attend a school listed as having a black enrollment of 100 percent. In light of this, Lena makes it a point to use travel to show her children it is "nice" and "acceptable" to have friends of all different races.

> I know when I went to my brother's wedding, who lives in Virginia, I commented—you know, I could have just kept it to my head, but I wanted to say out loud—how, you know, it's nice to see groups of people from different backgrounds together in a social environment and how I don't see that anymore [now that we live in Detroit], so that [my daughters] could be cognizant that, you know, it's OK, it's an acceptable thing. And as they grow, that they won't be timid—you know, I've even seen cases where people don't want to have white friends. They'll have a white friend, but they don't want to be known to be socializing with the white friend outside of their job or whatever else. I want them to know that that's not necessary; it's stupid. So, hopefully, they'll be all right.

It seems Lena's youngest daughter, Lenáe (ten), may be getting some of her mother's intended messages—that it is unnecessary to fall in line with the crowd in terms of racial separation, that she should not "look at other [cultures] as being foreign." When asked what she likes the best about who she is, Lenáe responds: "That I'm not like other people. I'm just weird. I like to try different things. I like different cultures . . . different types of foods. . . . I like Arabic food, Chinese food."

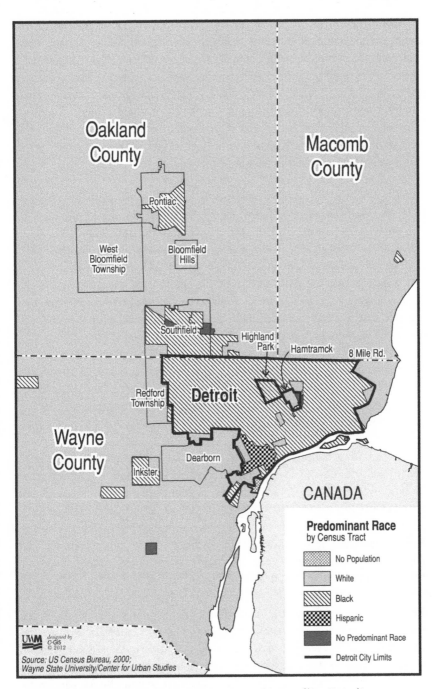

Legend:

Predominant Race
by Census Tract

- No Population
- White
- Black
- Hispanic
- No Predominant Race
- — Detroit City Limits

Source: US Census Bureau, 2000;
Wayne State University/Center for Urban Studies

MAP 3.1. Predominant race by 2000 census tract, Metropolitan Detroit area.

Wayne State University Center for Urban Studies 2000; US Census Bureau 2000. Map created by the Cartography and Geographic Information Science Center at the University of Wisconsin–Milwaukee.

Cora, mother of Kaiya (eleven) and Rayna (ten), also believes travel expands her daughters' horizons in terms of racial thinking, although they, and even she herself, are still confused about the relationship between race, nationality, ethnicity, culture, and religion. Note, for example, that Cora uses the term *Arabics* to refer to Arab people, even though the term *Arabic*, when used as a noun, refers to a language and not a people, and she tells her children she does not know whether "Arabics" are black or white. Although it does not necessarily clarify their thinking on the topic, Cora thinks travel nevertheless helps disrupt her children's assumptions about race.

> Like Arabics ... my kids don't really know how to deal with that community because that's a whole new race that has moved into our communities. And my kids don't know how to deal with Arabics now. . . . They be like, "Momma, well, are Arabics black or are they white?" You know. We've talked about this already. And they were like, well, my answer to that was like, "Look, I don't know. Because you see some dark Arabics, you see some light Arabics." But the majority you see that are over here are light. Then again, not no more, because when we went to, um, Cleveland, Ohio—we took them to Six Flags—we saw a lot of black Arabics. And my kids were like, "Momma, they wear the same thing that they wear in Dearborn. Why they not white?" I was like, "See. We're back to that again [*laughs*]. Because, see, there you go. There's no color in a nationality. I mean, we're just all human and without color" [*laughs*].

Cora's story highlights the reliance on an oversimplified black/white binary and the role of travel in problematizing (if not fully disrupting) that dichotomy. Notice that Cora first refers to Arabs as "a whole new race" but then reverts to defining them as either black or white based on skin tone, unable to move her children or herself away from the black/white dichotomy. She proffers that most Arab people "over here" are lighter skinned but suggests that might not be representative of the entire Arab population. Indeed, Andrew Shyrock and Ann Lin note the largest portion of the Arab population in Metropolitan Detroit is "Christian, suburban, and likely to identify as white" (2009, 58). In Dearborn, Michigan, in particular, however, the Arab population is mostly Muslim and "likely to identify as other" as opposed to white (Shyrock and Lin 2009, 58). Dearborn is a suburb that shares a sizable border with southwest Detroit and was established in the early twentieth century by Henry Ford as a residential community for white auto workers; black workers were relegated to Detroit proper or to the segregated community of Inkster, which Ford also helped establish and keep segregated (Babson 1986, 42). Today Dearborn's population is 35 percent "of Arab origin"

(Baker and Shyrock 2009, 17), earning Dearborn the moniker "the capital of Arab America" (Shyrock and Lin 2009, 58). It is this Muslim Arab population of Dearborn to which Cora's daughters compare the people they observe at the amusement park. Since Cora identifies them as "Arabic" solely because "they wear the same thing that they wear in Dearborn," it is possible some forms of Muslim dress symbolize "Arab" to Cora, causing her to mistakenly elide "Arab" and "Muslim," a common mistake in US popular thinking (Varisco 2007). Whatever the case may be, it is clear that, while this one experience alone did not seem enough to shake their reliance on a black/white dichotomy, seeing black people outside of the expected national, cultural, or religious delineations they had come to expect and Arab or Muslim people outside of the racial or ethnic delineations they had come to expect had an impact on Cora's girls. Cora took this as an opportunity to send two racial socialization messages: first, that nationality is different from race and that no single race has a monopoly on "Arabness" or "Americanness," and, second, her favored but largely inconsistent colorblind message, "We're just all human and without color." In this case, the ways in which place has shaped their understandings of race, ethnicity, culture, and religion are clear, as is the role of travel across space in unbalancing (at least partially) the children's (and Cora's) ideas about race.

Sarah also tells of travel outside of Detroit challenging her children's ideas about race, particularly what it means to be black or white. In their neighborhood, she says, her children's racial authenticity has been challenged based on their speech and, for her daughter Trisha, also based on her lighter skin tone and her attendance at one of Detroit's "Gifted and Talented" public schools. Note that Sarah says the extent of this depends on place—where they are within Detroit (known affectionately as "The D").

Depending on where we are in the 'hood, in The D, already [Trisha gets], "So you go to [a gifted and talented school]. Who do you think you are? You just want to be white. You just want to look like a little white girl, a little fake girl." Oh, she already gets that because we don't live too far from here. Like I said, we're still in the 'hood. . . . And so, to the people in our neighborhood, they see Elijah and Trisha as snobs, and that's so funny to me because that's so far from the truth. You see what I'm saying? So, she is, or they are, challenged on their authenticity. "Are you black and how black are you? Because, after all, you go to [a gifted and talented school]; you're lighter; you don't dress like us." Because we don't get into all that Fila, FUBU, and all that stuff. I'm serious, it seems they go along with being in a certain African American, you know, culture. But we don't get into that. And so, they are already challenged, just by the way they speak.

But Sarah finds it ironic that her children are accused of "want[ing] to be white" based on their speech in the context of Detroit because in another context their speech would be interpreted as "using that slang" or talking like they are "in the 'hood." In fact, she says, "My kids don't talk all that proper." She has told her children:

> "You don't even talk right. And you will find out just how much you don't *when you go to different places*." And when we went to Las Vegas, they were, like, corrected, and I was like, "See, told you so." Mmm hmm. . . . I told them; I said, "If you just use proper English, you would not have to switch up." Because I will get after Trisha for using too much slang. I said, "You know what? We go a lot of different places, and you're going to really get embarrassed using that slang so much." And when we were in Las Vegas, she had to catch herself a couple of times and she got embarrassed. I said, "See? It's not useful." I said, "Trisha, it's a whole big world out there," and I said, "We happen to live in Detroit in the 'hood, but guess what? You guys are going to be exposed to a lot of different things in the world, so why don't you just adopt a universal language? Stop!" I'm serious; I said, "Stop talking and looking like, you know, like you're from one place." You know? So, I hope they get it. Sometimes they get it; sometimes they don't (emphasis added).

As I will discuss in more detail in chapter 5, and as a plethora of existing studies already show, many African American parents encourage their children to switch codes—change styles of speech and self-presentation—based on their environment as a means of coping with racism (Bennet 2006; Harrison et al. 1990; Peters 1985; Smitherman 1997; Walker et al. 1995). Certainly, switching codes is about much more than language, but language is a part of it (Smitherman 1997). Several studies cite this bicultural message as perhaps the most common in African American racial socialization, arguing that black children need to learn "the information and skills necessary for upward mobility, career achievement, and financial independence in the American mainstream" while still "feel[ing] pride in their own ethnic culture" (Hale-Benson 1990, 211–212; Hamm 2001). Sarah may agree, and she certainly emphasizes both achievement and racial pride with her children, but she does not see what scholars call African American Language (AAL)—also sometimes referred to as "Black English" (Smitherman and Baugh 2002)—as part and parcel of that pride. Furthermore, she worries her children do not always remember to switch codes and says she therefore encourages them to "adopt a universal language." Sarah's use of the terms "universal language" and "proper English," seemingly to refer to English spoken by middle- and upper-class whites or to Standard English, is problematic in the sense that white English is as specific or particular as Black English, but only white

English gets privileged, normalized, and posited as "universal" and "proper" (Balibar 1990; Smitherman 2000; Tatum 2003). Geneva Smitherman argues that even the encouragement of "bi-dialectism," or the idea that "blacks . . . would have to learn white English although whites would not have to learn Black English," simply "discriminates against blacks because of the blackness of Black English" and ultimately falls under the paradigm of the "linguistics of white supremacy" (2000, 80). But Sarah believes her children should adopt only Standard English, arguing that any construction of blackness (or white-ness) based on a particular type of speech (or dress or behavior or skin tone) is limiting at best and essentializing at worst.

Here again, place is tied into both children's developing ideas about race and mothers' concerns about that process. In their neighborhood, Sarah's children's speech is critiqued as not black enough; in Las Vegas it is critiqued as too black. While she says she can tell them all she wants, she believes it is only through travel that her children realize that they, in her words, "don't even talk right," fulfilling her prediction that they would "find out . . . when [they] go to different places." Moreover, Sarah's main concern is that her children are *placing* themselves with their speech, identifying themselves as being "from one place," specifically, "Detroit in the 'hood." She is especially troubled about how this may impact her children when they "go to different places" outside Detroit. Of course, without the attachment of racialized (and racist) meaning to space, this would not be an issue. It is only through the ideological construction of black space as undesirable that being identifiable as "from one place" defined as a black space (in this case, "Detroit in the 'hood") could be conceived as a concern.

Conclusion

Although the children and mothers were *not* asked how travel or place entered into children's comprehensive racial learning, a good proportion of them raised place unsolicited, particularly through travel narratives. This chapter has highlighted such travel stories and argued that they reveal the ways in which place itself communicates apparently influential and enduring messages about race, influencing children's developing ideas about racially ascribed behaviors, racialized boundaries, racialized hostility, and the attachment of racialized (and classed) meanings to their city, as well as the material and psychological impact of such meanings. As eighth-grader Mahogany puts it, "I learn being black from everywhere I go."

Of course, place and travel are by no means the only influences on children's comprehensive racial learning—indeed, the children also mention parents, other family members, school (teachers and curriculum), media, peers, church, and neighbors as part of their process of developing ideas and identities. But as this chapter has shown, place is indeed an important player in this process, having heretofore been largely neglected in literature on how children learn race. In this chapter, place's central role has been evidenced through the ways in which place itself sends messages to children about race. In the next chapter, we will see how place shapes the messages mothers send their children, therefore taking an additional, overarching, but indirect role in children's comprehensive racial learning.

4

Place Matters

Shaping Mothers' Messages

While the last chapter looked at how place directly and actively teaches children about race, this chapter theorizes the indirect role of place in children's comprehensive racial learning. Specifically, I will argue that place influences what mothers choose to teach their children about race and racism. First, by comparing the racial socialization message of the mothers in this study with a smaller pilot sample of parents in the San Francisco Bay Area, I will argue that the Detroit mothers send fewer direct verbal messages about black history, leadership, creative expression, beauty, and more, not because they do not find such things important but because place does it for them. Second, the influence of place is further evidenced in the fact that, while all of the mothers suggested that place was their "partner" in teaching their children about race and racism, some mothers see it as a positive partner—providing a "racial safe space" for their children—while others consider it a detrimental partner— acting as a "false shield" and leaving their children unprepared for the racism they will confront if they leave Detroit. Although not entirely cut-and-dried, the mothers who themselves grew up in Detroit tend toward the former, while the mothers who grew up elsewhere are the strongest voices supporting the latter. Therefore, place shows yet another form of influence—whether or not the mother herself grew up in Detroit influences how she engages in racial socialization.

Two Types of Messages: Procultural and Responsive

Based on the mothers' interviews, I outline a model of maternal racial socialization using two broad categories—*responsive* and *procultural*—to describe the mothers' messages. As Diane Hughes and her colleagues (2006, 749) note, scholars in the field of racial socialization have yet to agree upon a common typology for discussing types of familial racial socialization messages. The model I propose here adds to the discussion (see, for example, Hughes 2003; Stevenson et al. 2005). For example, the broad categories of responsive and procultural racial socialization overlap with and build upon Howard Stevenson's (1995) discussion of "creative" and "reactive" racial socialization, Wade Boykin and Constance Ellison's (1995) discussion of "tricultural socialization," and Hughes's (2003) discussion of "cultural socialization" and "preparation for bias."

In my model, responsive racial socialization messages are those that parents use to counter negative notions of blackness coming from society. Procultural racial socialization messages focus on the value of African and African American heritage in and of itself and are not in response to racism. Some may argue that all racial socialization, even that about African American history, culture, and heritage, is in response to racism; otherwise, it would not be necessary. I posit we need a model that presents a balanced consideration of familial agency and structural constraints and recognizes that "normal Black behavior and consciousness is not merely a reaction to adverse environmental elements" (Parham et al. 1999, 43). As Ralph Ellison notes in his 1964 critique of Gunnar Myrdal's study of US race relations, *An American Dilemma*, African Americans have not "live[d] and develop[ed] for over three hundred years simply by *reacting*" (Ellison [1964] 1995, 315, emphasis in original). Stevenson (1995) makes a similar argument in relationship to racial socialization. He writes, "Instead of viewing racial socialization as preparing the child only for oppressive experiences (e.g., protective African American culture), it is proposed that these processes also include teaching children how to be proud of their culture because its substance is historic, African derived, culturally empowering, and not dependent on oppressive experiences" (1995, 51). Stevenson calls these latter types of messages "creative." In my model, some of the messages that Stevenson describes as "creative" could be understood as *either* responsive *or* procultural, depending upon the parent's purpose in sending such messages. Thus, the intent and context of each message is critical in determining whether it is procultural or responsive. For example, a family may discuss the achievements of African American inventors throughout history in order to highlight the greatness of African American heritage in and of itself, thus engaging in procultural racial socialization. The same family in another context may focus on the achievements of African American inventors throughout history in order to counter negative racial socialization messages their child has heard elsewhere about the alleged laziness or lower intellectual capacities of African Americans, thus engaging in responsive racial socialization. This model moves away from a reactionary construction, while still acknowledging the ways in which racialized social structures affect African American families' racial socialization practices.

"I Think It's Really the Environment":
Place and Procultural Racial Socialization

We will look further at responsive racial socialization in the next chapter; in this chapter I want to argue that place shapes the mothers' procultural messages, particularly the extent to which they choose to focus on procultural messages at all. The influence of place on maternal racial socialization priorities is evident when we compare the racial socialization priorities of mothers in Detroit with another set of African American parents. In 2000 and 2003, I conducted pilot interviews with a small sample of African American adults and children in the San Francisco Bay Area. The California sample was smaller than the Detroit sample but was similar in terms of educational attainment, employment status, and marital status. In contrast to the Detroit sample, however, all of the families interviewed in California were living in predominantly white or Latino areas.

In the Bay Area pilot study, the parents concentrated relatively equally on both procultural and responsive messages. However, in the Detroit study, with very few exceptions, the mothers focused almost exclusively on responsive messages, or "damage control." In fact, just two Detroit mothers, Audrey and Barbara, stressed procultural messages in their interviews. Does this mean that the other mothers in the Detroit study do not care about African American culture as much as the California parents? I argue no, that place simply takes care of the procultural messages for them. Karyn Lacy (2007) discusses this phenomenon at the neighborhood level in her study of middle-class African Americans living in suburbs of Washington, D.C. In the one predominantly white community she studied, black parents took "additional steps to expose their children to black spaces" (2007, 173). In the two predominantly black communities she studied, Lacy says, "The neighborhood serves as the construction site for black racial identity. The children in these areas develop an insider's sense of what it means to be black as they learn cultural cues through interaction with black neighbors. Thus, their parents believe that they do not have to actively nurture and build that identity in an overt way" (2007, 167). I argue a similar phenomenon is at play here. In the case of Detroit, however, the "construction site for black racial identity" expands beyond the neighborhood level to the city as a whole, including all levels of city government, schools, cultural institutions, and public spaces. And this not in a relatively small suburb, but in a large city of almost a million people at the time of this study. In this sense, Detroit provides a cultural context in which, unlike much of the United States, African American culture is "locally dominant" (Hartigan 1999). Audrey even refers to the city of Detroit as "Blacktown." In the city as a whole, Michelle says, the "main identity really is black. I think it's really the environment, because everybody around them is black." These mothers feel that, because black culture is omnipresent and implicit within everyday life in Detroit, its value is not something that needs to be explicitly emphasized in verbal racial socialization. The city itself sends positive messages about black history, leadership, creative expression, beauty, entrepreneurship, achievement, and so on. In contrast, the Bay Area parents who participated in the pilot interviews all say that they purposely seek out predominantly black spaces to which they can take their children to show them positive examples of black culture, leadership, and the diversity of experiences among African Americans. On the surface, this difference could appear to be due to levels of education, as the California pilots included a slightly higher percentage of college-educated parents. However, one-third of the mothers in the Detroit sample held a bachelor's degree or higher, but only one of these mothers mentioned procultural racial socialization in our interview.

Racial demographics, however, likely come into play. Five out of the six families in the California pilot sample were living in predominantly white areas at the time of our pilot interviews, and one was living in a city that was approximately one-quarter African American, one-quarter white, and one-half Latino. But, as I argued in chapter 1, Detroit's place character and its influence on racial socialization is about more than simple racial demographics. The city has had African American mayors, police chiefs, school superintendents, and other civic leaders since before the children in this study were born. The public school system also has included three African-centered schools since before these children were born, and in June 2006 the school board approved the planning of a broader "African-centered education curriculum program." Such educational programs are designed to encourage African American student achievement through the creation of relevant and supportive learning environments and a teaching philosophy focused on African core cultural values (Detroit Public Schools 2006). Many mothers say these are just a few of the aspects of everyday life in Detroit that implicitly teach their children to value African American culture, history, leadership, and achievements. Their children, as Natalie puts it, do not feel pressure to "act what they're not" or to devalue African American culture in favor of white culture. "Detroit is such a black city," Sharon explains, "[that] I probably don't emphasize being black so much [with my children]. They grew up in Detroit—very black." In this context, the Detroit mothers in this study entrust much of the procultural socialization of their children to the city itself.

The difference in the emphasis on procultural racial socialization messages between the parents in the Detroit and California samples is clear. For example, parents in the California pilot consistently emphasized the importance of the black church as a space for the affirmation of black cultural heritage and shared history, even if they were not religious. In contrast, mothers in the Detroit sample refer to churches as religious institutions, rather than as black cultural institutions. When the Detroit mothers do talk about race or ethnicity and the church, they emphasize that their church is racially mixed and is therefore a space in which their children have exposure to people who are *not* black. Sarah takes her children, Trisha (fourteen) and Elijah (twelve), to a predominantly black church but is excited that the church is more diverse than many of their other realms of daily interaction. "We go to church on Wednesday nights," she says. "We belong to a non-denominational church, again with the diversity—you might see anybody at our church. We have Arab Americans; we have—but it's predominantly black—but we do have, you know, white people that attend, some Hispanics, I think some Indian groups, Arab Americans, too. So I'm like, 'This is cool,' because this is like everybody is here." Gina, mother of twins Terri and Tyrone (thirteen), also mentions race and church, stressing that church is not about race or racial heritage but about religion. She says, "We done went to a white church before, so it's not a matter of where you go, it's just a matter of what you know." The only Detroit mother interviewed who remarked on the positive cultural aspect of black churches was Audrey, mother of Toussaint (eleven), but she was referring to her own upbringing in Detroit at a time when it was a whiter city. She does not, however, take her own children today, saying, "I'm not participating in those churches now. We've taken our spirituality to a different—in a different direction." For mothers in Detroit, then, church is very important as a religious and social institution but is not as significant as a specifically black institution, as it was for the parents in the California pilots. I posit this is because Detroit's place character makes the need for such institutions less salient in the minds of these mothers, as opposed to the California families, who were living in cities with very different place characters.

Families in the California pilots also emphasized the importance of extended family in racial socialization, saying, specifically, that they relied on extended family to provide a positive black environment. For example, one California mother said she and her husband make a point of taking their children to visit her husband's family in Mississippi every summer so that her children can "be around lots of black folks and just kind of absorb it all." The Detroit families also discuss the importance of extended family; fully two-thirds of the mothers interviewed say that they picked their current residential neighborhood based on its proximity to their parents or their in-laws. The difference is that the Detroit mothers do not articulate this focus on extended family as being part of their racial socialization. Extended families do clearly play a role in the comprehensive racial learning of the children in this study, both explicitly and implicitly (Winkler 2011). Algea Harrison and colleagues assert that the importance of African heritage is communicated to children through the "persistence of some African cultural patterns among contemporary African American families for both rural and urban areas," such as an emphasis on kinship and interdependence (1990, 354). Still, the Detroit mothers do not point to extended family as a specific "black space" in the way the California parents do, again indicating that Detroit's place character makes the need for such spaces less salient.

Margaret Caughy, Suzanne Randolph, and Patrica O'Campo studied the level of "Africentricity" in African American homes by observing the presence of certain toys, artwork, figurines, books, music, African American–oriented educational toys, pictures of family members, subscriptions to African American periodicals, and African fabric or clothing (2002, 40–41). Their findings "indicate that a home rich in African American culture . . . is associated with greater factual knowledge and better problem-solving skills among African American preschoolers even after adjusting for the confounding effects of family income and parent involvement" (Caughy et al. 2002, 50). Although their findings relate to children younger than those in this study, their point that African American artwork, toys, books, and other items serve as "racial socialization features of the home environment" (Caughy et al. 2002, 37) applies to all age levels. The parents in my California pilot studies also talked about surrounding their children with positive representations of blackness through black books, dolls, and artwork. The families in Detroit may very well surround their children with these same representations, but only two mothers mentioned such things as a part of the racial socialization of their children. Audrey says that she and her husband, Dumay, a medical doctor, make a point to "keep pictures of black people up on the walls." She continues, gesturing to her kitchen wall, "You'll see the JAMAs up here, Journal of the American Medical Association. Whenever there's a black person on the cover, Dumay takes it, you know, and puts it up there. We're going to do something with those one day. They don't always have black people on that cover, but when they do, we make a point of putting it up." The only other mother who mentions surrounding her children with black books and images was Gina, who shares that she started a "youth black book club" for her children because the books they were assigned in school had "nothing dealing with them. So on top of what they have to read in school, they have to read a book for me, too, that's dealing with black history."

Other than Audrey and Gina, however, none of the Detroit mothers mentioned the importance of giving their children black books, artwork, or dolls. In fact, the only mother who mentioned dolls at all, Bridget, says, "I think about how they have all the different color dolls now. You can buy a white doll or a black doll. What difference do it make? It's a doll. You play with them. They both do the same thing. You know, so I don't get into that separation anymore. I don't look at—you know, when I buy a toy, I just pick one up and buy it." Like most of the children in this study, Bridget's daughters, Rebecca (eleven) and Margaret (nine), attend a virtually all-black school, live in a zip code that is 98.7 percent black, and attend a predominantly black church. Bridget herself grew up in Detroit after the white flight of the 1960s and 1970s. Although it is possible that Bridget would not find African American–themed toys particularly important regardless of where she lived, I argue that the overall lack of explicit focus on such toys amongst the Detroit mothers in this study rests in the fact that Detroit provides an environment in which black beauty, intelligence, culture, and presence in general is normative and does not need to be taught through toys. The differences in the focus between the Detroit and San Francisco Bay Area parents does not mean mothers in Detroit do not purchase or use African American toys, books, and artwork. In fact, I saw evidence to the contrary during interviews in people's homes. Rather, I argue it means these items, and procultural messages in general, do not stick out in many of the mothers' minds as a salient part of their racial socialization practices because black cultural heritage is implicitly understood and valued in Detroit. I do not want to oversimplify here—clearly the dominant narrative of colorblindness, which inherently normalizes whiteness, is found in Detroit, as discussed in chapter 2. It certainly permeates national media and state-mandated curricula (A. Johnson 2006; J. Katz 2003), and most of the mothers in Detroit say they feel the need to counter these messages through responsive racial socialization, as I will explain in the next chapter. However, in terms of procultural racial socialization, it appears the Detroit mothers do not feel compelled to engage in this as directly with their children, not because they do not think it is important, but because place takes care of many of these messages, essentially acting as their partner in racial socialization. However, as we will see in the next section, the mothers are not in agreement about whether place is their friend or foe in this process.

Safe Haven or "False Shield"? Place as Freeing or Limiting (or Both)

Place influences what the mothers tell their children about race and racism in another way as well. Whether a mother sees Detroit's place character as a positive or negative influence on her children shapes her racial socialization messages. Specifically, although the mothers agree Detroit provides their children with an environment in which black culture is normalized, some mothers see this as a gift—a racial safe space or utopia—while other mothers see it as a cruel joke being played on their children which will, as Sharon puts it, "cripple" them when and if they decide to leave Detroit. Adding another layer of place influence, the split in mothers' views on this topic tends to break down along mothers' own place background—whether or not she herself grew up in Detroit. Of the nineteen mothers in this sample, fifteen grew up in Detroit and four did not. A majority of the mothers who were themselves raised in Detroit describe Detroit as a positive element of the racial socialization of their children. For these mothers, place serves as a shield, a sort of racial safe space, and they see it as a gift to their children. In contrast, the handful of mothers who grew up outside of Detroit describe Detroit as more negative in terms of racial socialization because they see it as homogenous and isolating. This is not a perfect dichotomy; mothers from each group mention both positives and negatives of the racialized space of Detroit. In the end, however, in terms of the racial socialization of their children, having grown up in Detroit or elsewhere seems to be correlated to their thinking on the topic. And these differences exist even though the two groups have similar demographic profiles in terms of income, education, and employment.

Place as Protective

Annette is the mother of thirteen-year-old Matthew and an eighteen-year-old daughter. When asked how she came to live in Detroit, she responds, "I was born and raised in Detroit . . . and continue to stay rooted here in Detroit, even though all of our friends have moved out to the suburbs." Annette says that, unlike the environment her friends have found in the suburbs, Detroit allows her children to blossom in a space where they will be comfortable and not constantly challenged based on race.

> For my kids, I want them to be a part of Detroit. And it's not that we live outside our home, either. The good thing is that they are not [*pause*] part of a small part of the minority [like they would be] outside of Detroit. They are within the majority within the city limits. And if we need that exposure, we can go get it. And then they can come back. It's not to say that they would be uncomfortable there [in the suburbs]. I just, I just prefer—I just think that to me Detroit is home. It always has been. I'm comfortable here. I don't feel like I got to fit in, got to have the right kind of this and the right kind of that. I don't—I don't know. I go by my friends' [homes in the suburbs] and enjoy it, but they always have their issues too.

Observe how, in the middle of this quotation, Annette switches from using the pronoun "they"—referring to her children—to the pronoun "I." She moves seamlessly between her own experiences growing up in Detroit and the experience she wants to provide for her children. Her firsthand understanding of growing up in Detroit and being "the majority within the city limits," as well as going outside of the city and feeling as if she has to work to fit in, has shaped how she sees place in relationship to the racial socialization of her children. Even though Annette would prefer to "live outside of [her] home, [in] a neighborhood that if we want to take walks at night, we can walk and we'll feel comfortable," she says she and her family do not particularly do so. Nevertheless, she says, her children feel "a part of Detroit." It seems that being a part of Detroit means, at least partially, to live in a city in which they are part of the racial majority and therefore are "comfortable" and "fit in." Annette believes Detroit will free her children from the burden of living life from a defensive standpoint, feeling they have to explain themselves or try to fit in. At the same time, she states, "I think real life is diversity," and her children may need exposure, either to people of other races or to the experience of being in the minority. Still, she thinks it is best to get that exposure through travel rather than moving to the suburbs. Many of her friends have chosen to live in the suburbs, she says, because of concerns about safety and schools. Although she agrees "the school systems aren't good," she believes it is possible to have access to both safe neighborhoods and decent schools within Detroit. "I support the public school system," she says. "I believe in schools of choice. I've driven my kids to the schools that I wanted them placed in." While moving to the suburbs may alleviate worries about safety or schools, her friends still "have their issues" there, too, such as their child being "the only African American child in the classroom" or "with maybe two African Americans in the class." She points out that her son Matthew (thirteen) affirmed this for her when he told his friend, who had recently moved to the suburbs and been put in the overwhelmingly white school there, "You better tell your momma to get you up out of there." When Annette asked him why he said this, he responded, "Wouldn't you be uncomfortable?" For all of these reasons, Annette sees Detroit as a protective space in which to raise her children.

Audrey also thinks living in Detroit is positive for her children's comprehensive racial learning. This is one reason why she and her husband, Dumay, have chosen Detroit (and, in the near future, the Caribbean) as their home. When asked if her choice about where to live has anything to do with how she wants to raise her children, Audrey responds:

> Mm hmm. That's one of the reasons why I haven't moved out. Because, you know, essentially, where we're going in [the Caribbean] is Blacktown. And Detroit is Blacktown, too. . . . I still [work] here, and I still, you know, I don't go out to Oakland County. I get treated differently in Oakland County. I don't want to go out there. But you know, I'm not running after the ducats [money], so thank God. Somebody else [Dumay] is working in the house. I guess if I *had* to [work in Oakland County] I would, but I, I can make that choice to not do that. So . . . yes. I want to be here, in Detroit, for my children.

Like Annette, Audrey slips between discussing the significance of place for her children and for herself. She begins and ends by saying that she has stayed in Detroit for her children because she wants to raise them in "Blacktown" and that when she and her husband do move their children away from Detroit, it will be to another "Blacktown." In between, she shifts to talking about her own experiences with wanting to stay in Detroit, despite being able to make more money in the suburbs, because she is not treated well in the suburbs and is more comfortable and fulfilled working in Detroit. Notice that Audrey, too, draws on her own experiences growing up in and living in Detroit to illustrate what she sees as the protective role of place in her children's comprehensive racial learning.

Another example comes from Desarae, who is the mother of twins Cara and Corey (thirteen). Desarae was born and raised in Detroit but was sent to live with family members in the South when she was sixteen years old.

> I left [Detroit] for about a year and a half. So I'd say between the ages maybe sixteen and a half to eighteen, I left. . . . That's when I realized what racism was, when I was a teenager, because living here in Detroit, I didn't know what it was. But when I went south, you know, I found out. And I remember it was hard for me because here I was, I'm going on seventeen, and I was being put in a certain category and I couldn't understand why. You know, I'm an A student just like Becky over here, but it's like, "But you can't do what Becky do." I'm like, "What you mean I can't do what Becky do?" So that's when I found what racism was. About seventeen. And I didn't like it because, to me, I had lived in Detroit. So I chose to come back to Detroit.

For Desarae, there is a clear connection between place and racism, so much so that she could not tolerate the racism in the South precisely *because* she had lived in Detroit. That short time outside Detroit was enough to show her that her hometown provided a unique shield from racism, and she does not want her children to be outside of that space. Perhaps having this experience as an adolescent—at school in the form of lowered expectations, racist presumptions about her capabilities, and academic exclusion—is another reason why Desarae connects it to the desire to protect her now-adolescent children from similar exposure. Recently, Desarae has considered relocating to a state with a warmer climate. "I don't know," she says. "I was thinking about maybe moving to Arizona or Florida. And somebody says, 'Well, you know they're very racist in Florida, especially Miami.'" So Desarae has decided to stay in Detroit because of the safe space from racism she believes it offers.

Other mothers who grew up in Detroit had analogous experiences and engage in similar reasoning, seeing racism as something that happens outside of Detroit. Describing how she came to live in Detroit, Gwen, mother of Tiara (twelve), says, "I was born and raised here in Detroit, Michigan. And I've been here for forty-six years. . . . I love it. I wouldn't go no place else. You know, I've traveled, my younger years, with my mother and stuff like that. But I would prefer to live in Detroit, Michigan, for the rest of my life." When asked about what she teaches her daughter about racism, she responds, "I haven't encountered the racism. I haven't really encountered that. . . . Now maybe if I go, if I take a trip to Georgia or something, you know, down South or something like that, where they say it's still going on, but here, up here, I don't think it's like that because I don't see it." Notice that Gwen identifies racism as "still going on" down South but not in Detroit. One might think that Gwen's answer was influenced by what she thought a white northerner might want to hear. However,

Gwen does not shy away from talking about racialized issues in the interview, saying that she teaches her daughter Tiara to be proud to be black and that Tiara "knows the difference between black and white" and would be able to handle any racism that comes her way because "she's very mature, so she knows." In fact, she says Tiara and her cousin critique systemic racism in the curriculum at their school, telling their mothers, "They don't even talk about black history; we don't even learn it!" So, while the cross-racial context of the interview may well have shaped Gwen's responses, I want to argue that place—Detroit itself—also played a role. The language Gwen uses—"I don't see it"—is similar to that we heard from Corey (thirteen) in chapter 3 when he said he did not think white people littered or sold drugs because, he said, "This far I've never seen it." There I made the argument that, due to the influence of place, it is only logical that most of the behaviors of any kind—positive, negative, or neutral—Corey has observed would have been performed by African Americans, not whites, Asians, Native Americans, or Latinos. Making a similar point here, I argue it is possible that Gwen's not seeing racism in Detroit has to do with place. As thirteen-year-old Corey puts it, "There is not a lot of racism in Detroit" because "it's not that many Caucasians in Detroit." Of course, a pure numeric majority alone does not protect a group from racism, as can be seen, for example, in South Africa under apartheid or New Orleans circa Hurricane Katrina (Brunsma et al. 2007; Durrheim et al. 2011; Marable and Clarke 2008; Wailoo et al. 2010). As I have argued, however, it is not only the predominantly black population or, more specifically, the relatively small proportion of whites, but also the civic, social, and cultural control of many institutions in Detroit by African Americans that leads to this unique place character.

Anita, mother of twelve-year-old Shani, also sees racism as something that happens outside of Detroit. She says about growing up in Detroit, "I don't remember too many white people around us. . . . Seriously, I didn't really want to consider [racism] until when I got to Eastern [Michigan University]. . . . And it was a big shock." Upon entering the university, which is about twenty-five miles from downtown Detroit and, in the late 1980s when Anita attended, had an undergraduate student body that was approximately 85 percent white and 7 percent black (Eastern Michigan University 2001, 26), Anita says she was shocked to experience racism. At first she was angered, both by the way she was treated and by the inequities she saw between the ways she and her white peers had been prepared for college. "They were taught more and that did make me mad. But, oh well, I got over it." Anita returned to Detroit to raise her children, she says, "Because this is someplace I know, I'm familiar with."

Julie did not move to Detroit out of familiarity or comfort—she is one of the four mothers in this study who did not grow up in Detroit—but she makes a parallel point, albeit from a different perspective. Julie, mother of Josh (ten), grew up in a smaller city in southeastern Michigan, and, while that city's population

was about a third African American, Julie's neighborhood, church, and schooling experiences were almost exclusively white until she reached high school.
Before she married Josh's stepfather and moved to Detroit, Julie was raising
Josh in that same community, where Josh's father, who is white, still lives. When
asked whether or not Josh had encountered racism at this point in his life, Julie
first talked about Josh's white aunt, whom she describes as "mentally ill," being
"really unruly, mean, nasty. . . . She would say, 'Well, you're black; you're not like
us.'" I then asked if Josh had experienced any racism since moving to Detroit, to
which Julie responded by describing teasing from Josh's black peers in Detroit—
being called "white," "Chinese," or "snowflake"—because of his light skin tone.
Following up one final time, I asked Julie if Josh had "experienced racism from
white people since [he has] been here [living in Detroit]," to which Julie replied,
"Uh uh. No. What white people?" Julie's rhetorical question points to the role of
place in Josh's comprehensive racial learning, calling attention to the way
Detroit essentially keeps children from frequent encounters with whites. Unlike
the other mothers who did not grow up in Detroit, though, Julie does not worry
about Detroit being a "false shield" from racism. This may be because her son
spends time with his white father, as well as his white paternal and black maternal grandparents, in the city where Julie raised Josh for the first several years of
his life. This city, which is approximately two-thirds white, has provided and
continues to provide Josh with plenty of exposure to white-dominated settings.
In fact, growing up in this same city, Julie thinks she was overly exposed to such
settings. Regarding the mistakes she thinks her parents made in her own
upbringing, she says, "I think that [racial] isolation wasn't good . . . that they
did with us. Not intentionally. I don't think [my mother] even thought about it.
I know she didn't think about it because I've talked to her about this. But
isolating us from other black kids. That she'd have at least raised us in a black
neighborhood if we were going to go to all-white other things. Or made sure we
went to the public black school in elementary from the get, if we were going
to be in the white neighborhood. But there needed to be more balance. And
there wasn't."

This led Julie to feel uncomfortable in predominantly black settings. After
going to private school through junior high, Julie then attended a public high
school. She says:

> When I got to public school, I, well, I always, um, I felt the way white
> people do that aren't from a black area or interracial area when they go
> into a all-black environment and they feel uncomfortable. You start to
> sweat a little bit. Oh my gosh. I stick out. I know I stick out. I look differ-
> ent. I talk different. I don't want to stick out, and I, so I feel that way. I
> would feel weird going to Sweetwater [Tavern], downtown [Detroit], or
> whatever that bar is, just because I don't—I don't have the right shoes.

I don't have the right jacket.... Right now, as an adult, I don't have the
right gear.... [And in high school] it was the same. Um, in high school,
it was, "You're not black enough." And so they—I got ixnayed. That was it.

Interestingly, Julie's language about feeling pressure to fit in and have the
"right" things parallels Annette's language, only Julie feels that pressure in predominantly black settings in Detroit, while Annette feels that way in the white
suburbs. Julie attributes this to the racialized spaces in which she was raised
and thinks moving her son to Detroit will help to shield him from facing these
problems. "I think it's important for him to learn how to socialize with his
people, with black people," she declares. "I'm so glad that he has the opportunity because I felt like I was at a disadvantage of not being around other
black kids. The only black kids I was around was my sister and my brother....
And I wanted [Josh] to be able to have a more of a piece of blackness than
I thought I could give him by myself."

Protected but Confined? Racism and Mobility

This notion of Detroit as a protective space raises an important issue: although
the mothers—especially those who grew up in Detroit, like Annette, Audrey,
Desarae, Gwen, and Anita—tend to see place as protective in terms of their
children's comprehensive racial learning, the feeling of being confined to
Detroit by the racism beyond its borders likely communicates a powerful message to their children. Indeed, as Doreen Massey argues, "mobility, and control
over mobility, both reflects and reinforces power" (1994, 150). This creates what
Massey calls a "power geometry" in which "different social groups have distinct
relationships to this anyway differentiated mobility: some people are more in
charge of it than others; some initiate flows and movement, others don't; some
are more on the receiving-end of it than others; some are effectively imprisoned
by it" (1994, 149). While they may not feel quite imprisoned, in listening to their
mother weigh their options about moving to a warmer climate, Desarae's
children, Cara and Corey, have no doubt received the message that racism puts
limits on their options and mobility. This only adds to those children's
own experiences with the racialization of space and the literal and figurative
policing of the boundaries between those spaces.

Pressures to stay in Detroit can also come from within. Sharon, mother of
Nina (thirteen), has friends who moved out to the suburbs and were told, "Oh,
you're a sell-out. You're leaving Detroit. You're betraying your race." This pressure, too, is not lost on children, who do not want to be seen as "sell-outs."
Of course, not only fears and attitudes, but persisting structural barriers limit the
freedom of mobility for African Americans in Detroit. Thomas Sugrue provides
evidence that, even in the contemporary period, "real estate steering and discrimination against blacks have persisted, as audits of brokers' racial practices

have demonstrated" (1996, 269; see also Squires and Kubrin 2006). All of this impacts children's comprehensive racial learning. Lionel Scott argues that racism can affect children not only when they experience it "directly," but also "vicariously, collectively, institutionally, and transgenerationally" (2003, 524). Therefore, the indirect consequences of racism—such as feeling essentially confined to one place—can have as much of an impact on children as direct confrontations with racism, like those from which Annette, Audrey, Desarae, and others are trying to protect their children by living in Detroit.

One mother and life-long Detroiter, Cora, has recently moved her daughters, Kaiya (eleven) and Rayna (ten), to a racially mixed neighborhood and says she will probably eventually move to "a predominantly all-white neighborhood . . . further out, over Eight Mile"[1]—outside of the city of Detroit—because she and her husband want more "elbow room." She does not want her children to feel that place restricts their mobility, but the idea of moving to a predominantly white area clearly causes anxiety for her children. "They just ask the question, you know, like, 'Mom, why do we got to move out there with all those white people? I mean, why can't we move where there's black people?' Like I told them, and my answer to that would basically be like, we're not moving where there's white people; we're moving where there are people. You know. And they're not on our elbows. We can flush our toilet and our neighbors don't hear [*laughs*]. I don't want them to feel like we're moving anywhere because of races. . . . Because they *did* ask." She adds, "I'm not doing this just to stress out my kids. I'm doing this because I like the elbow room. I like the land that you get, you know. And I don't care if my neighbors are green. I mean, they could be blue. I don't care." Here Cora adopts colorblind language to suggest her neighbors' race is insignificant to her. However, the idea of moving to a predominantly white area is clearly concerning her children—who, perhaps not coincidentally, were among the handful of children who were very guarded in their interviews with me. In fact, Cora and her husband recently moved their girls "from an all-black neighborhood—a community, not just our neighborhood, but community, because the school they went to basically was all black"—to their current neighborhood and school, both of which are about 85 percent black. This change caused racialized anxiety for her children, who were not used to being in neighborhoods and schools with this many white people—about 15 percent white. Cora relates, "They asked when we moved here, you know, 'Mom, did you all notice that our neighbors were white?' Hello! And Kaiya came to me and told me one time, she said, 'Momma, I don't know how I'm going to get along with this. Do you know that all of our—everybody in this neighborhood is white? The only ones black over here is Charlene,' which is my husband's cousin that lives down the street. I told her, 'No, it's not. You just haven't seen everybody over here.'"

Even though Cora and her family still live within the city of Detroit and in a neighborhood that is predominantly African American, the change in racial demographics—having some white neighbors at all—had a huge impact on her children, to the point Kaiya (eleven) perceived the neighborhood as all white and was not sure "how [she was] going to get along with this." Cora is aware that exposing her children to racism and racially based anxiety is one price to pay for mobility but, nevertheless, has plans to one day move her family "out over Eight Mile" to the predominantly white suburbs. Although this does not worry her, it evidently has her children concerned. Even if Cora and her husband are not allowing race to limit their mobility, place does impact their daughters' understandings of mobility. In this way, structural racism permeates the everyday lives of children in Detroit, even when place is protective in the sense of shielding them from individual encounters with racism.

Place as a "False Shield"

In contrast to many of the Detroit-born mothers who see place as protective, the mothers who did not grow up in Detroit—Sharon, Natalie, Lena, and Julie—are more likely to see place as detrimental to their children's comprehensive racial learning. In fact, Sharon describes it as crippling. Sharon grew up in Southern California but ended up in Detroit after marrying a Detroit native. "We were supposed to move [away]," she says with a laugh, pointing out that she has now lived in Detroit for fifteen years. Her oldest child, Nina—who was also interviewed for this study—is thirteen, and Sharon also has a ten-year-old son. When asked if she talks to her children about their racial identity, Sharon responds, "I probably don't emphasize being black so much. They grew up in Detroit: very black. I didn't grow up like that. I grew up in a multicultural environment. And so, to me, Detroit is very black and white. But I grew up with *everybody* [in Southern California]. So it's Hispanics and just every nationality. And I told [my children], they're really crippled because they're not experiencing a good, you know, diverse cultural experience. They're really crippled because of that."

In her own interview, Sharon's daughter Nina seems to confirm Sharon's point, insisting her mother never talks about anything "special or important about being African American." It's not necessary to talk to her children about their racial identity, Sharon says, because place does that for her. In fact, she thinks place may overdo it. That Detroit's demographics and place culture are "very black" and that the broader racial politics in metro Detroit are "very black and white" are points Sharon finds devastating to her children's comprehensive racial learning. She continues, "I'm telling them they're crippled because they're in this black world. And they have so many—you know, *everybody's* black. And I'm like, you know, that's not normal. You know, you're in this little spot, but that's not how it is. You go to some other places, and that's not how it is. You are not a majority, you are a minority. You know, so, I had to get them to understand that. But because, I think, I travel a lot with them and expose them to different experiences that they can kind of see that, yeah, this is how it is in Detroit. But that experience is just a Detroit experience."

Sharon's insistence that her children not see Detroit as normal is striking. She emphasizes that place—specifically, being in a "black world"—metaphorically "cripples" her children and that it is important for them to know they are "not a majority." Remember that Annette also talks about switching from being a "minority" in US society to being a "majority" in Detroit, but where Annette considers this empowering, Sharon sees it as a misrepresentation of reality and relies on travel to prove her point. As we saw in chapter 3, many mothers use travel to expand their children's horizons, particularly in terms of their ideas about race, but Sharon's specific motivation is to show her children that being "a majority" in a "black world" is "just a Detroit experience" and "not normal." She goes on to admit that she can see how other parents may see Detroit's place character as protective, saying:

> It can be [a shield from racism], but it's such a false shield because it doesn't prepare them for life. You know. For a lot of kids, when they went to school, and they went to an all-black school, they had all-black teachers, they had all-black administrators all their life; they're not prepared because you're not going to work with all blacks all your life. That's not—you know, that's very rare that all your life that's all you're ever going to work with. But then you only have met that one culture, so then when you meet somebody and they're different, you're looking at them like, "Whaaa? Uhhh! What's that? That's strange!"

Of course, residential segregation is common across the United States, and most white American children live in predominantly white areas and attend predominantly white schools (Charles 2003; A. Lewis 2003; Lipsitz 2011). However, because of structural and cultural racism, many of those white children may well work and function in similarly homogenous—or at least white-dominated—environments as adults. Sharon is clear, however, that this is much less likely for black children. For Sharon, this means Detroit is less like a racial safe haven and more like a dangerous trick that will leave her children vulnerable. Once again, she emphasizes that she thinks the Detroit experience is not normal and that this will hurt her children in the long run.

Natalie, mother of Kenny (thirteen), agrees. She grew up in a small city about an hour away from Detroit, with a population approximately half African American and half white. She moved to a suburb of Detroit for work, eventually moving to Detroit proper after meeting her husband, himself a Detroit native. She points back to place and her own experiences when discussing how she thinks growing up in Detroit may disadvantage her children. "In the city of Detroit," Natalie remarks, "it seems like a lot of the schools are segregated. I mean, like there's a lot of all-black schools, just from the schools that my kids attend. And I think it's important for different nationalities to be at all schools. Because . . . I went through a school system in [my hometown] where it was black and white, and I think that's important. I think that prepares kids for the real world." While place can provide some protection from racism, Natalie believes, it can also open children up to future problems. She even suggests Detroit does not represent "the real world," much as Sharon suggested Detroit was "not normal." In one sense, these mothers are correct that Detroit is unique in terms of its racial demographics and place character; in fact, even the mothers who are from Detroit and see it as positive for their children agree with this. And, certainly, wanting their children to learn to survive and prosper in the face of a racist society is central to racial socialization in African American families. In another sense, however, these comments could be read as denigrating or "othering" black spaces by referring to them as "not normal" or not "the real world" (Said 1978). These mothers do not necessarily suggest, however, that white-controlled spaces should be considered "normal" or "real," but rather that the United States is multiracial and that multiracial settings are what they consider "normal" and "real world" in this context. But much as Jacqueline Nassy Brown argues in her examination of race in Liverpool, England, that "a national politic of place . . . shapes race in that city" (2005, 8), it is indeed the political, social, and economic structures of the United States that shape racial formation in Detroit. In that sense, then, Detroit is a very real-world manifestation of racial realities in the United States. As Toni Morrison has argued, the universal (or "normal") is found in the particular (LeClair 1994, 124).

Ultimately, of course, it is up to the children to interpret their mothers' messages. Sharon's daughter, Nina (thirteen), who has been told she is "crippled because [she is] in this black world" and that it is "not normal" to live where "*everybody's* black," shows ambivalence in her racial attitudes. On the one hand, she talks about "help[ing] out the black community," resisting racism from white classmates, and insisting on wearing her hair natural even though her friends pressure her to have it straightened. ("I do not like straight hair. I hate it. My hair is naturally curly. Why can't I wear it the way I want to wear it?") On the other hand, she seems to take pride in "hav[ing] white in [her]" and being told she "can blend in with white people." Nina says the most attractive person she can think of is a member of an African American R&B group because "he has light skin." In response to a question about what, of everything she's learned about being black, is most important, she responds, "How to act. How, um, like that you don't have to, like—most people take black people as out-of-control people . . . loud, obnoxious." This response seems to reflect Evelyn Higginbotham's concept of a "politics of respectability," which equates "public behavior with individual self-respect and the advancement of African Americans as a group" (1993, 14). This, Higginbotham argues, was an ideology on which middle-class and elite black women historically drew because "they felt certain 'respectable' behavior in public would earn their people a measure of esteem from white America" (1993, 14). Similarly, in her statement here, Nina seems to suggest that, out of everything it means to be black, the most important is to disprove whites' racist stereotypes. Of her own friends, Nina says, "Here [in Detroit], I have mostly African American friends. But in Atlanta, they're Asian, some Caucasian, and then two black, maybe, because it's not like—it's a lot of black children in the community, but I usually don't talk to them." Although she does not explain why she does not talk to any of the black children in her grandmother's Atlanta neighborhood, even though there are "a lot," her indication that "how to act" is the most important thing to remember about being black may provide some insight. It seems very possible, then, that Sharon's message to her children that "they're crippled because they're in this black world" may be tied to a developing idea about blackness—or at least "the demeanor of ordinary African Americans" as undesirable or inferior, even if this is not Sharon's thinking or intent (White and White 1998, 222).

For Sharon, racial attitudes in Detroit are another part of her concern about raising her children there. She says that African Americans in Detroit "feel [racial] oppression, you know, in everything they do. They feel that their job, their this, their that, the schools, everything, it boils down to race. . . . I've never seen it anyplace else." She has lived in California, Atlanta, and other parts of Michigan but upholds that this racial outlook is, in her experience, unique to Detroit. Using Nina's father as an example, Sharon explains:

> What I see, like with Nina's father, is, "Oh, you know, that person looked at me wrong because I'm black." No. He may have looked at you wrong because he just didn't like you. He could look at everybody like that. You just don't know. And that's my perception, is that you don't just automatically assume, "Oh, he didn't open the door, you know, for me. But he opened it for all them." So? You know, why are you assuming that? I don't assume that because that's black. Now if they come to me and say something, then that's different. But, I see a lot of that in Detroit. Like, and I never experienced that in California. But certain people, everything that happens to them is—you know, so many things that happen to them: "I didn't get that job because I was black." "I didn't—" You know? [*Whining,*] "This happened to me. That clerk didn't help me. She walked away. She went over to help those white people." And I don't see in those same eyes. I'll say, "Oh, she must didn't see me," but I'm not going to assume it's because I'm black that I'm being ignored.

What Sharon characterizes as a tendency on the part of black Detroiters to assume racism is difficult to verify and could be attributable to any number of things. Sharon could have shaped her answer toward a colorblind script she might assume a white person would want to hear. (However, as I will discuss

shortly, her daughter Nina affirms that Sharon sends her these kinds of messages, although Nina herself is not sure she always agrees.) Or Sharon could
actually be seeing more open acknowledgment of racism in Detroit because
black Detroiters are, in fact, bearing the brunt of an incredible load of racism—
not necessarily different than that borne by other African Americans, but
distilled by place. That Sharon sees more of this response in Detroit could also
have to do with the empowerment Detroit's place character provides black
people there to feel comfortable openly bucking the national master narrative
of colorblindness. Whatever the reason, Sharon's perceptions of place and
localized attitudes about race are shaping how she socializes her daughter.

In light of Sharon's comments that she and Nina's father have decidedly different mindsets regarding racial issues, it is likely that Nina must negotiate two
different sets of parental racial socialization messages. When asked about this,
however, Sharon maintains that she has raised the children and they are likely
to reflect her own thinking on the topic. "[Nina] gets it from me," Sharon states.
"She's around me the most; hasn't been around as much with her father. So
they—I raised them. And they're mostly with me. So, mostly, probably, from me.
And she doesn't—I don't hear her saying those types of things. That, 'Oh, somebody said that's because of [race].'" In her interview, Nina does state that her
"parents are separated" and she lives with her mother, and many of her views do
match those of her mother. For example, she says she "wouldn't want to raise
[her] kids [in Detroit]" because "it's not diverse." On the other hand, Nina does
not shy away from noticing, naming, and discussing racism. For example, she
talks about experiencing racism at school from one of her only white classmates
and says that, while black teachers believed the black students when they
reported the incidents, "we had white teachers at the time too, and they were
like, 'Well, we don't think so.'" In this example, the racism from the classmate
was explicit—the kind of racism Beverly Tatum (2003) would call "active" and
"conscious"—and seemingly the only kind Nina's mother, Sharon, says she is
willing to acknowledge when she says, "Now if they come to me and say something, then that's different." But the racism from the white teachers, who
doubted their black students' claims, is potentially ambiguous, the type to
which Sharon referred when she said, "I'm not going to assume it's because I'm
black." The difference in approaches between Sharon and Nina reflects what
numerous studies have shown, that children's racial beliefs are not significantly
or reliably related to those of their parents (Hirschfield 2008; P. Katz 2003;
Patterson and Bigler 2006), and supports the theory behind comprehensive
racial learning, that the primary caregiver is just one of many influences on
how children develop their ideas about race, and not always the most influential one.

Lena, mother of Tanika (thirteen) and Lanáe (ten), also did not grow up in
Detroit. She spent most of her childhood in Colorado, but also in Texas, Hawaii,

Oklahoma, and the Philippines. She describes life growing up with her mother, whom she says was "a hippie" and "very Afrocentric," as full of "a lot of different kinds of people—white, black, African, what have you." When Lena was young, her mother "always tried to let [her children] know [about] African American history." Lena's father lived in another state, and, "being an educator," she says, "he always showed us how to—any situation that we came across—how to evaluate the situation." Lena says that both of her parents taught her to think critically about race and racism. She gives an example from one summer when she worked at a daycare center and a white child "always rubbed my skin . . . [trying to] kind of rub it off, and then finally she asked me why I was that brown." Lena continues, "I think, had my parents not educated me on [race and racism], then I guess I could have had a harsher response. But I understood that she just wanted to know and she didn't understand. So, they must have taught me well. I guess I should tell them that every now and then [laughs]." She adds, "I think they were great for me in that regard. I think I was always pretty proud, more or less, to be black."

As an adult, Lena joined the military and also "married a military man." They lived on the East Coast before moving to her husband's hometown of Detroit when their daughters were very young. Lena describes herself as "a military brat" and says that, because of this, she can live anywhere. However, she finds Detroit to be "a very strange city in regards to race." Having spent most of her childhood in areas where African Americans comprised a small minority of the population, Lena appreciates the sense of community Detroit provides for her children. However, she worries that "everything is so separate" racially and wishes that "there was more of a mix." She expresses concern that her daughters might pick up what she sees as Detroit's "close-minded" approach to race, in which "people tend to stay to themselves and look at other things as being foreign." Although Lena is raising her daughters in a different context than that in which she was raised, she feels that they still need the same racial socialization lessons that her parents taught her as a child: to know that racism exists and "to be cautious," but also to "know how to coexist" and "be willing to communicate with people from different backgrounds." Lena herself grew up in predominantly white, Latino, and Asian areas, so, she says, "I appreciate the fact that [my children] are around blacks more than I was because I feel that that might help in their interaction with other black folks. However," she continues:

> I wish it was more integrated because living in Detroit, being an outsider and coming in, to me, Detroit tends to be . . . a little set in their ways. And a lot of people think that everything in the world is the same as it is here in Detroit. And I think it is important for [my children] to know that you're going to have to—I mean, if you plan to or hope to succeed—then you're going to have to expand your horizons beyond Detroit, which

means you need to learn how to speak correctly. And so much of the speech pattern within the inner city is not correct, but because it's not emphasized because that's the way everybody speaks, then it's not something that anybody really addresses. So when you go out, later on in life, or when you go to write a paper, and you're so used to saying "they" instead of "their," you're going to write "they" instead of "their" almost subconsciously. So. . . . [In some ways] it's a hindrance against them.

Lena situates herself as an outsider vis-à-vis Detroit, and her view from that standpoint is much like Sharon's: Detroit is a place very different from anywhere she has lived previously, and it is critical to her children's racial socialization that they know that. Also, like Sharon's, Lena's concerns are based in preparing her children to function and succeed upon leaving Detroit (and it seems to be assumed that they will leave Detroit). While she does say she would prefer a more integrated environment for humanistic and interpersonal reasons—pointing out that "we're all essentially the same"—the concern she articulates more urgently is preparing her children to succeed in a US society that privileges and normalizes whiteness. Lena finds it unfortunate that her children should have to adjust their language based on environment. "I am pro-Ebonics," she says. "I feel it is a valid language." Indeed, "a massive body of research" exists showing that what scholars call African American Language is "a communication system with its own morphology, syntax, phonology, and rhetorical and semantic strategies" (Smitherman 2001, 28–30). However, Lena says, "Unfortunately, if you don't speak a certain way, then you are going to be perceived a certain way . . . and maybe be passed up for an interview or maybe thought of as being illiterate." As such, Lena says she is "on the fence" because, while she finds racist assumptions based on language offensive, she also does not want her children to have any strikes against them if they move beyond Detroit. In this sense, she sees place, while sometimes positive, as primarily "a hindrance against them."

Place also limits ideas about blackness, Lena believes. Raising her daughters in Detroit, she fears, circumscribes their ideas about the acceptable dreams, desires, and proclivities of "real" or "authentic" black people (Boyd 1997; E. Johnson 2003; Senna 1995). This fear, plus her own place-experience growing up, have led Lena to focus on racial socialization messages that "let [her daughters] know that it's OK to be who they are." Growing up in a smaller city in the western United States, Lena learned to love Latin and country western music. In Detroit, she finds that her racial identity is sometimes challenged by others because her musical tastes do not conform to narrow definitions of "what black folks like." She says, "[Because I'm] not from an urban environment, so often you hear people say, 'You're not black. Black folks don't listen to that kind of music. Black folks don't do this; black folks don't do that.'" Because of this, she says she emphasizes, both verbally and through her own behavior, a broader notion of what it means to be black. "I make it a point to, whatever kind of music I'm in the mood to listen to at that time, playing it regardless of where I am. . . . I'm hoping that they'll see that it's OK to be who you are regardless of where you are. You shouldn't have to hide certain things because it's not quote-unquote the black thing to do." Lena's repetition of the phrase "regardless of where you are/I am" here highlights the importance of place in this message. She does not simply want her daughters to be "OK [with] . . . who they are" in their home or when traveling, but even (and especially) when they are out and about in Detroit. She believes it is because she grew up outside of Detroit that this issue is particularly apparent to her. Moreover, her emphasis on teaching her children to unabashedly be themselves "regardless of where [they] are" highlights her understanding of place as influential in constructions of racial authenticity.

Julie, too, voices a critique of narrowly defined racial authenticity and says her position also comes from her experiences as an outsider. She worries that her son, Josh (ten), may be adopting the idea that blackness necessarily requires a particular aesthetic involving "flossing" fancy cars and clothing, which she cannot afford and of which she does not approve. "It is most definitely pushed in the black culture," she says, "to have certain shoes that are cool during, you know, whatever school at that time. . . . Just like I was saying, that I, I have problems going—I wouldn't go down and sit at the bar downtown because I wouldn't have the right shoes on to fit in with the black crowd. And I'd get the look up and down like, where'd you come from? I don't want to get that look. And I would. That's why I don't go. . . . [I teach Josh] you can wear whatever shoes you want. And what's cool is that you choose what you like, not what everybody else has. That's what I'm trying to encourage." It is clear Julie is attempting to both model and verbally encourage a broad definition of blackness, which is not characterized by popular trends, but by the ability to stand up for who one wants to be, while still embracing one's community and heritage. As we will see in chapter 6, encouraging a broad, inclusive conceptualization of blackness—particularly one that includes all skin tones—is actually among the racial socialization priorities of many of the mothers, including those from Detroit. However, what is unique about Lena's and Julie's approach is the explicit centrality of place in their articulation of this issue.

So we can see patterns emerging depending on whether or not the mothers grew up in Detroit, with those who did considering Detroit more of a positive influence in racial socialization and those who did not considering Detroit more of a negative influence. Again, though, this is not a perfect dichotomy—we heard mothers who grew up elsewhere acknowledge some of the positive influences of Detroit on their children, and a few mothers originally from Detroit also mention some of the negative influences of Detroit's racialized space on their children. For example, Sarah, who grew up in Detroit, drives her children, Trisha (fourteen) and Elijah (twelve), to charter and magnet schools each day because, she says, "I wanted to put them in a school that gave them a more, I guess, realistic view of the world. The neighborhood schools don't because it's all African American and the world is not like that. But you know what? You need to go to school with everybody; you need to go to school with people that have money, don't have money, black, white. You know, so you can get a better, a more worldview, realistic view." Although they do represent more racially diverse schools within the city of Detroit, the schools Sarah's children attend had enrollments that were 99.5 percent and 95.7 percent African American at the time of the interviews. In fact, two-thirds of the children in this study attended schools with African American enrollments equal to or higher than 95.7 percent. While Sarah made an extra effort to enroll her children in diverse schools that were not "all African American," these schools would still be considered black spaces in terms of enrollment, although it is important to note the argument that schools as institutions are in some ways "coded as white" regardless of their student demographics (A. Lewis 2003, 143).

Certainly, white children growing up in the suburbs may have even less exposure to black people than black children in Detroit do to whites. Yolanda, mother of Shaun (fifteen) and Travis (thirteen), points out that the problem of exposure goes both ways.

> If you always with the same thing, or the same people all the time, then that's all you know. That's like, when I worked out in the suburbs and stuff, I've had little white kids come up to me—you know, I wear blond hair and blue contacts—and they're looking at me like, "What the hell is going on?" I've had them touch me, like [looks confused and awestruck], you know? And then you look at the parent and say, "You need to get this baby out!" You know what I'm saying? Because when they step out there and they're on their own and they don't have a surrounding of just their people, then how are they going to know how to act?

Of course, white privilege and structural racism all but guarantee that this lack of exposure causes relatively few problems for whites in terms of life outcomes such as education, employment, health care, and housing (Rothenberg 2008; Wise 2008). For African American children, however, the story is quite the opposite (M. Brown et al. 2003; Feagin et al. 2001; Oliver and Shapiro 1995; Perry 2011). This is likely why the mothers who are not originally from Detroit and have lived most of their lives outside of Detroit are especially worried about their children learning how to function well in spaces coded as white.

Conclusion

Place, then, not only shapes children's comprehensive racial learning directly—as shown in the previous chapter—but also indirectly, by shaping mothers' racial socialization messages in several ways. First, Detroit's place character prompts many of the mothers to focus more on responsive racial socialization, leaving most of the procultural socialization up to the city itself. Second, whether a mother sees Detroit's place character as a positive or negative influence on her children shapes what she tells—or avoids telling—her children about race, racial identity, and racism. Finally, adding another dimension of place influence, having grown up in Detroit or elsewhere seems to shape the mothers' thinking on the topic. In particular, although all the mothers agree Detroit provides their children with a city environment in which black culture is normalized, mothers who themselves grew up in Detroit are more likely to see this as a gift—a racial safe space—while mothers who grew up elsewhere are more likely to see it primarily as abnormal and a detriment to their children in the long run.

5

Competing with Society

Responsive Racial Socialization

Michelle laughs freely when sharing stories about her thirteen-year-old daughter, Elina, and her ten-year-old son, Carlos, often beginning, "Now, *this* is *so* funny." Her pride in her children is clear as she shares details about their talents, interests, and personalities. "They just tickle me sometimes," she says, smiling. However, she becomes very serious when the topic turns to her deep concerns about how racism may impact her children's lives. Although she expresses uncertainty about when and how it is best to talk to Elina and Carlos about racism, she is unequivocal about her responsibility to do so. "As a parent," she says, "it's like arming them. You *have* to let them know that it's there because it's a way of protecting them. . . . You hate to teach it to them, but at the same time, if you're going to be able to keep them safe, they have to know." What Michelle describes here is what I call *responsive* racial socialization, which parents use in response to negative messages about blackness communicated to children through sources outside of the family.

African American youth receive a variety of often conflicting messages about race. This has led, as discussed in chapter 1, to something of a "family versus society" debate in the literature, in which scholars argue whether families or societal sources are most influential in children's racial learning. The framework introduced in this book—comprehensive racial learning—posits that children actively develop their ideas about race and racism by consciously and unconsciously sifting through, questioning, adopting, rejecting, internalizing, reframing, and making meaning of racialized messages from a wide variety of sources. The family, of course, is one of these sources and plays a role in children's comprehensive racial learning through racial socialization. The mothers in this study differ in their ideas about precisely when and how it is best to communicate messages about racial identity and racism to their children and what the exact content of these messages should be, but all except one report engaging in racial socialization. Two-thirds of the mothers indicate that they talk to their children about racial identity, and two-thirds say that they talk to their children about racism. Taken together, eighteen out of nineteen, or about 95 percent of the mothers, say that they talk to their children about either racial identity, racism, or both. (As we will see later in this chapter, the one mother who says she does not engage in racial socialization, Bridget, says she thinks perhaps she needs to begin doing so.) How does this compare to findings about the commonality of racial socialization among African American families in other studies? Using the data set from the 1979–1980 National Survey of Black Americans, which included 2,107 participants, Michael Thornton and colleagues found that "two out of three black parents (63.6%) indicate that they have said or acted in a manner to racially socialize children" (1990, 404). Carolyn Murray and Jelani Mandara reinforce this figure, writing, "A review of the literature indicates that about two-thirds of African American parents consciously race-socialize their children" (2002, 84). In their review of the literature, Anita Thomas and Suzette Speight found that current studies indicate "that approximately one half to two thirds of the parents report, when asked directly, that they do racially socialize their children" (1999, 154). However, in a 1997 study involving "94 African American parents of third-, fourth-, and fifth-grade children," Diane Hughes and Deborah Johnson found that 82.1 percent had "talked to child about unfair treatment due to race" at least once in the past year (2001, 981, 986). Hughes found that between 88 and 100 percent of the African American parents in her sample engaged in racial socialization (2003, 23). With regard to this Detroit sample, Thornton and colleagues' (1990) and Murray and Mandara's (2002) two-thirds figure holds if we are considering the discussion of racial identity and racism separately. However, when racial socialization is understood to include *either* messages regarding racial identity *or* messages regarding racism or both, the number jumps to about 95 percent, more like Hughes's (2003) figures.

In this study, regardless of income, household structure, marital status, education, or neighborhood, virtually all the mothers say they engage in some form of racial socialization. These mothers see much of their role as "damage control," or responsive racial socialization to fight the impact of negative societal messages on their children. In the previous chapter, I explained how the mothers in this study leave much of the other type of racial socialization—procultural, which focuses on the value of African and African American heritage in and of itself, and not in response to racism—to place. In this chapter, we will see that while place is certainly influential in their responsive messages as well, it cannot take care of responsive racial socialization for them. Racialized spaces and places within the United States are, after all, still "productions of the United States" and, therefore, reflect and are shaped by national constructions of race (J. Brown 2005, 8). Despite all of its uniqueness, then, and the ways in which it challenges certain hegemonic ideologies (such as the normalization of whiteness), Detroit still embodies and is molded by racial formation in the United States (Omi and Winant 1994), and the mothers' responsive racial socialization must deal with this reality.

This chapter will describe and illustrate these mothers' responsive racial socialization, which I break down into several categories: *protective*, in which mothers attempt to shield children from encounters with racism; *preparatory*, in which mothers explicitly educate children regarding the existence of racism and provide them with coping/adaptive mechanisms to deal with life in a racist society; and *critical*, in which mothers help children engage in critiques of racism so that they will neither internalize nor accept it. The fourth category, *inclusive definition of blackness*, in which mothers dispute homogenous understandings and portrayals of African Americans, will be examined in chapter 6.

"We Keep Them Insulated": Protective
Responsive Racial Socialization

First, several mothers say they try to shield their children from both individual and institutional racism or to at least delay their children's confrontation with either one for as long as they can. However, the ways in which they conceptualize and go about this take varying, sometimes divergent forms. They cite racially protective spaces, timing of racial socialization messages, and filtering media as components of their protective racial socialization. The first, racially protective spaces, is something touched upon in earlier chapters—that place can be protective in terms of children's exposure to racism. Seven of the mothers cite keeping their children in such spaces as something they consciously do to counter the effects of societal racism, part of their responsive racial socialization. As we heard in chapter 4, Annette, Audrey, Desarae, Gwen, Anita, and Julie all see Detroit, in some ways, as a shield from everyday encounters with racism.

For Audrey, attempting to delay her three sons' encounters with racism means choosing to live in Detroit, which she refers to as "Blacktown," and placing her children in a school which provides a racially protective space. This means not only a predominantly black space, which could be found at virtually any Detroit public school, but also a space in which the curriculum and materials are centered on black history, realities, and issues. "We chose an African-centered school," she says of herself and her husband, "because, unlike when I went to school, no one in the books that I read—See Susie run. Where is Spot? Spot jump?—Nobody in the book looked like me. . . . I wanted to put them in an environment that I knew it was going to be loving and embracing of them and their blackness and their energy and their melanin." Audrey seems to reference basal readers like *Dick and Jane*, which were widely used in US schools from 1930 through 1970 and did not have any African American characters until 1965 (Kismaric and Heiferman 1996). This kind of symbolic annihilation (Eichstedt and Small 2002; Klein and Shiffman 2009; Tuchman 1978), or "the way cultural production and media representations ignore, exclude, marginalize, or trivialize a particular group" (Merskin 1998, 335), is part of what mothers must address in responsive racial socialization. Audrey has chosen to do so by placing her children in a more protective educational space, which, in contrast to her own experiences in Detroit Public Schools, not only tolerates but celebrates and understands their racial and cultural identities.

This racially protective space not only reflects their own reality in the course materials, but also actively rejects the common stereotype that African American boys are "bad," dangerous, or misbehaved (Ferguson 2000; Kunjufu 2002; A. Lewis 2003; Noguera 2008). At her sons' school, Audrey says, "It won't be anybody making them sit down or stand in the hallway . . . [just] because of their energy level. . . . And even if there is discipline—and they do focus on self-control and self-discipline—it won't be because they just don't want to deal with this little black kid. You know? Or, 'He's bad!' Or whatever else it is." The racialized ideas about black boys as "bad" or difficult have serious implications for their schooling experiences and beyond. In an educational context, these preconceptions often translate into higher rates of detention, suspension, and assignment to special education (Kunjufu 2005; Noguera 2008; Schwarz 2011). Beyond school, these ideas can mean that employers, police, and other authority figures see black boys and men as insolent or threatening, leading to negative outcomes in employment, income, housing, health and well-being, incarceration, and even mortality (Clayton and Moore 2006; Geronimus 1998; Noguera 2008). By sending her sons to an African-centered school, Audrey is hoping to both avoid these problems while her children are school-aged and give them the tools to best respond to racialized expectations when they become men.

Lena's daughters, Tanika (thirteen) and Lanáe (ten), are in a school described by the National Center for Education Statistics as having a 100 percent black enrollment, but it is not an African-centered school. She has mixed feelings about the racially protective space of Detroit and the school her daughters attend. More racial diversity would be good for her children, she believes, and she has considered moving her family out to the suburbs in an attempt to find it. She has not done so, however, because she worries about her children losing the racially protective space, which she refers to as a "comfort zone."

> You don't want to go too far out of your comfort zone because then—
> I mean, unless you're a very strong person and feel like, "OK, I don't
> care; we're going to conquer any obstacle"—that's a big jump to make.

I mean, because I could go out somewhere, I don't know, Canton or somewhere . . . but am I really going to go out there? So. And then there's always the fear, and this is something that I have told the girls—so, I mean, life is so contradictory; it's not fair—that you still do have to be cautious [about racism]. . . . You know, I hear these stories about [Howell, Michigan, that] . . . it used to be where the KKK Grand Dragon [lived]. . . . So I don't want to teach the girls to think, "Oh, no, here comes the white people; let's hide, close the door, or whatever." But at the same time, you never know who is who and you have to be cautious.

Lena begins by talking about racially protective spaces as merely more comfortable for her family; they could move out to the suburbs, but it would be a struggle in terms of dealing with racism, prompting Lena to ask the rhetorical question, "Am I really going to go out there?" She quickly moves, however, into presenting racially protective spaces as potentially life-saving when she raises the specter of a high-ranking Ku Klux Klan leader living and holding rallies in Howell, a town about sixty miles northwest of Detroit. So racially protective spaces, like racial socialization in general, are about more than keeping children comfortable; they are also about keeping children physically and emotionally safe.

For Audrey, as much as she tries to keep her sons in racially protective spaces, she and her husband are not able to shield their children entirely from racism. She shares an example, still fresh in her mind, which occurred almost eight years before our interview. "I just remember being at an ATM," she recounts, "and my son Toussaint might have been three-and-a-half. And there was a white woman in front of me, and he was kind of moving close to her. And I'm like, I could see she was nervous, so I was bringing him back. And I said, 'You know, he's only three-and-a-half; he can't steal your PIN number.' And she's like, 'Well, you don't know how early they can start.'" Audrey admits that this and similar incidents, such as receiving poor service at white-run businesses, have exposed her son to racism and prompted him to ask, "Well, what's wrong with *us?*" However, she still believes she has succeeded in keeping her three sons "pretty much insulated from all of that." When asked to explain, she says, "We keep them close to us. We keep them really close to us. They're not going anywhere. If we go somewhere we've had an experience, or if it looks tricky, or if they're not waiting on us fast enough, we get the hell out of there. . . . I don't know how it affects [my oldest son, Toussaint]. He might be hurt. He might feel like 'Well what's wrong with *us?*'"

That Audrey repeats three times that she and her husband keep their sons literally close to them suggests this is an important part of her responsive racial socialization. Setting up a barrier from racism from the start is the first racial socialization step taken by many of the mothers, as discussed in chapter 4. Being in such a space, though, and even being near their parents much of the time, cannot fully keep children protected from racism. Audrey acknowledges this, and even though she tries to quickly remove her children from potentially "tricky" situations, she admits even the act of removing them can leave an impression, causing them to wonder whether they themselves are the problem. This reveals one of the imperfections in protective racial socialization: keeping children from the reality of racism is inevitably impossible. Despite public scripts claiming otherwise, the ideologies of white privilege and white supremacy are woven throughout society, even in relatively "safe" enclaves such as Detroit. Through protective racial socialization, however, parents are simply attempting to both minimize and delay their children's exposure to this. While this may be helpful emotionally to children, the previous chapter showed such protection from racism can also leave children especially unprepared and vulnerable when they do encounter racism.

Timing

Timing, too, can be used as protective racial socialization, but mothers employ it in divergent ways—some believe delaying contact with and knowledge of racism allows their children to maintain their innocence and not develop a victimized mentality; others believe early awareness of and tools to deal with racism are the best way to protect their children. Many feel conflicted; they want to avoid placing too great a burden on their children, but they also do not want their children to be caught unawares. This is consistent with findings in the racial socialization literature, which suggest this balancing act usually results in parents waiting until their children are adolescents to begin discussing racism with their children (Hughes et al. 2008; Suizzo et al. 2008). But children begin developing their ideas about race much earlier, and research shows children display racial biases by age three to five that do not necessarily resemble the racial attitudes of adults in their lives (Aboud 2008; Hirschfield 2008; P. Katz 2003; P. Katz and Kofkin 1997; Patterson and Bigler 2006; Van Ausdale and Feagin 2001). Waiting until their children are into adolescence to discuss these issues, then, means parents leave the children to cultivate these ideas without direct parental input (although, it should be noted, parents likely send nonverbal and/or unintentional messages throughout the child's life) (Lesane-Brown 2006).

Patrice and Bridget are mothers who have delayed talking to their children about racism because they believe the discussion might prejudice their children. Patrice, whose youngest daughter, Mahogany, is fifteen years old, says, "I never really talked to her about that because [pause]—I know she young, but I just never really said nothing to her about that. I tell her to love everybody. You know. I can't say I told her nothing about that yet. I really haven't. You know. All I told her you supposed to love everybody, whether they be purple, black, green, whatever." Patrice presumes talking to Mahogany about racism may cause her to have animosity toward people of other races. This idea that talking to children or youth about race and racism in any manner will poison their minds or put ideas in their heads is surprisingly common in popular culture and goes along with the notion of children as blank slates (Van Ausdale and Feagin 2001). This portrait of children as passive, empty vessels simply waiting to be filled with information from adults is contrary to the theoretical model of comprehensive racial learning, which posits children as active in the creation of their ideas about race. Moreover, research shows the "empty vessel" model is simply not correct (Aboud 2008; Hirschfield 2008; P. Katz 2003; Katz and Kofkin 1997; Patterson and Bigler 2006; Van Ausdale and Feagin 2001).

Patrice's daughter Mahogany seems to struggle a great deal with understanding racism, at times critiquing it and at times appearing to internalize it. As I argued at the beginning of chapter 2, where I examined Mahogany's case in detail, much of her apparent rationalization of racism—blaming black people themselves for the racism directed toward them—is directly in line with colorblind ideology, which claims race neutrality but actually normalizes whiteness. While I am not suggesting Mahogany's ideas are directly attributable to Patrice's silence about racism and general colorblind missives, parents are certainly one component of children's comprehensive racial learning. The contradiction between her own real-world experiences with racism and her mother's colorblind messages and silence about racism may well contribute to Mahogany's apparent confusion.

Bridget, mother of Rebecca (eleven) and Margaret (nine), is the only mother in the study who says she never talks to her children about either racial identity or racism in any way. She has avoided the topic, she says, because she worries about prejudicing them or going against her Christian faith, which she says teaches not to "look at people because [of] the color of their skin." However, Bridget is beginning to rethink her silence in the wake of an experience her nine-year-old daughter, Margaret, had at school. When I asked her, "Do you feel like you have to prepare your kids to deal with racism at all?" she responded, "I—not really. I think maybe I could give them a little more information about it because I know Margaret, I think it was, was in a class one day, and she said, um, I think she said the little boy said he didn't like her because she was black." So Bridget is inclined toward the colorblind ideology she believes her faith dictates, but as her daughters begin to have racialized experiences outside of the home, she is reconsidering her approach. As I have argued here, whether she does so may well impact her children's understandings of and responses to racism.

Perhaps relevant, both Bridget and Patrice fall in the lowest income bracket in this study. With annual incomes of less than $15,000, both are struggling to raise their children on state assistance and live well below the poverty threshold. One completed the eleventh grade while the other completed some college courses. These points raise the issue of power relationships in the interview context. Both women are older than I and were being interviewed in their own neighborhood in the home of an acquaintance; however, I am a white woman, and I was the one asking most of the questions and recording their responses. So there were multiple identities and factors in the interview context that could have shaped their responses, perhaps toward what they thought someone in my position would want to hear, that race does not matter. It is important to note, however, that the two other mothers with similar socioeconomic profiles talked openly about preparing their children to deal with racism.

Other mothers believe that their children are just too young to recognize racism, even when they are confronted with it. Barbara is proactive in talking to her youngest daughter, Brianna (fourteen), about the historical struggles of black people. However, while she firmly believes racism is alive and well today, Barbara thinks Brianna is just too young to recognize it in its contemporary, more covert form.

[Brianna does not notice covert racism] yet because all Brianna gets is Disney Channel and videos. She hasn't seen it yet. She hasn't even seen it. Now she knows what is going on in terms of politics and everything, but we don't look at the racism or anything as far as that. We talk about who's the best candidate and what they say. . . . So, we haven't—I haven't pushed that issue, but I would like to know what she knows or what she thinks she knows. But, ah, no she doesn't. She doesn't see any of that yet. Even with Girl Scouts—going to different things and it's mostly white girls—[Brianna and her friends] don't see it because they're so—they're still little girls. They're so busy laughing and joking and playing with each other; they don't even see if the [white] girls are ignoring them or whatever. They don't see it. They don't see it.

First, that Barbara claims Brianna does not recognize racism because she is only exposed to the Disney Channel and music videos is curious since both have been highly criticized for racism via omission, misrepresentation, and presenting a very narrow range of images of African Americans (Giroux and Pollack 2010; Holtzman 2000; Lugo-Lugo and Bloodsworth-Lugo 2009; Perry 2003). Second, Barbara claims that Brianna is politically aware but makes no connections between politics and race. However, she then continues that she does not actually know what Brianna "knows or what she thinks she knows" about race, racism, and politics. Third, Barbara does not think Brianna and her Girl Scout troop friends, all of whom are African American, notice any racism when they travel to predominantly white Girl Scouting events in other parts of the state.

The evidence presented in chapter 2, however, would suggest otherwise. That chapter showed the common experience among children in this study: when they travel outside of Detroit, this serves as their first and primary exposure to direct interpersonal racism. Although Brianna did not discuss Girl Scout trips in her interview, the only example she gave of experiencing racism occurred outside of Detroit when she and her mother were ignored by a suburban mall store clerk who helped the white customers before helping them. Taken together, these three points show Brianna not only is old enough to recognize and understand racism, but is already doing so in some instances. Moreover, she is certainly being exposed to racialized images and ideas through television shows and music videos, and research shows that the critical skills gained through racial socialization could help recognize and challenge those racialized ideas (D. Johnson 2001; L. Scott 2003).

This is exactly what Lena points out when discussing her desire to start the conversation with her ten- and thirteen-year-old daughters. Although she has given some thought to whether they can really comprehend the intricacies of race and racism at their ages, she thinks it is better to foster discussion early than to essentially acquiesce to outside sources. Regarding a public television documentary, *Race: The Power of an Illusion*, which explores the historical construction of race and racism, Lena says:

> I meant to tape it, actually. So that I could make them watch it, whether they wanted to or not [*laughs*]. I think that kind of stuff is important. . . . And they may not have liked it, but I would have made them watch it. And it may have even been too deep for them, but at least they would have seen this, that, or the other, and if they had any questions, then we could have discussed whatever. And it still may have been too deep for them, but at least, you know, I am a strong believer that—you know how they'll say that you can't teach, "Oh, you can't teach this to so-and-so because he's too young, or they're too young"? Well, if you don't teach it to them, then, you know, how do you know what their capability is and what they will and what they won't absorb? So it's better to at least try than not to try and then later on wonder why they are the way they are.

Lena concedes her children may not understand everything about racism but says she cannot know if she does not try. Further, she says it is better to plant the seeds now and hope they can draw on the information later, even if they do not fully comprehend it now.

Sarah agrees and says one advantage of starting the conversation while Trisha (fourteen) and Elijah (twelve) are young is that they are still interested in and seeking out her opinion. When asked about how she thinks forces outside of the family affect how her children learn about race and racism, she answers:

> They learn about [race and racism] from all of those different influences and experiences [modeled behavior, television, church, place], but the one thing I can say about our relationship—the relationship I have with my kids—they always come back to me, and they'll ask me. And when they come and ask me, I'm like, "Oh good! They're still asking me!" So that I get a chance to share with them my beliefs, my values. And I know that they're going to go out and test what I tell them, you know, against the world, their friends, TV, what they see, the media; but I just feel like, *while they're young* I have an opportunity, so I'm getting all that I can get in! [*Laughs.*] You know, with positive experiences where I'm trying to teach them, and, hopefully, you know, they'll turn out to be just some decent people (emphasis added).

Sarah describes her position in her children's comprehensive racial learning as a source of ideas, but also a sounding board off of which her children can bounce notions they pick up from other sources, in the process of forming their own viewpoints. Understanding her children will make up their own minds, she nevertheless wants to get her message in and believes she only has so much time to do so before she holds less sway over their ideas.

While the research supports the importance of beginning racial socialization early (Caughy et al. 2004; Suizzo et al. 2008), is it possible to overdo early protective racial socialization? Michelle and Audrey are worried that their early and frequent messages might backfire or have unintended effects. Michelle has mixed feelings about this. Although she sees her early start with racial socialization as a way to help empower them, she now worries that she may have "prejudiced" Carlos (ten) and Elina (twelve).

> They know what it is; they know that it exists. They know that people will treat you differently—good or bad—because of race. I think they have an image of it—of white being privileged and black not being. . . . I mean, racism as an institution, they actually understand it. I mean, they do. They do know that you will be treated better, or not, because you're white. They know that. So that they'll notice if we go in a store, and they're conscious if people are staring at them, if it's a mostly white environment. "Well, why are they looking at me? Because they think I'm going to steal something?" And unfortunately, it's an assumption of negativity. I mean, you know, I hate to say it, but it's already programmed into them—racism as an institution—that they'll experience it in some form and that they'll just be treated differently because of it. I guess I've prejudiced them [*sigh*].

Michelle now wonders if she began too early, when her children may not have been able to understand the nuances of racialized oppression. For example, she worries that they think uncritically about why whites have disproportional access to fancy homes and may simply think of it as deserved. "We see these really nice houses," she says, "and Elina is like, 'White people live there.' So, [now they think] only white people live in nice houses." Michelle sees this as one sign that her children, and particularly Elina, may be internalizing her message about "white being privileged and black not being" to mean that "white is better." Elina, she says, "has hit a 'white is better' mode in her life" where she thinks only white people are attractive or can have and deserve nice homes. Both of her children have started using the racialized term *ghetto* to describe negative behaviors. Worried, perhaps, either that her early start caused her to overdo her message or that the nuances of structural and cultural racism are simply too complex for her children to fully grasp, Michelle is now trying to neutralize some of her early racial socialization, opining, "I've actually found myself having to counteract it now that they're getting older."

Audrey also wants to begin racial socialization with her three boys, Toussaint (eleven) and two younger boys, at a very early age. She shares that her own parents did not teach her about racism when she was a child, and, consequently, she says, her "feelings were hurt" when she began to experience racism. This led her to believe earlier racial socialization would be better for her own children. However, she worries she may be starting too early or emphasizing racial socialization too much. "Sometimes they tell me, 'Look, Ma, my self-esteem is intact. You know, I am, I'm all right. We don't need to go there. You know, I realize this. You know, you don't have to keep talking about African people, African, African. I understand that.' So, I don't know. Maybe I'm doing them a disservice. It's like, 'We don't have to do this all the time, do we?' So they may reject it after a while. I don't know." This again brings us back to the finding that many parents agonize over when and how frequently to engage in racial socialization (Suizzo et al. 2008), not wanting to overburden their children, make them feel victimized, or, as in Audrey's case, cause them to rebel against possibly heavy-handed messages. It is not clear whether there is a precise way to determine the optimal time to begin racial socialization. Developmental psychologists agree children begin to recognize and develop ideas and bias related to race at a very young age and, therefore, recommend talking to children about racial identity and racism early. However, those discussions need to be age-appropriate, which can be difficult for parents to know or finesse since this is not a topic addressed in your average parenting book or class, nor modeled well in early childhood education or society more generally (Tatum 2003). In the absence of societal discussion of this topic, the timing of racial socialization messages seems to depend largely on parental opinions about children's readiness, which research suggests is generally underestimated (Hirschfield 2008; Van Ausdale and Feagin 2001).

Filtering Media

Mothers realize that they do not have control over all of the racial socialization messages that their children receive during their daily lives, but many work to filter the sources over which they do have control. The most often cited source mentioned in this regard is television. About one-third of the mothers articulate their desire to shield their children from negative messages about blackness by filtering their children's television access. However, these mothers all admit that they cannot fully shield their children from powerful media messages about race. For example, Audrey tries to shield her sons from negative messages about black people on television but acknowledges that some of these messages may nevertheless get through to them. She worries about the general aesthetic put forth in the media that encourages a racial hierarchy with white people at the top and black people at the bottom.

> I try to focus on and tape programs that have black people on, so I can put it on the television: *Gulla Gulla Island* or some of those earlier shows from those early years. But [the general aesthetic on television], it's like in the same book that I'm describing to you, where they call black people the "Ethiopian" or "Negroid race." . . . I bought it at an antique shop and it was from the 1800s. But it's like when they're talking about the Caucasoid race, it says, "In no other race is the mark of beauty so high and so noble a bearing." And that's what comes across [in the media]. And then it's like, about the African people it says, "In no other human—the ties to humanity are slim and tenuous at best." You know? I think that that still comes across through the media.

Here, Audrey argues that the contemporary mainstream media reinforce the same ideas about racial superiority and inferiority that were prominent in the antebellum period. Because she finds this to be overwhelmingly the case, she makes it a point to record the few shows she feels portray black people accurately, positively, and holistically. She admits, though, that she finds it overwhelming to try to monitor and protect her sons from all of the racialized messages in the media. "I don't monitor it as much as I should," she says. "I should monitor it more . . . television, all together. But I don't. But you know, they're mostly watching cartoons and that sort of thing. . . . But which ones, and what are they putting into [Toussaint's] head, I don't really know. I should watch it more closely." It is telling to hear Audrey admit this, since she is so vigilant about protecting her son from exposure to racism. As we have heard, she keeps her children physically close to her as much as possible in order to shield them from racism and has Toussaint in an African-centered school in hopes of keeping him from the racism in textbooks, curriculum, and teacher expectations that she experienced as a child. While she acknowledges the predominance of cultural racism in media in general (Holtzman 2000; Klein and Shiffman 2009; Tatum 2003), she is a very busy working mother with three young children (one still in diapers) and a husband who works long hours. Essentially, she is not able to filter all of the media her sons consume.

Julie finds herself in a similar situation. Although she monitors her son Josh's (ten) television consumption closely and is very strict about prohibiting music videos, she knows he will see them at his friends' houses. In particular, she worries about Josh wanting to portray "hardness," or a particular notion of black masculinity as tough and street-smart (Boyd 1997; Noguera 2008; Orelus 2010), which will be examined in more depth in chapter 6. She thinks that Josh's desire to exude "hardness" comes from pressure from his peers and from music videos on television. Although she cannot control what Josh's peers say and do at school, Julie does feel that she can shield Josh from some of these racial stereotypes by limiting his television access. "Hardness has been an issue with him at school. . . . So I've tried to downplay it as, you know, that's *not* cool. Being hard is not cool. But that's what's on the videos, and I don't—I don't know. You know, I was in the bathtub and I heard him; I heard a video of rap music. And I flipped open that door butt naked and wet. 'You better turn that off!' You know, I don't let him watch the videos. And I know he sees it other places. He catches it here and there." Julie's story of rushing out of the bath illustrates her high level of commitment to her restrictions on music videos. Still, she cannot fully shield her son because he "sees it other places" besides her home, and she believes "he's going to get it from his peers."

Annette also wants to limit her son Matthew's (thirteen) viewing of music videos in order to shield him from the racial stereotypes contained therein; however, she feels unable to do so because her husband likes to watch videos with their son. "I totally agree [that videos contain gendered racialized stereotypes]," she says. "I don't particularly like him watching videos. I can't say much with Dad sitting there going [*mimicking*], 'Hey did you see such and such?' So [*laughs*]."

Anita, the mother of Shani (twelve) and an older teenage daughter, worries about what music videos suggest to her daughters about black womanhood. When asked what lessons she thinks her daughters take away from music videos, Anita replies, "I think—you know what? I'm not sure about that question. I think maybe to a certain degree that they—that it keeps these girls thinking that they have to dress up with stuff like that. You know. But other than that—that's the only image I can see that [videos are] trying to give them at all. But I try to limit them watching videos. Like I know as soon as they get up—turn a video on. I know when they get out of school I let them, you know, but that—when the first thing they [do is turn on videos]—no. Because they will try. No. No. You know, that's just too much videos right there." Although Anita admits her daughters watch a great deal of music videos, the only problematic messages she worries about therein are those about how women should dress. While this is a significant concern, it is only one of many, many racialized (and gendered) messages prominent in music videos likely to be shown on BET and MTV.[1] It does not appear that Annette or Anita is working to help her children critique media images in the same way Julie is. It is important to note that other mothers in this study choose, rather than trying to keep their children away from racialized media images altogether, simply to help them process and critique media images, which we will explore later in the chapter in the section on critical responsive racial socialization.

"You Have to Let Them Know It's There": Preparatory Responsive Racial Socialization

Although mothers do try to shield their children from encounters with racism for as long as possible, preparation for racism is really the top racial socialization priority among mothers in this study. While two-thirds of the mothers say they have already talked directly to their children about racism, all but two of the mothers say they need to prepare their children for dealing with racism in the future. Even these two mothers make statements in their interviews to show that they do, in fact, send some preparatory messages to their children. Moreover, one of these two mothers—Bridget—reports regretting and reconsidering her neglect of preparatory racial socialization after her daughter recently reported experiencing racism at school. In one way or another, then, it appears the mothers in this study agree with Michelle's statement that, "as a black parent, [the existence of racism] is something you teach, you know, just to keep [your children] safe."

How to Recognize and Respond to Today's Racism

Most of the mothers report that their children know about the history of black people's struggles in the United States, but many worry that their children do not understand the nuances and manifestations of present-day racism and racialized inequality. As we saw in chapter 2, the children's interviews confirm the children tend of think of racism as historical in nature. While only two of the twenty-eight children said that they think that racism no longer exists, they think of it as dissipating and not as serious as in the past. The mothers say it is important that their children know that racism may have changed over time but that it still exists. Yolanda, mother of Travis (thirteen) and Shaun (fifteen), says she tried to make this clear to her boys but is not sure they get it. "I think my kids, along with the other kids, are like, 'This is the year 2003. It's not going to happen. That was back in the old days.' But it ain't back in the old days. It still happens. But they just don't publicize it like they used to. That used to be the thing, but now there's just so much other stuff. So I tell them, you know, you gotta watch out; you gotta be careful." In fact, Yolanda's description of her children's thinking matches what her son Travis (thirteen) said in his interview: "[Racism] still exists, but it ain't that much of an issue no more. . . . It changed at a certain level, like it really don't hurt people anymore like it used to."

Barbara also worries her child is naive about present-day racism. She says Brianna (fourteen) "doesn't see any of that yet." However, Barbara thinks that Brianna needs to be able to recognize the character of today's racism in order to protect herself from it.

> Personally, I tell her that I think racism still exists, but it exists in a dif-
> ferent way. And I told her that she has never really had to face it in any
> way, but there's so many things—and we talk about the Emmett Till, and
> we talk about the Malcolm X, and we talk about the Martin Luther King,
> and we see all the different things that come on [TV], and she reads a
> lot. But I also tell her that it also exists, kind of under the cover, with
> different companies, with different schools, and you have to be aware of
> how someone treats you and how they talk to you. I say, "You're going to
> be on the job and this person may not like you, and they might—you have
> to always cover your butt and make sure you're doing what you're
> supposed to do."

Barbara's description of "under the cover" racism matches Michael Omi and Howard Winant's (1994) conceptualization of racism in the post–civil rights era as racial hegemony, where racism is not obvious and overt, but subtly coded into institutions. Based on the evidence presented in chapter 2 that the children conceptualize race and racism as things of the past, the mothers are justifiably worried their children may find it more difficult to recognize this current type of racism. Recent scholarship also shows children "exposed to a color-blind mindset" are less likely to recognize racism and racial bias, even in its most obvious forms (Apfelbaum et al. 2010). It is understandable, then, that these mothers deem it critical to show their children racism still exists, although it may be manifested in different forms from those it took historically.

Also important is Barbara's admonition that her daughter will have to work twice as hard as her white counterparts and "cover [her] butt," or make no mistakes on the job. Previous studies have found this to be a common preparatory racial socialization message (Hughes and Chen 1999; Peters 1985), although in this study it is most often emphasized with boys, as will be explored in more detail in chapter 6. But here it is important in the context of awareness of and preparation for a more subtle, institutional racism. Barbara is letting her daughter know that racism is not likely to be open and obvious in the workplace and, therefore, will be more difficult for Brianna to prove. Thus, Barbara suggests her daughter must be aware of its more subtle forms and do her best to mitigate their impact on her by creating an impeccable record beyond reproach.

Lena believes not only that racism still exists, but that it is unlikely to ever be eliminated because it is inherent within our social structure. She cites as an example Jane Elliot's famous 1968 "Eye of the Storm" experiment. Elliot, a third-grade teacher, temporarily awarded superiority and privilege to her blue-eyed students and inferiority and disadvantage to her brown-eyed students, creating instant social inequality in her all-white classroom. "Unfortunately," Lena explains, "it's the ruling class that makes the rules, and you have to assimilate regardless of who the ruling class is. There's always going to be some form of racism or prejudice. I don't think we'll ever be away from that. And what that one study proved—you know, the blue eyes against the brown eyes—shows that no matter what, there's always going to be some kind of distinction to pit people against each other, unfortunately. So, you know, racism is not going to just go away—and I try to show the girls [that]."

According to Michelle, although racism may have changed over time, its dangers are nevertheless acute. She sees preparatory racial socialization as "arming" her children.

> As a parent, it's like arming them. You *have* to let them know that it's there, because it's a way of protecting them. And you need to have them cognizant that things—bad or good—will happen to them because of it. So, you hate to teach it to them, but at the same time, if you're able to keep them safe, they have to know. They have to know that if you go a certain place, it might be physically endangering to you. You have to let them know that sometimes really unfair things are going to happen to them, not because they've done something wrong; it's just how somebody perceives them. And you have to let them know that some of the things they want they can't have just because of who they are. So, you maybe teach it to them because it's something you have to, because it's just part, it's just as much a part as teaching kids not to put their hand in the fire because it will burn you. You know, I think, as a black parent, it's something you teach, you know, just to keep them safe.

This description of "arming" one's children is akin to the scholarly concept of racial socialization as a process of "armoring" children in preparation for encounters with racism (Bell and Nkomo 1998). The war analogy is significant; children must be lovingly prepared for a highly racially hostile world.

Even mothers like Cora, who primarily utilizes colorblind rhetoric with her children, and Desarae, who initially insists she does not talk to her children about racism at all, see it as part of their duty to prepare their children for racism. Though both heavily emphasize universalistic messages in the racial socialization of their children and express the desire to move to areas more racially diverse than Detroit, both nevertheless remember being blindsided by racism in their own childhoods and want to prevent their children from facing similar pain. Cora says:

[A] few of my [white] friends going to school, their parents didn't accept me because I was black. And it kind of hurt. Don't get me wrong; it hurt because I didn't think it was fair to me to judge me by my color of my skin, knowing that . . . your daughter or your son may be the best friend I ever had. You know, but their parents did have that racism thing going on. And that hurted a lot. . . . And that's why I try to be as open as I can with [my children]. You know, if you have a problem, come to me. Let's talk about it. And especially when it comes down to racism because I don't want to put you out here in a world that you don't understand. You know. People will judge you by your color. You know. And it's bad, don't get me wrong, and I wish it didn't happen, because really we're all the same. If I put a cut on my hand, put a cut on your hand, how are we going to bleed? The color of our blood is the same. So I mean, it should matter because the color of our skin? No.

Cora clings to the ideology of colorblindness throughout her interview, paralleling the color of black and white people's blood, stating, "I am color blind." She points out that she has white neighbors and insists, "I refuse to move in a one-sided neighborhood," adding, "and I don't care if my neighbors are green. I mean, they could be blue. I don't care." She notes, "My older brother is mixed and my husband is mixed," and she proudly says of her eldest son, "I can honestly feel like I've raised him well because I see that, you know, he had a couple of girlfriends that were black; he had a couple of girlfriends that were white." However, she ultimately shows she feels it is necessary to prepare Kaiya (eleven) and Rayna (ten) for racism. Her statement to her daughters, "I don't want to put you out here in a world that you don't understand," is particularly poignant because it reveals she must prepare her girls for the world as it is, rather than as she lives it or as she wishes it would be.

Desarae, mother of twins Corey and Cara (thirteen), says she does not "dwell on racism," which seems to mean she does not raise the issue with her children. However, she says she will have to do so now that her children are involved in activities that will take them outside of Detroit. She herself never experienced racism growing up in Detroit until her mother sent her to live in the South when she was a teenager, and she wishes her mother had prepared her for the racism she encountered there.

DESARAE: So since I don't dwell on racism, it will have to be certain instances, like now Cara's going to find out because now she's on the cheer team and they're going to be going to different states. So she's—I'm going to have to let her know, "Well, you know, sometimes you're going to go places and people are going to judge you, but that doesn't mean that you're a bad person. I don't want you to feel bad about yourself. It's just some people are ignorant." You know, I can't think of anything to tell them but that's just ignorance; and when a person is like that, you don't agitate them, you know, because you never know how far they'll take it. Just, you know, walk away.

ERIN: Do you feel like that was something you wish your mom had told you before you went to [the South]?

DESARAE: Yeah. You know what? That was something that I was mad about. I said, "Why would you send me down here and you know how these people are?"

Problematic but not uncommon is Desarae's statement that, because she does not "dwell on racism," she can only discuss it with her children when a specific incidence arises. She is among the mothers who—like many of the children (see chapter 2)—adopt the colorblind notion that discussing racism at all is equivalent to dwelling on it. But the reality of these mothers' lives often forces them to recognize and confront racism. Such is the case here, where Desarae was blindsided by racism as a teenager because her own mother did not prepare her or, in Desarae's own terms, "dwell on racism." Although Desarae finds herself following her mother's example, the sting of her own experiences with racism as a teen is causing her to reconsider this silence about racism and instead prepare her children for its existence.

"You've Got to Learn How to Flip-Flop": Dual Consciousness/Biculturalism

Having ensured their children know racism is alive and well, these mothers then work to give their children a repertoire of adaptive behaviors to help them cope with it. A majority cite the ability of their children to function successfully in both white and black cultural realms as the most important coping tool they can give to their children. In this kind of racial socialization, sometimes called dual consciousness or biculturalism, African American families encourage their children to embrace their own culture but be able to participate in that of whites in order to advance in society (Boykin and Ellison 1995; Harrison et al. 1990; Peters 1985; Walker et al. 1995). In other words, they want to enable their children to "cross borders" between "different sociocultural worlds" (Stanton-Salazar 1997, 22). In her study looking at how black and white parents socialize their children around the issue of cross-racial friendships, Jill Hamm found that black parents "approached [the issue] from a position of necessity occasioned by their ethnic minority status in American society," noting that, "in the longer term, their children ran the risk of economic and social problems if they could not relate to members of the culturally defining group" (2001, 90). Barbara affirms this, saying it is just a fact of life that her daughter Brianna (fourteen) must learn to move back and forth between black and white realms because she cannot stay sheltered in exclusively black spaces forever. "How can I put this?" she asks. "OK, you can't go to a black college because it's so far away and I can't afford it. So you have to learn how to interact. You really do."

For Julie, this ability to not only function, but thrive in both predominantly black *and* predominantly white settings is a critical part of what she wants to give her son, Josh (ten). She explains, "One of my gifts is for him to be able [to be] in a room with all black people and know who he is. And love all the black people being around him and enjoy what they are, and not be intimidated or afraid of it. And to be able to walk into a white room, next door, and sit in that room and love who they are and still be comfortable with who he is. I want him to be able to go in each room and not have a problem." Julie was raised in a pre-dominantly white environment and says that she always felt uncomfortable and out of place in black spaces. Therefore, she sees comfort in what she calls "flip-flopping" between different types of environments as not only a necessity but a true "gift" for her son.

Cora, too, wants Kaiya (eleven) and Rayna (ten) to be able to feel comfort-able with white and black people and says this is one reason why she and her husband recently moved them to one of Detroit's more racially mixed neigh-borhoods. While Cora thinks the new environment will eventually help her children negotiate white and black social realms with ease, she notes that they are still in transition. One of the messages she sends her daughters is that they need to be aware of their surroundings and behave accordingly. To her children she says, "And you living in a mixed neighborhood now. . . . You don't want to run out there and say [*taunting*], 'White girl, white girl, white girl' or 'White boy, white boy.' *Believe me*, you don't want to do it in this neighborhood!" In other words, she believes their neighborhood, while still predominantly (about 85 percent) black, serves as somewhat of a white space within the context of Detroit (in fact, her daughter indicates as much when they first move in, opining to her mother that it seems "everybody in this neighborhood is white"). In this space, Cora teaches her daughters to be able to switch language and behavior based on with whom they find themselves dealing.

Yolanda is less focused on comfort and more on survival in her bicultural socialization. Of her sons, Shaun (fifteen) and Travis (thirteen), she says:

> I teach them, you know, even in like the way that they dress and the way that they conduct themselves. You're not going to walk around with your clothes slouchy. You can't grow your hair because you can't comb it. And you see these guys—and I will tell them. My girlfriend's nephew just today, he has long hair; he was getting it braided . . . [and] his hair was all wild; his pants was baggy. I said, "If I seen you come in my place of

business, I would be watching you because you look crazy." You know what I'm saying? So, if you want people—you have to look respectable and you have to put that extra effort forth because people look at you and think, "This is a black boy," you know? "He going to take my stuff." So I teach them: you have to prove you're different. You have to be hard-working, respectable, clean, and decent. That's what you have to be. That's what I teach them. You know, this is what you have to do. You can't be acting no damn fool, walking around with your pants hanging off your butt, your shoes untied. You know? You just can't do that. . . . [You need to do this] to be able to survive. If you at work and you need to be a certain way, then that's the way you be. If you outside playing and you need to be a little tougher or whatever, you know, don't bitch up.

While she wants her sons to be able to function in a work environment, which she identifies as a white realm even if not all of the people working there are white, Yolanda also wants to be sure that her boys can hold their own in black realms, particularly on their own block—a tree-lined street of modest single-family homes in a working-class neighborhood on Detroit's west side. There are certainly gendered aspects of her preparatory messages here. These will be explored in more depth in chapter 6, but let me make two points briefly here. First, I want to highlight Yolanda's ideas that switching repertoires into a white realm may require behavior that would be considered "soft" in a black realm and that switching repertoires back into a black realm requires the admonition that her sons be careful they "don't bitch up." While the notion of white as "soft" and black as "hard" may be true for girls as well, the pressure is stronger on boys to be hard in order to survive, as Yolanda stresses. Even the statement that failing to put forth a hard persona would be equivalent to essentially losing one's masculinity, but only in a black space and not in a white space, highlights the significance of both place and gender in the practice of and preparation for racism, as well as in the development of racial identity. Second, I want to highlight Yolanda's statement that people (and here she does not seem to be talking only about white people) are fearful of black boys who dress or wear their hair a certain way and that this fear is justified ("I would be watching you," she says). Here Yolanda dips into the controversial terrain of the politics of respectability (Higginbotham 1993). She asserts the onus is on her sons "to prove [they are] different . . . hardworking, respectable, clean, decent," rather than on society to disrupt the racist notion of the normative black boy as dangerous, lazy, untrustworthy, dirty, or indecent, especially when engaging in highly prevalent fashion trends such as sagging their pants or leaving the laces on their shoes loose. (Of course, many white boys in cities and suburbs across the country follow these same trends without the same assumptions being attached.)

For many of the mothers, a large part of the ability to "cross borders" is dependent upon language. They believe their children need to be able to, as Michelle says, "speak the vernacular" but also know when to "adopt the white voice." What Michelle calls "the vernacular" is perhaps more accurately described as African American Language (AAL), but is also sometimes referred to as "Black English, Black Language, African American Vernacular English, Ebonics, and African American English" (Smitherman and Baugh 2002). Geneva Smitherman notes that African American language is "*not* 'broken English,' nor is it sloppy speech"; rather, she continues, it is a "systematic, rule-governed, and predictable" language (2001, 29).

In his memorandum and opinion regarding the 1979 Michigan court case *Martin Luther King Junior Elementary School Children, et al., v. Ann Arbor School District Board,* Judge Charles Joiner wrote: "It is clear that black children who succeed, and many do, learn to be bilingual. They retain fluency in 'black English' to maintain status in the community and they become fluent in standard English to succeed in the general society" (quoted in Smitherman 2001, 33). Smitherman (1997) gives the term "switching codes" to this practice of changing language repertoires based on environment and argues that it is critical to African American achievement in mainstream American institutions. Lena agrees that her daughters will need to learn how to "switch codes" in order to succeed in most colleges and professions. "If they can't speak properly," she says, "if they can't construct a sentence without using our little idioms, then you're already going to—I mean, not saying that you won't still succeed, but it's going to be harder depending on where you plan to go in life. If you're going to be a movie star, then you do whatever you want. But if you want to be an engineer or [*laughs*], you know, a business executive, then they're going to expect—and it's sad that you should have to change, but unfortunately we do."

As we heard in chapter 4, Lena believes it is particularly necessary to emphasize language specifically because of place, because she and her husband are raising their girls in Detroit. Even though she values AAL and bemoans the fact that African Americans should have to switch codes at all, she sees it as inevitable, something all African American children must learn. Those in Detroit, she thinks, are at a particular disadvantage because they are not forced to switch codes on a regular basis. "It's not emphasized because that's the way everybody speaks," she says, "[so] it's not something that anybody really addresses." She worries that place may hinder her daughters from learning to "switch codes" and that their speech and writing will be erroneously interpreted as "sloppy."

The connection between place and language may be one reason why so many mothers in this study put particular emphasis on preparing their children to switch codes. Julie ties this issue to place, contrasting her experience growing up attending an all-white school in a predominantly white city to her son Josh's (ten) experience after moving to Detroit at age eight. She worries that Josh's failure to learn when it is appropriate to switch codes, or in her words "flip-flop," is "a Detroit thing."

> I grew up with an educator, my mom, who didn't ever, you know—we didn't speak slang at home. I didn't. I went to an all-white private school. All the kids were from the country. There was no slang spoken at school. I got to a [more integrated] public [high] school, and then kids said, "Why do you talk like that?" I said, "Talk like what? What are you talking about?" I didn't cuss. And so I raised Josh without slang because that's how I talk most of the time. And he does an extreme of, you know, he just will—he won't say his consonant sounds.... It's a Detroit thing.... [Since he moved to Detroit] he's really learned how to do the talk, so they don't give him a hard time about that. But [it bothers me] a little bit because I want him to be able to talk. So that he can work, first. And then do that for fun with your friends, but you've got to learn how to flip-flop. And he doesn't flip-flop very well. He doesn't flip-flop very well at all. We'll be with my family, or at a family gathering, and he—you know. And I'm like, no, you can't—you've got to clean it up. You're not with your friends. I'm not your friend. You can't talk to me that way.... So I don't mind it so much as I have a problem with it not being used correctly. So I, I get on Josh. I say, "You know, you can't use it until you figure out how to use it, or when it's OK."

Julie seems to uncritically equate AAL with "slang," cursing, not being able to talk, and corrupt language, telling Josh he needs to "clean it up" at family gatherings with her extended family who live in the small city where she was raised. She clearly considers AAL to be supplemental and tells Josh she will forbid him to use it at all if he cannot learn to "flip-flop." Julie wants her son to be able to have cultural currency with his black peers, something she did not feel she had because she failed to "do the talk," but she clearly prioritizes Standard English. This message that he should be comfortable in his racial identity but dismiss AAL may be confusing for Josh, since Smitherman argues that the devaluing of AAL also inherently devalues black people themselves "because of the blackness of Black English" (2000, 143).

For the most part, Sarah agrees with Julie, encouraging her children, Trisha (fourteen) and Elijah (twelve), to "just use proper English," rather than having to switch codes. As we saw in chapter 4, she also ties this to place, pointing out the irony that, in Detroit, speech considered "talking white" is actually not "proper English" at all. "[My kids] don't even talk right," she says. "[They] don't talk all that proper." Still, in the context of Detroit, Trisha's and Elijah's speech has been interpreted to mean that they "want to be white." Despite the fact that they may sometimes get teased or challenged because they "use proper English," Sarah encourages her children not to have to switch codes. "Well, I told them," she says, "if you just use proper English, you would not have to switch up. . . . You're going to really get embarrassed using that slang so much. . . . Why don't you just adopt a universal language?" As discussed in more detail in chapter 4, Sarah, like Julie, seems to equate AAL with slang, calling Standard English "proper" and "universal." The positioning of a very particular kind of English, typically spoken in an overwhelmingly white section of the American Midwest (Labov et al. 2006), as universal facilitates racist exclusions through the normalization of whiteness (Balibar 1990). On the other hand, Sarah is very conscious and critical of the normalization and privileging of whiteness in many ways throughout her interview and in the racial socialization of her children (for example, see Sarah's critique of media images of whiteness in the next section). It seems Sarah's encouraging her children to adopt what she sees as a more universal presentation of self—one that was not closely associated with Detroit or "the 'hood"—is an attempt to prepare them to cope with the racist assumptions tied to speech and place.

Michelle agrees, telling Elina (thirteen) and Carlos (ten) that "people identify what you are . . . what your qualifications are" based upon speech and that they can therefore use language to counteract racist expectations. She encourages her children to adjust their language, or "flip the script," depending upon their environment. "[I tell my kids,] 'Flip the script. You know, if you're in there [with white people], talk just like them.' I was like, 'Adopt the white voice.' And [my kids] learn. They know. Depending on where you are, change your tone. Change how you speak." Stating explicitly that this does not preclude them from embracing and valuing AAL, she says, "You know, it's like, if anybody questions you, show your intelligence. Yeah, OK, fine, we can be home and you can drop the '-ing' from every word you know! It can be 'goin',' 'fixin',' 'we fixin' to go,' 'my mama and them,' 'we be clubbin',' [laughs], OK? Look, be Ebonically how you feel. And then, when you're in a social situation [snaps her fingers], flip the script. Clean up the language. You know, make it light on yourself." Here again, while Michelle says she values AAL, she links intelligence and "clean" language to Standard English, thereby implicitly linking the opposite qualities to AAL. As we saw with Josh, this likely sends Michelle's children mixed messages, implying they should both embrace and reject, value and devalue AAL. Despite these conflicting messages, Michelle says she just wants to make interracial interactions easier for her children and teach them that "language is a weapon, and it's also a shield."

Unlike some of the other mothers, who equate Standard English with intelligence without problematizing that assumption, Lena finds it contemptible her children should have to adjust their language based on environment. "I am pro-Ebonics," she says. "I feel it is a valid language." She continues:

> I also don't appreciate the fact that it's OK for a Jewish American from New York to say "tish," "tush" or—what's another common Yiddish phrase?—"chutzpah" or whatever; that's totally acceptable. Or an Italian American from the East or someone from Boston, they speak with their own particular cadence and they have their own words and so on and so forth, and no one looks upon them as being any less intelligent or any less anything because they speak that way. But if you hear an African American speak, if you hear a Latino speak, or if you hear somebody from the South that has a drawl, you automatically assume that they're ignorant, you know, whatever, because they can't speak. That bothers me; it's a double standard. So that bothers me. However, we lived how we lived. I'm not Sabrina [the witch]. I can't wiggle my nose and make everything the way I think it should be. And unfortunately, if you don't speak a certain way, then you are going to be perceived a certain way. And unfortunately, because most people don't speak correct English—not that I speak correct English, but a more acceptable form of English—then they're going to maybe be passed up for an interview or, maybe again, thought of as being illiterate: when you hear people say "pacifically" instead of "specifically" [laughs], or any number of phrases that we have perverted and have become acceptable in our community but aren't correct. So if you decide to step out of this little society here to go somewhere else or to do something else, then that's going to count against you.

Lena gives a clear critique of the racialized and placed assumptions about intelligence attached to language, linguistic styles, and accents, pointing out that equally unique styles of speech—for example, Yiddish-infused, accented English used by New York Jewish Americans and what she terms Ebonics—trigger entirely different presumptions about their speakers. The struggle, however, is between this clearly logical argument and the practical truth that many Americans do, in fact, make presumptions about intelligence based on speech. This puts mothers in a bind. Do they prepare their children for society as it is or as it should be? Audrey says her parents chose the latter and it ultimately hurt her a great deal. "I don't know if they were shielding me," she says, "or if they were living in a world that they wished it was like." Either way, it ended up leaving her vulnerable and, she says, "It did change the way, or it gave me an idea how I would do it personally once I had kids." Ultimately, most mothers in this study choose, like Audrey, to prepare their children for the reality of society but to teach them to be critical of that reality. This brings us to the next type of responsive racial socialization message.

"Think It Through": Critical Responsive Messages

In addition to protecting their children from and preparing their children for encounters with racism, some African American families also communicate a critique of racism as part of racial socialization. Virtually all mothers in this study encourage their children to deconstruct and critique racism in one way or another by teaching them to resist the internalization of racist ideas, to think critically about race in US society, and to always treat others fairly, even when they are not treated with fairness themselves.

Resist Absorption of Racist Ideas

Among the most common messages the mothers report are those meant to discourage their children from internalizing racist stereotypes. Indeed, Algea Harrison and colleagues argue that African American families work to discredit the "negative portrayals of [their] ethnic group" through racial socialization (1990, 354). Several of the mothers pick specific racialized stereotypes to refute in both words and actions. For example, Barbara cautions Brianna (fourteen) against buying into racist stereotypes about black female-headed households being deficient. She explains, "I was upset because I had listened to something on the radio, and I was like, 'Why is it that when you are a black female and single, they feel that you are not capable of doing anything or not knowing how to do anything or you're such a poor, poor woman?' I'm like, *why?* I teach my kids, you know, all the kids that. [The people on the radio are] like, 'You know that child's mom *is* single.' You know? And I'm like, why is it just because you come from a single-parent family and you're a black female and your son or daughter get in trouble, that that marks you?" Barbara speaks to racial hegemony here—to the coded, cultural racism prevalent in US society. From the 1965 Moynihan Report, which blamed problems faced by African Americans on female-headed households, to a 2011 "Marriage Pledge" signed by major candidates for the Republican presidential primary, which suggests African American children were better off under enslavement because they were purportedly "more likely to be raised by [a] mother and father" (Haberman 2011), this demonizing of single black mothers is widespread. Barbara, who has raised both of her daughters on her own, wants Brianna to recognize this as racism and critique it as such, rather than internalizing it.

Yolanda believes that simply by being married, working, having cars, and not ever having received food stamps, she is modeling for Travis (thirteen) and Shaun (fifteen) a critique of the notion of black women as "Welfare Queens" (Hancock 2004; Perry 2011). She explains, "I don't think that my kids even know what welfare is. You know what I'm saying? Because we all—all my friends—we work. We're not stereotypical. We all got husbands we live with; I've been with my husband for fifteen years. You know? You know, we have the same things that the white people on TV have! You know? Your mama and daddy go to work every day, you know, you got a couple of cars, you know, everything! And we never got food stamps, you know, so they don't know what it is." Although it is clearly not her intent, Yolanda's message could be reinforcing the negative stereotypes she means to reject. By simply saying, "Look at us, we don't fit the stereotype," without adding further critique of the stereotype itself, Yolanda may in some ways bolster the idea that single mothers or families who accept food stamps or people who are unable to find work are lazy drains on the system, rather than encouraging her sons to look at the structural and social issues that create such circumstances. To be fair to Yolanda, she does critique structural racism later in her interview, pointing out she thinks it is problematic but understandable when "a person who's just like in poverty that don't have nothing" says to his or her children, "Them white motherfuckers don't want me to have shit!" Such critiques of institutional racism are necessary, she says, but she worries that when parents "say it like that . . . they're not really explaining it to their kids."

Similarly, Gina targets the racist notion that intelligence and race are interlinked, but her delivery may be confusing for her twins Terri and Tyrone (thirteen). She says, "I teaches them that you are black. And no matter what nobody to tell you, you're black. You're not black ignorant, you know. Because most people associate—well, not most people. But there are some people out there who associate black with being ignorant. And an ignorant person is an uneducated person. So I mean . . . I teach them [that] at home." While Gina means to directly refute racist stereotypes, the idea that there is an established category of "black-ignorant," of which her children are not a part, could shore up racist notions of blackness in general, motivating her children to think of themselves as "exceptions to the rule," rather than critiquing the racist idea itself (Gaertner and Dovidio 2005). Neither of Gina's two interviewed children, however, reflects this. Tyrone (thirteen), for example, criticizes this idea. "Like . . . with my teacher at my school," Tyrone explains, "she doesn't like black people, and she's black. I don't get that. . . . She think black people are bad or something."

Psychologists have shown that people rely on stereotypes much more than most would like to believe, but that these stereotypes often function subconsciously (Operario and Fiske 1998; Wheeler and Fiske 2005). The first step to fighting them, then, is to recognize that we have unknowingly internalized them. Natalie struggles with this herself and very frankly shares her experiences with her son Matthew (thirteen) and older daughter. "They have heard me say that young black guys have a bad reputation, and I said, and I've found myself falling into the category of not even speaking to young black guys, especially if their pants are sagging or they have French braids, or if they just look like what the news or the television stereotypes as a hood." Natalie explains she struggled to recognize the ways in which she had internalized racism of this sort and now works to actively fight those ideas. "I said [to my children], 'And now I make it a habit to smile and to speak to young black men because they're human! Right? And it's OK to be nice to everybody. Everybody's not a hoodlum.' And although we've been given that information a lot by the news—because on the news, I tell them, if it wasn't for bad news, there wouldn't be any news." In being honest about her own psychology, Natalie hopes to help her children not only recognize racialized images as problematic rather than truthful, but also pinpoint the origins of such ideas and the ulterior motives behind their propagation.

One idea several mothers work especially diligently to combat in their children is the notion that it is better to be white than black. Although the mothers were not asked specific questions about racialized stereotypes—in fact, they were only asked very broad questions regarding what they tell their children about racial identity and racism—six mothers independently raised the concern that their children have articulated the opinion it is better to be white than black. Their children, it seems, are responding to both white standards of beauty and to the perception that life would be easier as a white person.

Audrey admits that her friends have teased her about her children's apparent fondness for white people. She hypothesizes this gravitation toward white people might come from her own light skin, from television, or might just be "the beginning of the oppression cycle."

> I think that [the idea that white people are better or more beautiful than black people] still comes across through the media. And even though my black friends, they—when we go to camp in the summertimes, my children gravitate, especially the middle son, you know, to the white swim instructor, life guard—and they'll come up to me, even the older black people, and say, "Your kids love them some white folks, don't they?" And I laugh. But I say—and the baby does it too on this; he just, he'll go to, you know [white people]—I don't know where that comes from. I think, you know, look at me. I'm light skinned. So maybe it looks like mommy to him. I don't know what it is. But I, I, I just laugh. You know. I just laugh and say, "Well, I don't know what to say." But, so, I don't really know where it comes from, but I know it is the beginning of the oppression cycle. . . . I mean, people that are accusing me of raising my children, you know, to embrace white women, that's fine. I mean, they didn't say that particularly; they just, they just point that out. But they have their children at Country Day [an elite, predominantly white private school in the suburbs] and these other places. But my, my children know and respect themselves and their culture.

Audrey seems to struggle with where the idea that white is better could originate for her children. She suggests perhaps it is because of her own light skin tone, which may make sense for her two younger sons. The youngest, whom she refers to as "the baby" in this quotation, is just twenty-two months old and, developmentally, likely relates more to skin tone than to racial identity or Africanness (Murray and Mandara 2002). Her middle son, whom she says especially gravitates to the white swim instructor, is six and a half and not quite yet at the developmental stage in which he would recognize race constancy (the idea that things like race and gender are relatively fixed and do not change over time) or more abstract ideas like racial identity (Hughes 1997; Lefrançois 1995; Murray and Mandara 2002). However, he is at an age at which studies show prowhite bias among African American children is declining (P. Katz and Kofkin 1997). Audrey also sends her two school-aged sons to an African-centered school and appears to find irony in the fact that friends who send their children to elite, predominantly white private schools would accuse her of teaching her children to embrace or aspire to whiteness. She laughs off their comments and says, "That's fine," but clearly does not find the idea itself to be fine. Instead, she asserts that her sons "respect themselves and their culture." While the youngest two may not be old enough developmentally to fully understand the concept of culture and identity, her eldest son, Toussaint (eleven), expresses a clear, positive, African-centered identity, as well as sophisticated critical thinking about racialized inequities in society. Even he, however, at one point told his mother he wished he could be white. Audrey sees this as an inevitable part of growing up black in the United States. "Because of television and societal pressures," she maintains, "[my children] have said to me, 'I wish I was white.' And you know, we, we just have to work through it. And eventually they come through it. But they have to go through that. [We] just tell them that—we give them an idea of their history and where they came from."

So even living in Detroit and attending an African-centered school, both of which Audrey sees as racially protective spaces, Audrey's boys have all expressed at one point or another the idea that it is better to be white. That both Audrey and the scholarly literature ultimately attribute this to racism in media and society more broadly (Giroux and Pollack 2010; Graves 1999; P. Katz 2003; P. Katz and Kofkin 1997; Murray and Mandara 2002) shows that, essentially, there is likely no such thing as an impenetrable racial safe space in the United States. Even so, Audrey says they "work through it," with Audrey and her husband working to counter this idea by teaching their sons to think critically about the sources of and reasons behind it.

This idea can be stubborn, Michelle has found as she has tried to dissuade her oldest child, Elina (thirteen), from the blanket statement that white men are "cuter." She discloses that "[Elina is] at some scary point that's actually been kind of disturbing to me because she has hit a 'white is better' mode in her life.

She has verbally decided that she is going to have a white boyfriend, and she's going to marry white, and she just naturally thinks that white men are cuter to like. She just put it out there like that." In response, Michelle encouraged Elina to question her assumptions. She continues, "So I'm like, 'OK, why do you think this [that white men are cuter]?' She's like, 'Well, because, they are!' She said, 'Like, look at TV!' [*Laughs.*] And we had to have this discussion. She's like, 'Because the guys on TV are always like cute.' And . . . I said, 'But, Elina, you know, TV is not real. Everybody does not look like those guys. That's why those guys are on TV.'" When Elina remains skeptical, Michelle guides her through a critical thinking process, asking her to draw upon her own life experiences instead of relying on media portrayals. "So I actually had to make her *say* this and think it through. I said, 'Well, think about it. When you're at the mall, when we're walking through the mall and you see all those white people, do all the white guys look really, really cute to you?' She's like, 'Well, no, not all of them. Some of them look good.' I was like, 'Well, right, because that's regular people.' I said, 'Regular people are all shapes and kinds, baby, so every white guy is just not cute because he's white.' She was like, 'Hmmm. Well, yeah.'" Sensing Elina is still not entirely convinced, Michelle encourages her to think about all of the attractive black men she knows. "So I was like—I started naming black guys, and she was like, 'Well, he's cute. He's cute.' So I had to get her to concede, that, OK, black guys are cute."

What deeply concerns Michelle is her belief that Elina's blanket preference is indicative of underlying ideas about race. Even after Michelle got Elina to concede that not all white men are attractive and that black men are also attractive, Michelle says, "Still, she was like, 'OK, well, but I still think I want a white boyfriend.' So, OK. So, somewhere in her head, white has become an ideal thing. I'm not going to stop her from being attracted to white kids, but somewhere in her it's gotten incorporated that white's better, which is a little disturbing to me." In this case, the racialization of space combines with media images to create the conditions under which Elina's ideas developed. Not coming across many white boys or men in her everyday life, her ideas about white boys and men became tied to Hollywood actors.

The idea that white features, if not white people, are more attractive came up in several interviews. Anita bemoans this attitude taking root in her daughter Shani (twelve). "Because I know for a while, it was like, she wanted [*imitating child's voice*], 'I want my hair to be like my [white] teacher's.' Her hair wasn't soft and long enough. You know, blah, blah. You fine just like you are, and this is what you gonna have. You get what you get." Perhaps not unrelated, when Shani was asked to name the most attractive person she could think of, she said rapper Lil' Fizz, at the time a member of the popular R&B group B2K. Shani's explanation for her choice was this: "I like his dimples and his skin color and his long pretty hair." Lil' Fizz is relatively light skinned—although, of course, such assessments are subjective, he is arguably the lightest-skinned member of the four-person group—and at the time wore his wavy hair in a low ponytail, as opposed to the other young men in the group, who wore their hair in cornrows, in twists, or closely cropped. Anita says she works to teach her daughter that pride and beauty are not part of a zero-sum equation; she wants Shani to be able to appreciate the beauty of people in different races without that translating into a degradation of the beauty of blackness or of her pride in her own race and appearance. Still, Shani wavers when asked if she thinks she is attractive. "I don't know," she says, "because there's like some people be hating, saying I'm ugly, then the boys who say I'm cute. So I wouldn't know." When asked to choose one feature she likes, she responds, "[Pause.] Um. [Pause.] Let me see. It's nothing." It is possible she is simply being modest, although most children in this study felt comfortable saying they think they are attractive; Shani is one of only three children who did not answer in the affirmative when asked this question. It is also possible she does not think she is attractive for any number of reasons besides skin tone or hair texture. From Anita's account, however, and from Shani's own insistent assertion she is "not all black," it seems Anita may be right to worry, as do other mothers, that she must work particularly hard to counter the insidious message that white is better.

Cora's daughter Kaiya (eleven) has wished aloud she were white. While Kaiya says this is because of her hair, Cora interprets this to mean Kaiya believes life is easier for whites.

> I heard [Kaiya] tell me one time, she was like, "I wish I was white." . . . I was like, "Wait a minute. Why do you wish you were white?" She was like, "Because then my hair'd be straight and it won't hurt when I comb it out." [Laughs.] . . . That's what she basically was saying [that life is easier for whites]. And I told her, I said, "You know what, let me introduce you to some people that are white and are struggling just as you are." And which we have. You know, I mean, I've introduced her to—because a lot of my friends are white. . . . And I told her, I said, "You know, look! Aren't they struggling? They're struggling worse than we are."

Cora does not address the structural reality of white privilege and the impact it has on white Americans' everyday realities (McIntosh 1990; Wise 2008), nor does she explain what she means by "struggling" among her white friends, but she uses their troubles to try to counter Kaiya's belief it would be easier to be white. She also does not directly address Kaiya's desire for straight hair, an aesthetic mark of whiteness. It is possible, of course, that her white friends' struggles are also aesthetic, but Cora appears to have interpreted Kaiya's pronounced wish to be white as about more than hair.

In a different twist on the same theme, Yolanda says Travis (thirteen) and Shaun (fifteen) have internalized the stereotype that white people have everything under control, while black people are scrambling to get it together. She thinks a lot of people still teach this but makes it a point to expose the falsehood to her sons. Like Cora, she points out to her children that there are plenty of white people who struggle. "It's always been," she says, "and I still believe people always teach that being white is better. Where it's not necessary. Like, I tell my kids, it's a lot of white people get on welfare. . . . I say, that's where they get 'poor white trash' from, or 'trailer trash' or whatever. It's just that certain people just think that they're superior, and they're not. They're no better than. And they're always one step away from being just like you." For Yolanda, the idea "that being white is better" seems to be tied more to economic measures than to beauty. This may be because Yolanda has only sons, whereas the mothers addressing issues like standards of beauty have daughters. She does not seem to critically address why, on the whole, whites do hold significantly more wealth than blacks in the United States, or why blacks are disproportionately in poverty (Kochhar et al. 2011; Oliver and Shapiro 1995). Instead, like Cora, she teaches her sons that there are just as many whites as blacks struggling. Although it is possible Yolanda may be reinforcing another set of stereotypes with the terms "poor white trash" and "trailer trash," her purpose is to refute racist notions that most whites are rich or that most welfare recipients are black. Again, the racialization of place may play a role here, in that the poor people the children see are likely to be black simply because most of the people they see, period, are likely to be black. Their mother raises the notion of mobile-home parks as one place poor white people can be found, but there are no such parks within the 139-square-mile city of Detroit (although there are several in nearby working-class suburbs). Once again, place is likely impacting the boys' personal experience and, therefore, the development of their ideas, akin to Corey's (thirteen) denial that white people litter or sell drugs because, he says, "This far I've never seen it."

Sarah believes the perception that it is easier to be white, or that white people "have it going on," comes from the media, and she has to help her daughter Trisha (fourteen) critically unpack these media images.

> We had this conversation this summer where Trisha said it was better to be white. And that upset me. I said, "Where did you get that from?" She said, "It just seems like it's better. It just seems like they don't go through what we go through, and it just seems better. And they always act like they have it going on." I said, "Trisha, that's perception." And I explained it to her that, "The reason why you think that is because of what you see on TV constantly, what you see in your teen magazines, and what you hear on the news." And I said, "And that is, you know, coloring your perception." And she didn't get it. And then I just broke it down to her a little bit. I said, "Think about it; every time you see something on TV and

it's whites, it's good. And then every time you see something on TV and it's black, they're acting a fool or it's bad. So you begin to think that's the way black people act and that's the way white people act."

Like the other mothers confronting this, Sarah expresses pain at hearing that her daughter may be internalizing the idea that "white is better." To fight this, she focuses on teaching critical thinking to help Trisha work through the differences between a white-biased perception and reality. Much like Yolanda, though, Sarah does not seem here to address Trisha's point about white people not having to "go through what [black people] go through." While Trisha's statement is broad, the racialized nature of US society certainly makes it true (not simply a perception) on many levels. However, although she does not pick up that point here, it is clear in Sarah's interview, as well as in those with her children, that she is indeed teaching them to recognize and critique such structural racism.

Another tool mothers use to help their children resist internalizing racial ideas is an emphasis on pride in oneself and in African American history. As discussed in chapter 4, many of the mothers underscore racial and cultural pride as a part of procultural socialization. Let me be clear, though, that accentuating racial and cultural pride can also be used as part of responsive socialization if the purpose of the message is to react to and critique the racism their children do or will encounter. For example, to help her daughter Shani (twelve) reject the idea that it would be better to be white, Anita stresses cultural pride, encouraging her daughter: "Keep your head high, whatever your color." For Gwen, the mother of twelve-year-old Tiara, the very first response she gave when asked about what, if anything, she tells her daughter about being black was this: "To be proud, that, you know, that she's black. And [pause] it's nothing to be ashamed of, that you're black. And try not to, try not to judge other people, you know [pause]. I don't want to say that there's no, that there's no [difference between black and white]. What am I trying to say here? [Pause.] Don't be ashamed of being black." Implied within Gwen's response is the fact that there are forces likely to tell Shani she should be ashamed of her race in one way or another.

Desarae points out other racial and ethnic groups in the United States who also receive these messages and respond by "stick[ing] together" and having pride in their culture. She holds these groups up as models for her twins, Cara and Corey (thirteen). "I try to teach them to have pride in theirself," she says. "I try to teach them have self-respect, values, and morals. And you should have these regardless of what culture, what race. I think if you look at, like, Chinese or Arabic, they stick together. . . . And I try to teach them, you know, don't think you're better, or don't think that someone is better than you." In this case, pride and racial solidarity are being offered as tools to critique and cope with racism.

She also believes balance is important; while she wants to critique racist messages by telling her children that they are as good as everyone else, she also wants to be sure that her children do not interpret her encouragement of pride to mean that they are better than others.

Working as an educator in a city that is much more diverse than the environments in which her children operate on a daily basis, Annette uses her experiences to engage her son Matthew (thirteen) and older daughter, Tanya, in a critique of racism. As a teacher, she sees the impact racism can have upon young people and hopes to mitigate this for her children by teaching them to take pride in themselves. She says, "I have stressed, because of where I work—in my building there's twenty-six different languages alone, it's a melting pot of diversity—and I come home and I will share things with both Matthew and I have with Tanya, in terms of racism and how it's unfair and just how ignorant it is. [I am] telling them to believe in themselves. Whatever they do, believe in it."

Similarly, when asked what, if anything, she tells her daughter Mahogany (fifteen) about racism, Patrice says, "I told her you could be whatever you want to be. You know, if you wanted to really go to college, you can. You got to make up in your mind, you know; do your best and try to get there. You know, she the only one can get herself there. You know, I know it cost money. I ain't talking about money. But you know, you do good, you get scholarships and stuff, you always get to college. If you really want to go. If that's your goal, you can do. You know, don't let nobody tell you anything different or stop you, or anything. You can do anything you can do out of life. You can get it. And you can do it. Anything." Although Patrice does not mention it directly in this quotation, this is her response to a question about what she teaches her daughter regarding racism. As such, it is clear that she views her messages to be a part of her responsive racial socialization.

Annette also encourages her children not to buy into racist ideas about their abilities. Her eldest child was recently accepted to the University of Michigan and has expressed doubts about her abilities, worrying that she may have been admitted due to affirmative action. "I say take your twenty points and keep going," Annette says, "because in the long run it won't matter. . . . It just gets you in the door. Then you prove yourself."[2]

The idea in all of these messages is to teach children not to internalize the racism that suggests they are unable to achieve. By disproving specific racialized stereotypes and encouraging racial pride, the mothers engage in a critique of racism as part of the responsive racial socialization of their children. This is imperative, they argue, so that their children know, as Audrey puts it, "that they are strong and that they have a purpose and that they're not second-class citizens." These messages are crucial because of the preponderance of racist stereotypes endorsed by the broader American society.

Encouraging Critical Thinking

Eventually, of course, the mothers want their children to be able to critique racism on their own. To this end, they encourage the development of critical thinking skills in their children (Aboud 2008), particularly through discussions with their children about television, music, and language (Tatum 2003). In fact, we have already encountered situations in which mothers coached their children through critical processing of racialized images on television. For example, Sarah helped her daughter Trisha (fourteen) think through how she came to think it would be better to be white because of the biased, racialized images on television. Natalie helped Kenny (thirteen) recognize the ulterior motives behind television news portrayals of young black men as thugs. Yolanda said she and her husband are living examples that not all black people are like those on television. Here, Yolanda expresses further frustration with images of African Americans on television, noting that even Black History Month documentaries require critical thinking and additional research because the producers "try to sugar-coat stuff." Yolanda teaches her Travis (thirteen) and Shaun (fifteen) to learn to critique what they see and hear, do further research, and decide for themselves instead of being passive consumers. "I don't just say, 'Sit here and here and we're going to watch this and you got to learn from this!' . . . I try to take the sugar-coating away and let you see the real, what I feel is real. And then I tell you what I know. If you need a little bit more research, I can research it for you, I can help you with it, or you can talk to somebody else, and then *you* can decide because you're smart enough to decide once you get the facts, to know what's right and what's wrong. [Be critical] of everything. Don't trust everything." Yolanda adds that it might "sound bad" that she is teaching her sons to question all ideas that are presented to them as fact, but it is the best way she knows to engage in racial socialization because "if we see something on TV, I can explain it to them, but I can't just give them an example."

In fact, the use of racialized media representations as an impetus for critical racial socialization came up repeatedly. When asked what, if anything, she tells her children about racism, Cora responds:

CORA: When certain incidents come on the news, I let them watch the news, you know, and I don't want them to look at it one-sided. You know, I try to get their opinion on—like the guy that they just beat up that was, um, that had a confrontation with the police.

ERIN: In Cincinnati?[3]

CORA: Yeah. When they show the police on there, they was like, "Momma, he's black, though!"

ERIN: The other—the officer?

CORA: One of the officers that were in there, he was black, at the bottom [of the television screen]. And they—because I couldn't tell, I was like, "For real?" They were like, "Yeah, Momma! He was actually beating up that black man, too." I was like, well, I don't think that they were—they meant to use extreme force like they did. You know, it's a bad situation that the man did die. But I try to explain it to them not so much as the way that the news tried to explain it. I tried to explain it to them more of on a basis, maybe they did use excessive force that wasn't really necessary, you know, or then again, maybe they just used force because of the way that he was fighting back. You know. Just trying to keep their minds still rolling on it.

Cora wants to be sure that her daughters have the critical thinking skills to examine media representations from a variety of viewpoints and come to their own conclusions, and she considers this part of her racial socialization practice. Of course, her processing of this particular news story could also be seen as harmful to her girls' critical thinking, almost trying to talk them out of examining the complicated ways in which race and power come together in police brutality (Correll et al. 2007; Worden 1996). According to Cora, however, her ultimate goal is simply to get the girls to consider all angles.

Some mothers specifically mention music and music videos and teaching their children to critique the racialized images they see therein. Both Barbara and her adult daughter help her younger daughter, Brianna (fourteen), to understand that the images of black women in music videos are not something to which Brianna should aspire. "I'm always saying," Barbara remarks, "and even her big sister [says]—the way you dress and the way you act is how people respond to you. The videos are just because they're trying to sell records. So we *always* talk about that." Now, Barbara says, "[Brianna] knows that, looking at a video, that is not cute!"

Julie does not allow her son Josh (ten) to watch music videos at home, but she is aware that he does see them and listen to music she finds objectionable when he is with his peers or his uncle, who lives nearby. In these cases, she hopes having taught him to think critically about the racialized and gendered images portrayed in some will keep him from internalizing those ideas. Because Josh spends a lot of time with his stepfather and uncle, she says, "I get on [them] for the music and the songs that they choose. You know what they're saying—turn that off! I don't want my son growing up thinking that women are just bitches and hoes. I'm not a piece of ass. No! . . . [Josh] does know what a pimp is. And I point out the prostitute on the corner, and I tell him what her job is. And what the pimp is, and that's what you're talking about. That's what you're listening to? You think that's OK? These poor women. It's so sad, how they feel about themselves and what they allow to happen to their bodies." Because she thinks the glorification of pimping in some music dehumanizes both black men and women, Julie encourages Josh to think about the real people and consequences behind the language. She also tries to get him to critique the idea that "authentic" black men need to be uncaring or "hard," like pimps. She explains, "We talk about how being 'hard'—and I don't, I just, I don't think it's cool at all. And I think, um, almost a *good* bad thing is that [Josh's uncle] is so—[he] tries, [he] portrays this hardness. And Josh and I really see that as not cool. He's not cool. You know, that's clear to us. That's not cool. That's stupid. So I think that it keeps [Josh], hopefully, from that." Julie believes that her son's uncle is such a caricature of hypermasculinity that Josh sees through it as a farce. This, she says, makes it "a good bad thing"; bad because he is modeling this behavior for Josh, but good because, she believes, Josh can see it is not cool.

However, while Julie says it is "clear to *us*" that this behavior is stupid, Josh seems a little ambivalent. Josh's friends at school have formed a group they call the P-Unit, short for Pimp Unit and fashioned after the rap group the G-Unit (short for Guerrilla Unit). In his interview, Josh says that the purpose of his group is "just to have a group and so nobody knows all our secrets and stuff" and that he did not want the group to be called P-Unit. "I said, I wouldn't want *my* group to be called Pimp Unit because I'm not an owner of prostitutes, and I probably wouldn't ever want to be." However, he does not think his friends have been taught to think critically about the reality behind the use of terms like "pimp" and "ho." "[They get the terminology] probably from the music. . . . Probably they've never met one [a real pimp], I don't think. But their uncles and stuff probably call themselves pimps and stuff like that just to make their—the younger kids feel like they're heroes and stuff like that." It is interesting the extent to which Julie's responsive socialization seems to have worked its way into Josh's thinking here. He points to the stark and unpleasant reality of prostitution, saying he would not want to identify with such a thing. But he is also understanding of his friends' use of the term, thinking they are not using it literally and just got it from music or from older men in their lives who use it to elevate their own status. He also says, specifically, that his friends probably got this from their uncles, which is interesting given that Julie clearly holds up Josh's uncle to him as an example of someone pretending to be "hard" or a pimp. Josh seems to be a little conflicted about this overall, though. First he says he is in the P-Unit group, then later says, "I'm not really in it," pointing out that other kids make fun of the group and call it the "Peed Unit." He also says he "*probably* wouldn't ever want to be [an owner of prostitutes]" (emphasis added). So, he is clearly working through these issues in his own comprehensive racial learning process, negotiating the pull of ideas from his mother, his friends, and music and popular culture.

Critical racial socialization extends to other types of language as well. Part of critiquing racist ideas, several mothers argue, involves critiquing racialized language. Audrey says that she and her husband talk about African and African American history with their sons but that they make important linguistic distinctions. "We give them an idea of their history and where they came from," Audrey says. "We give them an idea of enslavement. We don't call it slavery. It's enslavement. It's like, no, you weren't a slave, you were *en*slaved. And the distinction between that."

Mothers Michelle, Barbara, and Sarah all raise the racial implications of the word *ghetto*, which many children use without being aware that it is racialized. "So, it's like, now we've got the phrase, 'Oh, you are so ghetto!'" Michelle says, "which basically means acting in some untoward behavior, or, you know, something that's not properly conducted or straight and narrow." Michelle works explicitly to help her children think through why they use a racialized term to talk about something that is not race based. Although this is not an indication of what language they use with their peers, neither of Michelle's two children used the term in their interviews, both of which were relatively long and during which each child was very talkative and open to discussing racialized experiences. Barbara says she tries to intervene not only with her daughter but with other kids whom she hears using the term. "When the kids say 'ghetto,' I say, 'Do you know what the definition of *ghetto* is?!' And then my daughter will say, 'The ghetto is when everybody of the same nationality lives in one place.' I say, 'Right!' I say, 'So we gonna find another word for when people act a certain way.'"

Sarah, on the other hand, does not necessarily have an issue with her children using the word *ghetto*, but wants her children to use it only if they understand it not to be specific to black people. She hopes that her children can think of the word as "not about being black [but about] a cultural thing." She expounds, "We say, 'ghetto.' You know? Like we say, 'Oh, that is so ghetto, will you stop?' . . . It's like it's a catch-all for everything. Like, 'Baby, don't be so ghetto.' And what we're saying is, what we're saying when we say that is don't act, like, culturally unacceptable. And it was interesting, too, because one time we were watching a talk show—it was one of those talk shows, it was either *Jerry Springer* or either *Ricki Lake*. And [Trisha] made the comment; she said, 'White people are ghetto, too!' I said, 'See, so it's not about a black and white thing.'" Pleased that her children understand that not all black people act in any single way and that people of any race can act in a way that is "culturally unacceptable," Sarah nevertheless points out the racialized nature of the word. She continues, "What it does, really, if we could just talk about that word, it really will identify where a person is culturally. And it's a catch-all for everything that's undesirable. When you're acting *too* black, if I could say that. You don't want to be, you know, ghetto because that's an undesirable black trait. And so, but when [Trisha] said that, I was pleased that she got it that it's not about being black; it's a cultural thing."

It is noteworthy, and potentially confusing to her children, that Sarah defines *ghetto* as meaning "when you're acting too black" and "an undesirable black trait" but also says "it's not about being black." Because she understands the term to mean "everything that's undesirable"—or, as Michelle put it, "untoward behavior"—Sarah is proud that her children recognize all racial groups are equally likely (or unlikely) to engage in undesirable or untoward behavior. On the other hand, she does not appear here to critique the racialized nature of the word itself, nor the significance of using a term so closely tied to race in general and black people in particular to describe "everything that's undesirable." Sarah's primary concern is that her children understand that the term can apply to people from any racial group *and* that it does not apply to all African Americans, regardless of where they live.

Derogatory names are Lena's main concern, and she is worried her children will not learn to think critically about their use because they are growing up in Detroit. Firmly tying this issue to place, Lena, who is not originally from Detroit, complains, "A lot people . . . here in Detroit, I think, are racist." She finds herself continually critiquing racialized language used around her children so that they will not adopt the corresponding ideas.

> My mother-in-law used to constantly say, "Oh, well, you know, Whitey at work," so and so and so and so. "Oh, but I'm not racist," or "I'm not prejudiced." Then why are you going to use a derogatory term? Right? I mean, why couldn't you just say, "This lady at work," or "This white lady at work," or "This Caucasian" or whatever, without having to say "Whitey"? It's derogatory. So how can you not be prejudiced or racial, but you use a derogatory term? I don't like the term *A-rab*. Firstly, "A-rab" is wrong! I mean, if you're going to say it, say "Arab." Firstly. [*Laughs.*] But secondly, not everybody that's from the Middle East is Arabic! But it's a derogatory term for the most part, when people say ["A-rab"] or "camel jockey" or whatever. Don't! You know? So, if I use that term, can I still say that I'm open-minded and I'm not prejudiced or racist if I'm going around calling people derogatory names?

For Lena, then, the critical racial socialization takes on a spatialized priority; actively helping her children critique racialized language is necessary, she believes, because no one else around them is going to do so. Of course, the use of derogatory racial terms is neither universal in nor unique to Detroit. But Lena believes Detroit's history, its demographics, and what she sees as its geographical isolation contribute to the problem. She expounds, "Detroit is the country, in the middle of the city. OK, most of the people here migrated—and this is whether they're black or white, actually, so the white people are just as country as the black folks—most people migrated here from the South for the better jobs, but they kept their South mentality. . . . And to me, it's just, it's just a very racially tainted city. And I don't know if that's because this is not a major throughway in the United States—because, unless you're trying to come to Michigan, you're not going to pass through Michigan—so maybe because we're isolated a little, maybe that's why it is."

It is true that most African Americans in Detroit today descend from those who came north as part of the Great Migration in the first half of the twentieth century, but this is true for many northern cities (J. Franklin and Moss 1997). Lena believes there is something about Detroit—perhaps its geographical location or being surrounded by the Great Lakes or the fact that there has not been a significant influx of people in the last forty years as the auto industry has declined—that makes it more insular than other cities. Conjecturing that this has led to an uncritical, "racially tainted" way of thinking, Lena proffers that raising her children in Detroit means she must be especially vigilant about teaching her children to scrutinize racialized language.

Perhaps Natalie best sums up the wishes of the mothers in this study to encourage their children to think critically about racialized issues. While her first instinct is to tell her son Kenny (thirteen) and his younger sisters what she thinks about a given incident, she instead encourages them to do their own critical thinking. She explains, "Just [as] cases . . . arise, like on TV or just with the track team—because there's black and white kids. And at church, we have white families at our church. So, if something comes up, then we'll talk about it, if it's a racial issue. And then I'll try to tell them—I may ask them, 'How would you have handled it?' And then I'll tell them how I would have handled it. And then sometimes I would just tell them my opinion, but I've learned to listen to what they're thinking first and then share with them what I think they should do." By asking critical questions, Natalie helps her children learn how to process and critique racism. Ultimately, many of the mothers, like Natalie, employ the Socratic method, teaching their children lessons about racism by getting them to think critically about the world around them.

"Don't Lose Your Humanity about It": Individual Character and Fairness

Another part of critical racial socialization is a focus on universal values, such as individual character and fairness. David Demo and Michael Hughes (1990) found that "individualistic and/or universalistic" messages are an important part of racial socialization, and Michael Thornton and colleagues (1990) note that African American families emphasize "human values" in addition to more specific racial values. While some studies find these messages to be correlated with a general "silence" about race (Hughes and Chen 1997), most mothers in this study instead combine this type of message with those already mentioned. They recognize the necessity of preparing their children for racism but also want their children to recognize people as individuals. This serves as a critique of racism, showing it is neither logical nor humane to generalize too broadly about people based on race. Michelle articulates how she balances preparing her children for the inevitability of racism with emphasizing that they ought to approach people as individuals. "I guess with my kids," she says, "I'm trying to teach them that, you know, you're going to have to grow up and be a little alert, but, you know, don't lose your humanity about it. Don't just assume that all of them are like that." Anita agrees, saying, "I mean, yeah, sometimes . . . something [about race or racism] might come up. Yeah. But otherwise, I really teach them that—what's that called? You know—we all the same. That's really what I teach them. So it's kind of, they get both." By "both" Anita means both direct discussion about racial identity and racism as well as universalistic messages.

Cora, too, prepares her children for racism while also admonishing them not to assume all black people are on their side or all white people are against them. "[Helping my kids figure out the reality of racism] has a lot to do with taking them out, you know, and really letting them look at the world. You know. Don't look at it through rose-colored glasses. You just better look at the world and pay attention to what you're looking at. Because I don't think it matters whether you're white or black as to how a person is going to treat you. You know, I mean I've been treated by blacks just as wrong as I have been by whites." Yolanda agrees and adds that treating people as individuals will not only help her children protect themselves, but also help them develop more fulfilling relationships.

> I tell them it's good white people and it's bad white people. You know? Ah, and the bad ones you will know because they will let you know. You just stay away from them. Just, you know? But it's good and bad people in all races; don't just think all black people are good, because they're not. And we have a thing where we went with Arabic people when the 9/11 thing happened, but don't, you know—everybody you meet, you meet them for theirselves, *not* because of what color they are or whatever. Because the school that they go to is a multiracial school. . . . They have a lot of Hispanic, a lot of Arabic people. . . . I just tell them, as it goes, take each person for each person. Because it could be another person from another race that could be exposed to you as a sister or brother, to where a person of your same race will fuck you up.

Thus, the mothers use universalistic messages about individual character to balance out the racial socialization of their children. These universal messages help their children to reconcile messages about the existence of racism and unique racial identities with messages critiquing racism because these universalistic messages focus, as Michelle phrases it, on being "a little alert" about racism without "los[ing] your humanity."

Fairness, too, is primary in the critique of racist messages included by these mothers as part of responsive racial socialization. The mothers say that, although their children might be judged on the basis of their race, they should nevertheless, as Gwen, mother of Tiara (twelve), puts it, "try not to judge other people" in return. Delores expresses this individualistic message when asked how, if at all, she socializes her daughter Kaneka (thirteen) about racism: "Oh, she already know about all of that. But you don't be racist back. You just pray for them people. Because they're some sad people." Acknowledging her daughter must be prepared to deal with racism, Delores believes she must nevertheless learn that she should not "be racist back" (although, in psychological terms, Delores is referring racial prejudice here, not racism) (Operario and Fiske 1998).

Patrice echoes Delores's point, saying, "I told [Mahogany] you supposed to love everybody, whether they be purple, black, green, whatever. And I tell her people will treat you bad, but you got to—just because they treat you bad, you don't treat them bad." Both women appear to take a partially colorblind approach (earlier, Delores says, "You can be purple; you still human"); they do prepare their children for racism but encourage them not to pay any attention to race in their own treatment of others. Lena concurs, stating that she tells her children "to accept everybody, more or less, as who they are." She continues, "We just happen to be black, and in some cases people don't like that, for whatever reason, but, you know, you still have to—you can't assume that everyone is going to treat you differently because of the color of your skin. But because of that, you also need to be cognizant not to treat other people a certain way because of the color of their skin because then you're just perpetuating the same thing."

This kind of message, while acknowledging the existence of racism, critiques its logic and instead emphasizes the idea of human equality. This echoes Marie Peters's (1985, 165) pioneering work on racial socialization, in which she found that African American families "encourage honesty and fair play" even though, because of their children's racial status, it will not always be returned. The mothers admit that it can be, as Cora puts it, "very confusing" for children that they "are supposed to treat people equally even though people don't always treat [them] equally." Some say faith or religion helps their children better understand this universalistic message. Desarae says the basic Christian tenet you must "treat people the way you want people to treat you" helps her children adopt fairness even in the face of racism. Bridget tells her daughters they need to treat everyone fairly, regardless of how others might treat them, because "God's way is not to hate. So we have to be the image of him. We have to do what his word says." She adds, "And that's what I try to teach my daughters. Even though somebody might be mean to you, or call you out of your name, don't worry about it. Ask God to fix them and pray. You know, don't look at people because the color of their skin because that's not right and God doesn't like that."

Similarly, Annette cites religion when explaining how she and her husband teach their son Matthew (thirteen) about fairness in the face of racism.

> [Matthew] thinks things aren't fair. And Matthew's playing sports, you know. Sometimes the coach will say something and [Matthew] doesn't like it and he doesn't understand and I said, "Welcome to the game of life." This is what happens. And it's not you personally sometimes, but it's just that you got a little more color than they. . . . That's just how things go. But then some things are not fair in life. But that's the way it happens and there's—you have no control really. . . . [But a sense of fairness] is being instilled in him. We go to church every Sunday. He knows right from wrong. And it's being preached to him constantly. No, life isn't fair. No, they probably shouldn't have done that to you. But I don't expect you to do that back to them. So, I think he listens.

While Annette prepares her son to encounter racism, but not to internalize it ("It's not you personally . . . it's just that you got a little more color"), she also believes his religious training helps teach him to nevertheless treat others fairly and not to retaliate. Faith, then, serves as a means of reinforcing her critical racial socialization messages about individual character.

By encouraging their children to refute racial stereotypes, resist absorbing racist ideas, think critically about racialized representations, and treat people as individuals and with fairness, all of the mothers engage in a critique of racism as an aspect of responsive racial socialization. This is meant not only to prepare children to encounter bias (Hughes and Chen 1997), but to help them problematize the system of racism in the process.

"How Do You Know What . . . They Will and What They Won't Absorb?": Comparing Children's and Mothers' Reports

Of course, *comprehensive racial learning* posits children as the central players in creating their own ideas about race and racism, so it is important to look at how the children process and make meaning of their mothers' messages. Overall, the mothers report engaging in more racial socialization than the children report receiving. All but one of the mothers (eighteen out of nineteen, or about 95 percent) say they talk to their children about racial identity, racism, or both. However, only three-quarters of the children (twenty-one of twenty-eight) say their parents talk to them about racial identity, racism, or both. The inconsistencies may be due to an actual communication gap between mothers and children, or perhaps the mothers or children felt there was a "correct" answer they "should" be giving—either that mothers felt they should be talking to their children about these things even if they were not, or that children felt maybe their mothers should not be talking to them about these things even if they were. The difference could also reflect the mothers' relative ease with answering open-ended questions as compared to the children. It is possible that the amount of abstract thinking involved in answering a question like "Do your parents ever talk to you about being black?" was more difficult for some of the children than for the mothers, although it should be noted there is no particular age pattern in terms of which children's responses matched those of their mothers.

Looking at maternal and youth responses within individual families, children were more likely to match their mothers' responses regarding racial identity (three-quarters of the children did so) than racism (half of the children did so). Again, this could be because of the social mores around the topic of racism; participants may have thought a white researcher would be more approving of talk about racial identity than discussion of racism. The inconsistencies, however, do not follow any particular pattern by age or gender of child (see tables 5.1 and 5.2).

Most of the inconsistencies within families occur when a mother says that she is sending a racial socialization message, but the child denies this. However, there are five cases in which the mother says that she *is not* sending a particular

TABLE 5.1

Comparison of maternal and child responses by age

Age of child	Number of children who match their mothers on racial identity question, # yes/total	Number of children who match their mothers on racism question, # yes/total
9	1/1	1/1
10	3/4	1/4
11	2/3	3/3
12	2/3	1/3
13	7/11	5/11
14	2/2	1/2
15	2/2	1/2
Total	19/26*	13/26*

*Although there are twenty-eight children in this study, there are two child-parent dyads for which there is not enough information to make this comparison.

TABLE 5.2

Comparison of maternal and child responses by gender

Gender of child	Number of children who match their mothers on racial identity question, # yes/total	Number of children who match their mothers on racism question, # yes/total
Girls	11/16	8/16
Boys	8/10	5/10
Total	19/26*	13/26*

*Although there are twenty-eight children in this study, there are two child-parent dyads for which there is not enough information to make this comparison.

racial socialization message, but the child says she *is*. For example, Gina says she does not talk to her twins, Terri and Tyrone (thirteen), about racism at all, but both of them say she does.

GINA: I really haven't [talked to my kids about racism]. I just talk about every-day life. Um, they haven't had to endure it. And their teachers that is white doesn't treat them no different than she would a white student. All I see is, as long as they're trying to educate them—I mean, we read, we read a lot of black books. And that's just, I just do that because I tell them you need to know about yourself before you can know about somebody else. That's what I tell them about it.

ERIN: OK. So you guys talk about history and stuff like that?

GINA: Yeah. I started them on a youth black book club. So, and that's because they don't—I mean, they wasn't reading enough in school. They were teaching them everything that was in those books. And when they have a literature book to read it was always whatever was in that course outline. It was never nothing dealing with them. So on top of what they have to read in school, they have to read a book for me, too, that's dealing with black history.

While Gina says that she does not talk about racism with her children, she immediately adds that the curriculum her children are given in school is racially biased in that it excludes materials and lessons reflecting black experiences. Gina therefore has her children read "black books" because their school's curriculum contains "nothing dealing with them." Thus, Gina's children may answer in the affirmative when asked if their mother teaches them about racism because they infer such lessons from their mother's critique of the school curriculum and materials.

It is likely this distinction between direct and indirect teachings accounts for some of the inconsistencies, but it is also likely some mothers send unintended messages to their children. Yolanda wants Travis (thirteen) and Shaun (fifteen) to listen to what she tells them about race but not model their behaviors on hers. While she encourages her boys not to make assumptions based on race, she says she does not always follow her own advice. "You know," she admits, "I don't know how to model nothing. You know, if you're going to go by my example—because it has been times where they have seen me, and I be like, 'Ooo, I can't stand that white motherfucker.' You know what I'm saying? Or different stuff like that. But then I have to tell them, 'It's just, it's not because he's white, it's because, you know. And I called him out like that because I can. Because I'm sure he would call me a black bitch if he didn't think I'd hear it.' You know what I'm saying? But, I just have to tell them because I can't . . . I can't just give them an example. I just got to be flat out." This "do as I say, not as I do" approach is certainly not unique to Yolanda—although she is perhaps more self-aware and honest about her experiences with it—but is something with which virtually all parents have struggled. In all cases, it results in children receiving unintended or mixed messages. Here, it could account for some of the inconsistencies between maternal and youth reports of racial socialization.

Conclusion

In their comprehensive racial learning processes, young people actively develop their ideas about race and racism by negotiating, reframing, and making meaning of all of the racialized messages they encounter, including those from the family. I break down the messages from family, called racial socialization, into two broad categories: procultural and responsive. While the mothers in this study leave much of the procultural racial socialization to Detroit itself, they believe they must directly and consciously engage in responsive racial socialization, which they see as "damage control" in response to negative societal messages. Strategies of responsive racial socialization include shielding children from direct experiences with racism, preparing children to deal with racism, and teaching children to critique negative messages about blackness. The mothers certainly are not monolithic in their ideas about responsive racial socialization, but all except one report engaging in it, and even she says she believes she needs to begin.

Of course, the children are the central players in creating their own racial identities, attitudes, and strategies for dealing with racism. The purpose of sharing the mothers' practices is not to suggest that they determine their children's ideas, but rather that they are one part of the equation. Place, again, is another part of the puzzle, influencing mothers' responsive racial socialization by shaping how they approach issues like protecting their children from racist encounters, enabling them to switch codes as a way of coping with racism, or combating the idea that it is better to be white.

Even the most optimistic mothers concede that racism is so ingrained in US culture and society that, despite their best efforts, their children may, as Lena says, "internalize it anyway." The mothers themselves, then, realize family is not all-powerful in this process. Indeed, racial socialization itself cannot enable African American children to overcome all of the structural barriers racism places in their paths. What racial socialization can and does do, however, is create a critical point of intervention in which parents are empowered to insert themselves into their children's comprehensive racial learning and help them negotiate racialized messages from the larger society.

6

Black Is Black?

Gender, Skin Tone, and Comprehensive Racial Learning

Despite important exceptions (T. L. Brown et al. 2010; McHale et al. 2006; A. Thomas and King 2007), few studies systematically explore the impact of African American children's gender and skin tone on their ideas about race or their parents' racial socialization messages (Hughes et al. 2008; Lesane-Brown 2006; Stevenson et al. 2005; T. Williams and Davidson 2009). Research on racial identity among multiracial adults, as well as the racial socialization practiced by their families, does a much more thorough job of exploring the impact of skin tone and gender on each process (Funderburg 1994; O'Donoghue 2005; Rockquemore and Laszloffy 2005; Tatum 2003; Twine 2006), but this has not extended to literature on African American children with two black parents.[1] In some studies, both gender identity and racial identity are considered, but as separate entities, neglecting the intersectionality of these constructs (e.g., Buckley and Carter 2005; Mandara et al. 2005). Black feminist scholarship urges us not to ignore the importance of intersectionality, or the ways in which identities and oppressions interact, in scholarly analysis (Collins 1991), including in scholarship on young children (K. Scott 2003). In this chapter, I argue that gender and skin tone come together with place to shape children's notions of race, racial identity, and racial authenticity, as well as their ideas about, experiences with, and preparation for racism.

Perceptions of Race, Racial Identity, and Racial Authenticity

First I will unpack the many ways in which gender and skin tone shape children's ideas about race. Here, we consider how skin tone and gender enter into mothers' messages about race and racial identity, as well as children's ideas about attractiveness, racial authenticity, and belonging. Throughout, place is always an overarching influence, guiding and tailoring these messages and ideas.

"It's OK to Be Who You Are": Inclusive Definition of Blackness

The fourth and final type of responsive racial socialization revealed through the mothers' interviews is an emphasis on an inclusive definition of blackness. Unlike the other categories of responsive racial socialization, which primarily deal with racism from mainstream white society, this category deals primarily with intraracial challenges regarding racial authenticity. While E. Patrick Johnson points out that "there are ways in which authenticating discourse enables marginalized people to counter oppressive representations of themselves" (2003, 3), the mothers here are concerned with those notions of "authentic blackness" that they see as limiting for their children. Many of these ideas originate in (and serve to further) white supremacist ideologies (Russell et al. 1993), and fully two-thirds of the mothers discuss encouraging their children to reject these ideas.

We have already heard from mothers who encourage their children to defy and dispute narrow definitions of blackness. For example, Sarah said her daughter Trisha (fourteen) is challenged on her racial authenticity by people in their neighborhood who taunt, "Who do you think you are? You just want to be white. You just want to look like a little white girl, a little fake girl. . . . Are you black and how black are you? Because, after all, you go to [a 'Gifted and Talented' school],[2] you're lighter, you don't dress like us." Challenges, too, come based on the way Trisha speaks, although Sarah counters, "My kids don't talk all that proper." In the face of this kind of questioning, Sarah works to give her children an understanding that racial identity is not defined by speech or dress or skin tone. She believes a strong sense of self-identity is a tool she can give her children to prepare them for both internal and external challenges based on notions of race. She hopes this will help them to be secure in themselves, adding, "I don't want them to feel like they're inferior because I sincerely believe that I'm raising just some dynamic people."

We also heard from Julie, who worries her son Josh (ten) will feel out of place, as she does, if he does not "have the right shoes on to fit in with the black crowd." But she says, "[I teach Josh] you can wear whatever shoes you want. And what's cool is that you choose what you like, not what everybody else has." Like Sarah, Julie wants her children to know their racial identity is not defined by their fashion choices, that they can stand up for who they want to be while still embracing their community and heritage.

Another example comes from Lena, who laments what she sees as an all-too-common definition of blackness in which, "if you are outside the box in any way, shape, or form, then, you know, the eyebrows are raised."

> So often you hear people say, "You're not black. Black folks don't listen to that kind of music. Black folks don't do this; black folks don't do that." And you hear that. It's a message that—I don't know where we get it

from—where we'll tell our kids, "Oh honey, you can grow up and you can be whatever you want to be! They sky is the limit!" But if they're talking about skiing, "Black folks don't ski!" So how can you give your child a message that they can do whatever they want, and then the first time they do something, play hockey or something, then you tell them that they can't do it? So, in regards to music, I listen to all kinds of music and I try to tell [my children] that it's OK. If you enjoy it, it doesn't matter what, you know, Tom, Dick, or Harry thinks, you have to be true to yourself and you have to do what makes you happy, regardless of what other people say. . . . You shouldn't have to hide certain things because it's not quote-unquote the black thing to do.

In encouraging a definition of blackness that is wide in scope, these three mothers inherently critique racist notions that being black means one can only have a limited set of affinities, proclivities, and abilities. They want their children to have strong black identities that can withstand challenges, both internal and external. By modeling secure, dynamic black identities, these mothers hope to provide their children with powerful examples of the heterogeneity of African American life.

"Black Is Black"

Another issue in this type of responsive racial socialization is skin tone. All interviewed children were asked how they would describe themselves if they were talking on the phone to an out-of-state relative whom they had never met in person. (This was before the days of broad participation in social networking websites, which now facilitate young people posting pictures of themselves online.) Eleven of the twenty-eight children responded with physical descriptions of themselves, and of those eleven, seven included a description of their skin tone. Significantly, the children who referred to their skin tone in response to this question were only those who described themselves as on one end of the spectrum or the other. This suggests skin tone is more salient for the children who are seen as outliers or as different—the lightest-skinned children, who are often called "white" and report regular challenges to their racial authenticity, and the darkest-skinned children, who are called "black" in a derogatory way, with reference to their skin tone, not their racial identity.

The mothers back up this finding. All but one say skin tone is an issue in the racial socialization of their children. They lament the higher value placed on lighter skin, as Audrey says, "even within our community," and the idea among some that it is not considered favorable, as Michelle puts it, "to be really *dark* dark. You never want to be a Hershey chocolate dark." On the other hand, some mothers also noted light skin can also be a disadvantage within the black community in terms of, as Audrey says, "people challenging [you] and

[your] blackness" because of it. The mothers were almost universally disapprov-ing of both notions—that "lighter is better" and that one has to be a certain shade of brown before being considered "authentically black." Thus, the mothers' interviews revealed a focus on an inclusive definition of blackness grounded in the belief that neither racial identity nor worth is determined by skin tone.

Natalie, mother of Matthew (thirteen), remarks, "My son and my two younger daughters—if a black person is light-skinned, they say that that person is white. And I'm trying to get them to understand that that's not the case. Black people come in different shades." Michelle agrees, saying she has had to assure her daughter Elina (thirteen) that her lighter complexion does not make her any less black, regardless of what her peers might say. Michelle explains, "Elina was like, 'Well, am I white? Because so-and-so says I'm white because I'm light-skinned.' This was when she was probably, like, seven. You know? And I'm like, 'No, you're black.' And then she was like, 'Well, then, if I'm black, then how come I'm light?' [*Laughs.*] And I was like, I said, 'Well, one, because your father is black Puerto Rican and he's light, so your color kind of comes from both.' I was like, 'But you know, essentially, you're black.' [*Laughs.*] . . . I said, 'So, look, you *are* black. Don't worry about it.'"

In this case, Elina is being challenged explicitly based on her skin tone, not her father's ethnicity (since, as Michelle points out, racially he is still identified as black). Michelle's messages are intended to build a positive black identity in Elina strong enough to withstand challenges based on skin tone and to reassure her that her racial identity is not reliant upon skin color. She could perhaps be seen as neglecting or erasing her children's Puerto Rican heritage, but she says her children are very aware of that heritage, and interviews with Elina and Carlos confirm this. Michelle points out the role place plays in her children's racial identity and the fact that it is sometimes challenged based on their skin tone.

> I think it's just like that just because of where they are. Because every-body else around them is black. I mean, they don't know any other biracial people. They don't know any other Hispanic people. Everybody's black. You know, their mama's black; their grandma's black; their grandpa's black. You know, they know, amorphously, sort of out there in the world, they've got these Hispanic, Puerto Rican people, but they've never met them. So, I think it [their black identity] is a self-concept that's just there because everybody else around them is that, so that's just what they primarily identify as. I mean, I think if you press them for it, they'll be like, "Oh, well, yeah, my dad is Puerto Rican and I'm Puerto Rican, too," but I think their main identity really is black, and I think it's really environment because everybody around them is black. As far as, I guess they pretty much feel like they look like everybody else.

Yolanda also encourages her sons not to make judgments about people's race based on skin tone alone. She scoffs at the notion that "all black people look alike," noting that even within their immediate family there is wide variation in skin tone.

Because there could be somebody Arab darker than [my sons]. You know what I'm saying? You don't just assume. I've seen white people with nappy-ass hair. So you don't just assume what somebody is because of the color of their skin. And I tell them about how I used say, "White people used to say all black people look alike. You could look at our family! We could all sit in the same room, we have the same characteristics, but we're not all the same color; we don't all have the same kind of hair; we don't all have anything." So, never assume what somebody is by the way that they look. Like I said, I got blond hair and blue eyes—well, most days. I got contacts and I bought them! So what the hell am I?

Using skin tone, hair form, and hair and eye color to make her point, Yolanda challenges her sons to think critically about how they define blackness. Again, metropolitan Detroit's large Arab population comes into play in racial socialization, here helping Yolanda make the point against eliding race with skin color. While some may argue Yolanda's own decision to wear a straight, blond weave in her hair or blue contact lenses could be read as reinforcing the idea that "white is better" (Rondilla and Spickard 2007; Russell et al. 1993), she vehemently denies this, arguing blackness or racial authenticity is not about hair or eye color.

Sharon teaches Nina (thirteen) and her younger brother that they are black regardless of the white and Native American members of her family tree. She remarks, "I've been able to explain, I guess, different colors [to my children]. And I explain to them their ethnic background. So that, you know, on this side of your family this grandfather, he's white. My great-grandmother is Indian. You know, and explain that we come from a hodge-podge, but you are black. You are African American. . . . There's all different, these different shades in my family. There's *light* light, you know, and there's dark, you know. And so they, they can see, you know, it's like, look at all your cousins, you know. There's all different colors. It doesn't matter." Sharon's children, like many African Americans, have mixed racial backgrounds, but she teaches them they are still black, as are all of their cousins of various shades. Some may critique Sharon's message as an affirmation of the "one-drop rule" or the rule of hypodescent, which has its origins in the US system of slavery as a means of reinforcing the economic and political power of slaveholders (Davis 2001; A. Johnson 2006). Sharon and many of the other mothers here, however, see themselves as sending a unifying message, meant to affirm membership, belongingness, and pride and to avoid the creation of separate, hierarchical categories of dark-skinned and light-skinned African Americans.

Gina, mother of twins Terri and Tyrone (thirteen), says her children unfortunately do hurl insults at each other based on complexions. She uses the "black is black" message to quell such arguments.

> Oh, they argue because, I think, Nick and Terri is the most fairest-skinned ones out of my [four] kids. And you know when they argue, they always be somehow, "Well, you black!" And I be like, "Well, both of you all, all of y'all are black!" It's just a matter of whichever way the chromosome went. One of you all got lighter and one of you all got darker. Because I'm dark but all their dads is light. So they do argue about it, but I tell them it ain't nothing but two true races, black and white. So their color is just color, you still black. . . . I mean, my pastor's daughter is really [light]—she got the hair and everything. But her grandfather was white. So that's why. So, they do look at things like that. But I done told them she's still black.

Gina's quote is important on a number of levels. First, it illustrates the common message among the mothers that skin tone and particulars of racial and ethnic heritage do not lessen one's racial authenticity. She mentions their pastor's daughter, who has light skin, straight hair, and one white grandparent, but emphasizes "she's still black." Second, it shows, despite her urging to the contrary, that her children do notice skin tone and use it as an indicator of status or authenticity. Third, Gina proffers the idea that there are "two true races, black and white." This reinforces a point I have made throughout this book, but especially in chapter 3, that these interviews evidence a restrictive construction of race, overly reliant on a black-white binary. Detroit at the time of these interviews was 1 percent Asian and around 5 percent Latino (US Census Bureau 2000d), although that population was concentrated in an area of southwest Detroit called "Mexican Town," an area of the city unusual in that it is 50 percent Latino and only one-quarter African American (C. Williams 2008). As also discussed in chapter 3, the greater Detroit area has the largest Arab population in North America, although more than 90 percent of this population lives in the suburbs, and only 1.6 percent of the city of Detroit's population is Arab (Schopmeyer 2000; Shyrock and Abraham 2000). Among the mothers and children in this study, many explicitly identify both Latinos and, especially, Arabs as white. On the other hand, four mothers say this dichotomy has been loosening since September 11, 2001, as Arab Americans became the targets of racial profiling. Nevertheless, Audrey points out that certain segments of the Middle Eastern community in Metropolitan Detroit are still thought of as white, saying, "The Chaldean American community has become white, for all intents and purposes. . . . Even they consider themselves white after a while." It is true that in the 2000 census "the vast majority of Arabs reported their race as White and no other race" (US Census Bureau 2003a), and Chaldeans, "a close-knit community of Iraqi Catholics who own a majority of Detroit's small grocery and liquor stores" (Shyrock and Abraham 2000, 20), may especially be read as such. But other mothers say their children are not sure what to make of Arab Americans since they do not fit well into their children's conceptualization of race as a black/white dichotomy. For example, in chapter 3 we heard a mother named Cora say that her children ask her, "Momma, well, are Arabics [sic] black or are they white?" Instead of problematizing the idea of a black/white dichotomy of race, Cora simply tells her children she's not sure because some Arab Americans are light-skinned and some are dark-skinned. She ends by reverting instead to colorblind rhetoric, telling her children, "We're just all human and without color." These and other interview excerpts illustrate how place influences definitions of race. While the construction of race as a black/white dichotomy is deeply rooted at the national level (Celious and Oyserman 2001; Denton and Massey 1989; Spickard and Daniel 2004), some argue it remains especially rigid in the Midwest, where levels of racial diversity and interracial marriage and cohabitation are lower than in other regions (Fernandez 2008; US Census Bureau 2003c, 12, 2008b; Wang 2012, 45–46).

We can see the impact of Metropolitan Detroit's hyper-segregation on this dichotomous conceptualization of race, as well as the fact that the children also reflect this way of thinking in some of the interviews. For example, Desarae offers a story in which her daughter, Cara (thirteen), indoctrinates a friend new to Detroit.

My daughter had a friend who asked her, "Well, you have good hair. I thought all black people had bad hair?" And she was like, "Well, no, we all don't—we all have different, just like we've got different skin, we have different hair." But see, this was a biracial child that had always lived in the suburbs. I think the mother died and [the child] had to come live with the father, so the child was put in a black neighborhood and really didn't know how to interact. So my daughter kind of told her, "Well, I tell you what, just stick by me and I'll let you know who's good, who's bad, who to play with, who not to." And [Cara] basically said, "You know, people going to look at you and they going to ask you, 'Are you white? Are you black?' So you got to figure out which one are you? Are you white or are you black?" And the girl's like, "Well, I don't know what I am." [Cara] said, "What do you mean you don't know what you are?" She said, "I'm just me." Because her parent taught her that she's both. They say, "You are, you are black and you are white." So this child, I think, my daughter helped her define her identity because she didn't know what she was. And when you're in a black neighborhood, my daughter told her, "You

know what? You black if you ain't white. Maybe in the white neighborhoods you could be white, but you're in a black neighborhood. I think
you better tell them you black."

Cara is genuinely trying to help her new friend fit in and thrive in her new
neighborhood by pushing her to accept the idea that "black is black" and that
having a strong black identity will help her face challenges to her authenticity
from within her new community. At the same time, this anecdote highlights the
constraints borne out of such a bifurcated conceptualization of race. For Cara's
friend, there may well be positive and negative psychological and social
consequences to any decision she makes (Rockquemore and Laszloffy 2005;
C. B. Williams 1999).

Lighter Is Not Better

Colorism, or the idea within any given racial group that lighter skin is better,
is well documented by scholars (Hochschild and Weaver 2007; Rondilla and
Spickard 2007; Russell et al. 1993). This "intraracial system of inequality . . .
bestows privilege and value on physical attributes that are closer to white"
(Wilder and Cain 2011, 578). As we have already heard, several interviewees
make mention of this in relation to beauty and attractiveness as well as access
to education, employment, and privilege. Many mothers say they emphasize
solidarity and a strong, positive black identity in order to dismiss this notion,
but many of the children reveal the idea is alive and well. One example comes
from Patrice, who says she has had to fight colorism with her daughter,
Mahogany (fifteen), who has been teased for having dark skin.

PATRICE: You know, people have called her "black" in the days. And I told her
that's why I called her, named her Mahogany. Because that's a black name,
you know. You black. And um, that's a good name for you. I say black is
beautiful. Don't let nobody tell you anything different.

ERIN: So you think people call her black because of skin tone? Because of skin
color?

PATRICE: Yeah. Because she's very dark skinned. . . . She had told me somebody,
"They called me black in school," and different stuff like that, and I tell
her don't worry about it because, I tell her, "They just mad because you're
beautiful." That's what I tell her.

Lena says many of her daughters' peers refuse to go outside in the summertime because they do not want their skin to darken, bringing to mind the title
of Marita Golden's (2004) book, *Don't Play in the Sun: One Woman's Journey
through the Color Complex.* She points out that black models and actresses with
lighter skin and more "Anglofied features" are portrayed as more beautiful in

the media, adding that "Michael Jackson didn't help it any." For her part, Lena tries to model the opposite value for her children, telling them that skin tone is irrelevant to beauty and that they should go outside and enjoy the sunshine.

ERIN: Do you think that the skin tone of your children affects ways in which you need to prepare them for racism or teach them about racial identity?

LENA: Unfortunately, yes. But more so, not from the Caucasian-to-black standpoint, but from the black-to-black standpoint because, regardless of what anybody says, people are still color struck. I mean, there are more and more African Americans that are darker that are getting prominence, whether it be TV—well, I'm talking specifically, I guess, about the show biz industry. But for the most part, it's still, even if it is a darker-skinned person, a lot of times they still had more Anglofied features, a narrower nose or different color eyes or something. So, it still plays a major role. When Alek Wek—I think that's her name, the Sudanese model—a lot of people cannot find anything, a lot of black people especially, can't find anything pretty about her at all because she's just so dark. So, I mean, it's still an issue. I coach a softball team in the summertime with my oldest girl. I tried to get my neighbor on the team. She's darker. She didn't want to play because she didn't want to get any darker. . . . Which, you know, was the last thing on my mind. Obviously, I mean, it's still, unfortunately, an issue. . . .

ERIN: So do you think—I'm wondering; as a parent, to what extent do you feel like you can counter that and to what extent do you feel like they internalize it anyway?

LENA: I think they're going to internalize it anyway. So I can say whatever I'm going to say, without drilling it into their head, and hope that some time, at some point, it will trigger a response. You know, our parents tell us all kinds of things and we don't necessarily listen to it at the time. But hopefully, somewhere down the line, it will ring a bell. I know I had a problem with color growing up, partially because I didn't grow up in an all-black area. Also, my mother and my brothers were lighter than me. And people would make comments and, you know, I remember those comments. I still stayed outside because, you know, back in the day you had no choice; you went outside. Now it's to the point where I like to get darker. Summertime, I'm out there in the sun. And my kids look at me and they think I'm a little crazy or whatever else, and maybe that's my own way of combating part of it, with the fact that they know that in the summertime I'm looking to get a tan versus hiding from the sun.

Returning to the "family versus society" struggle highlighted in the previous chapter, Lena is not optimistic she can compete with media and other social forces enough to fully prevent her daughters from internalizing the idea that lighter skin is better. Interestingly, Lena begins by calling this a problem "from the black-to-black standpoint" but later also acknowledges the role of mainstream media, which is controlled almost exclusively by whites. Here she speaks to African American internalization of racist ideas that have their origins in white society (Harrell 1999; Swim and Stangor 1998). Although certainly such internalization is not universal (Crocker and Quinn 1998; Harrell 1999; Swim and Stangor 1998), Lena thinks both the overwhelming presence of the idea that "lighter is better" in mainstream media and its adoption by many African Americans will mean that her children internalize these ideas despite her best efforts to the contrary. Still, she talks to her daughters about it and continues to model behaviors for them, in hopes that "at some point, it will trigger a response."

Anita, too, models for her daughter Shani (twelve) the idea that all shades are beautiful. "I guess because I'm darker than both my kids," she reflects, "so I just . . . I carry myself with confidence, so I just teach them the same way. Keep your head high, whatever your color. You know? I'm saying you're no cuter than me! I'm just as fine as you! [*Laughs.*]" Annette, too, worries that her son Matthew (thirteen) and his older sister might think they are better than others because they have lighter skin. Unlike Anita, though, Annette decides to avoid the issue because she worries discussing it might put ideas in their heads. She explains, "I think skin tone has, in the African American race, it has a great deal to do with [racial identity and how others treat you] in terms of within your own race and outside of your own race. . . . I have not [discussed it with my children]. Sometimes, just not knowing about something is better to me. I don't explain that because both of my children, I think, are not—they're not dark skinned, but they're medium-fair skinned. I don't want them to think that their color is better than any other." Avoiding discussing issues of race with children, however, does not prevent them from developing ideas (Hirschfield 2008; Patterson and Bigler, 2006; Tatum 2003), and messages about skin tone are undoubtedly reaching her children through media, peers, schools, or nonverbal family messages (R. Hall 2008; Wilder and Cain 2011). Annette acknowledges that skin tone has played a role in her own professional life, saying that her lighter skin often makes her white colleagues think of her as "an exception," or different from other African Americans, and leads her black colleagues to accuse her of not being authentically black. Both of these assumptions, Annette says, have "really hurt my feelings." This hurt has led Annette to avoid the topic of skin tone with her children, hoping she will not corrupt their thinking. As comprehensive racial learning asserts, however, parents are not the only (or even necessarily the primary) source for children's ideas, and even Annette's silence on the topic likely sends children its own message—not that skin tone is not important, but that it is not considered an acceptable topic of discussion (Tatum 2003).

Sarah's experiences with racial socialization and skin tone underscore both the complex issue of colorism and the tension between family and society in children's comprehensive racial learning. Sarah decided to remove her daughter Trisha (fourteen) from a prestigious school of choice because the school was "validating" the idea that "lighter is better."

> With Trisha, she went to another really good school [a "Gifted and Talented" middle school].[3] And [this school]—all the kids from [this school] go to [a "Gifted and Talented" high school] or they go to private schools afterwards. But most of the kids at [this school] are light-skinned, or they're mulatto. A lot of mulatto, a lot of mixed kids, interracial kids, we call them mixed. . . . So, when I first got there, it *bugged me!* Oh, it got on my nerves so bad! I said, "So why are all the little yellow kids going here?!" I said, "OK, so here we go again." And the principal, I said, "Oh, it makes perfect sense; look at the principal!" She was really into that whole light-skinned thing. . . . And I said, you know what? This is not cool because I didn't see very many kids there who looked like my son [Elijah]. And so, it seems like—no, not it seems like—at that school they used to validate that. To the point where Trisha came home one day and she made a derogatory comment toward Elijah because Elijah was darker. I said, "Hold up, wait a minute! Mmm mmm." I said, "Trisha, just because you're lighter, it doesn't mean that you're better." And I had to tell her where that came from, and I had to break it down in a way that she would receive it, or could receive it, meaning the lighter you are, you know, back in the day during slavery times, it meant you were closer to white and therefore you were better and more acceptable. And I said, "And honey, those same beliefs have somehow entered into society today and they're still prevalent." I said, "But Trisha, that's not the case!" I said, "You're grandma is really dark, and you love your grandma, so now what?" I mean, my mother is like really dark. I said, "So do you think you're better?" She said, "No, but, you know, in school . . ." And it just really, *really* confused her. And I had to really decide whether or not I was going to keep her in that school because I didn't want her to get the wrong message.

Sarah eventually decided to pull her daughter out of this school because of what she saw as its validation of lighter skin as superior. Ironically, in this quote, she does not appear to be critiquing her own use of skin tone as an indicator of belongingness, such as in her exclamation, "So why are all the little yellow kids going here?!" In using "yellow" as a descriptor for light-skinned children or "mulatto" for biracial children, Sarah could be seen as belittling such children, since these terms have been identified as offensive and exclusionary

(Davis 2001; Russell et al. 1993). Despite this, I understand Sarah's main critique to be not about lighter-skinned children's authenticity or belongingness, but rather about the societal phenomena of lighter-skinned African American children or biracial children having more opportunity for a higher-quality education than darker-skinned children. Sarah's response may also be tied to Beverly Greene's (1990) finding that African American parents are especially protective of their darker-skinned children in relationship to racism.

Sarah extends her critique to the relationship between skin tone and educational and economic opportunities, saying, "It's interesting because there is a relationship between color—whether we want to admit it or not—and socio-economics. It just simply is. You know, it seems—but we know why it is, because the lighter-skinned people get more of the opportunities and then they can take advantage of the opportunities and da da da da, and then the money—OK, so we understand that. . . . And so there are a lot of people who are darker, who haven't gone to school, who haven't finished high school, you know, haven't gone to college." Although this is certainly not an absolute truism contemporarily or historically (Small 2004a, 2004b), it does bear out in much of the research (Russell et al. 1993) and, on a smaller scale, within this study sample in terms of poverty and education. While 21 percent of the families in this study (four out of nineteen) live below the poverty line, a much-higher 60 percent of the children who describe themselves as dark-skinned (three out of five) do. In addition, while only 25 percent (seven out of twenty-eight) of the children in this sample attend neighborhood schools, which are the least prestigious of the four types of schools attended by children in this study,[4] 80 percent (four out of five) of the children who describe themselves as dark-skinned attend neighborhood schools.

Sarah is angered by the apparent inequity in opportunities between lighter- and darker-skinned black children in Detroit Public Schools and also because she had to make a choice between the best academic school for her children and placing them in an environment that did not privilege lighter skin. She continues:

> So I pulled them out [of the "Gifted and Talented" middle school], and what I was so disappointed about was, when I took them to [a neighborhood school], the principal was very dark, and so I thought she was going to be cool. And I was telling her my experience at [the "Gifted and Talented"/examination school] and I said, "Why does everything that we have that's good, as African Americans, why does it have to be associated with that whole light-skinned culture?" I said, "Why?" And so, she looked at me like, "Why don't you just grow up?" And she said . . . something like, "Certain things you just have to hold dear to you." I'm like, "What do you mean by that?" And so she said, "Listen, [the 'Gifted and Talented'/

examination school] is a good school; that was the best school that your daughter could have went to. You were probably going to school with a lot of important county members." And I said, "Yeah, she was." "And a lot of the police officials and city officials." And I said, "Yeah. But that's not supposed to get racial, the way I understand it." And I said, "Well, this is really tough for me." And she said, "You know what? That's just the way it is." And this was coming from an educated woman—very dynamic, I picked up. And she was dark-complected. So, it just hit me that somehow in her life, in her mind, she had justified it and come to terms with it and it was OK. And I just was totally confused. And I was like, "Wow."

Again in this quote, Sarah does not appear reflexive about her own reliance on skin tone as a sign of identity or ideas, saying about the principal at the neighborhood school, "She was very dark, and so I thought she was going to be cool." Sarah's point seems to be, however, that she was disappointed but not especially surprised when the first principal, whom she saw as benefiting from light-skin privilege, seemed uncritical of that privilege; but she was quite surprised when the second principal, whom she saw as being oppressed by that privilege, seemed just as uncritical. The fact that, from her point of view, someone oppressed by the system would simply advise her to accept the system was both confusing and dismaying. Still, Sarah believes having her children in a school that does not so explicitly validate colorism will ultimately be best for her children's comprehensive racial learning.

Sarah goes on to disclose that, while the racial socialization she received from her own mother may have made her "a little bit defensive and a little bit suspicious" in terms of searching out light-skin privilege, she sees real evidence in the Detroit Public Schools that colorism is alive and well, even at Trisha's new school. Sarah remarks, "Because she has light skin and all that, [Trisha] is considered to be attractive. I would never tell her to use it to your advantage, but I know, because of the way she looks, it is an advantage. It is. It just is." Nevertheless, Sarah continues to emphasize a strong, positive black identity, regardless of skin tone. She tells her children that lighter skin does not make a person better but recognizes that external social influences are telling her children otherwise.

Skin tone also comes into play in young people's ideas about attractiveness. As explained in chapter 2, children in this study were asked who was the best-looking person of whom they could think and why that person was the most attractive. Of the twenty-six children who named someone, twenty-five named an African American person and one named a Puerto Rican American. Two girls also each mentioned white male musical celebrities, but only after first citing black male musical celebrities. All were asked to explain why they named that person as most attractive. The most common reasons cited were long hair, face, skin color, eyes, and personality. Skin tone was mentioned four times, with light skin and dark skin cited equally. Elijah (twelve) and Trisha (fourteen), siblings whose mother and grandmother give explicit and frequent messages about the beauty of and pride in dark skin, both cite dark skin as a reason for attractiveness. Trisha, who is light-skinned, picks her aunt because of her dreadlocks and "chocolate" skin, and Elijah picks a girl at school with "dark" skin and dark hair. However, he also mentions her long hair and light eyes, both often associated with more anglicized features. Shani (twelve) and Nina (thirteen) both choose rapper Lil' Fizz as most attractive and point to his light skin as one reason why. As mentioned previously, Lil' Fizz was a member of an R&B group popular at the time of these interviews and wore his wavy hair in a low ponytail, as opposed to the other young men in the group, who wore their hair in cornrows, in twists, or closely cropped. When asked what she likes about the way Lil' Fizz looks, Nina replies, "He has light skin. His hair. . . . His eyes are a different color. His hair is all wavy and cute." Indeed, while only two children mention light skin color, several cite long hair and/or light eyes, which are traits often associated with lighter skin or mixed racial heritage. Long hair on both men and women is by far the most cited reason for attractiveness, with nine boys and girls referencing it. Eyes are also commonly named, and all of the children who do so discuss eyes that reflect more Anglo features in color or shape. Matthew (thirteen) talks about his girlfriend's "green eyes," Nina (thirteen) mentions that Lil' Fizz's eyes are a "different color" from those of most black men, and Toussaint (eleven) talks about his grandmother's "almond-shaped" eyes. Elijah (twelve) thinks a girl at school is beautiful because of her "dark skin" and "long . . . jet-black hair," but he also adds, "And her eyes change color, just like my sister. . . . If she cry, her eyes turn blue. And then, if she reflects on the sun, it's orange. And if it's like a dark day, they're really hazel." Again, the revered eyes seem to be those that are not typically African and are more typically European.

The children seem less likely to focus on Anglicized features when talking about themselves, although they are mentioned. All but three interviewees answered in the affirmative when asked if they thought they were attractive. One child, Corey (thirteen), says no, but adds that other people think he is attractive and says, "My momma tells me that girls like light-skinned people." Two girls, Shani (twelve) and Tiara (twelve), say that they are not sure whether or not they are attractive but that they do not think they are ugly. Again, the most commonly named reason for attractiveness is long hair, cited by six girls. Other reasons given include body/figure (listed by three girls), because other people say so (listed by two boys and one girl), and just overall (listed by four girls and one boy). Only Tyrone (thirteen) says his skin color, which he describes as "dark," is what makes him handsome. Two girls cite their eye color—Trisha (fourteen), who has light eyes, and Terri (thirteen), who says, "[I like] my eyes, mostly. They're not green or blue, but they're black eyes." Terri seems to feel she has to qualify her statement, explaining that she thinks she is attractive because of her eyes, despite the fact that they are "black eyes."

The children's responses suggest that skin tone or racialized features play a role in notions of attractiveness. It is interesting to consider whether some of the most-cited celebrities, including musical artists Bow Wow, Lil' Fizz, and Raz B, would be called "white" due to their light skin if they were classmates or peers of the interviewees. Richard Harvey and colleagues found that, among black college students, those at a predominantly black university "placed significantly higher importance on skin tone," especially in relation to attractiveness, than their peers at a predominantly white university (2005, 237). Understanding that these children are much younger and that a university is not the same as a city, it is nevertheless possible that skin tone becomes especially salient for the children in this study in the context of their operating within predominantly black realms of daily interaction. Still, the overwhelming majority of the children say that they think they are attractive, and the only three interviewees who were not sure of their own attractiveness fell across the spectrum of skin shades.

Of course, skin tone influences ideas beyond those about attractiveness. Several children share that, in their experience, lighter-skinned people enjoy favored status and/or think they are better than darker-skinned people. Thirteen-year-old Kaneka, who describes herself as dark-skinned, says that the light-skinned girls at school think that they can boss everyone else around. "When we was in the gym room, everybody was talking," she explains, "there was this girl named Jennifer [who] wanted everybody to shut up because she was, like, light-skinned and she had long hair. So she was telling everybody to shut up, and we said no. So I went up there, and I was like, 'We ain't got to shut up,' and then she hit me. And I didn't feel it, and then she hit me. I was like, 'Did you just hit me?' And she hit me again. And that's when I just started hitting in her face." Note that, for Kaneka, the skin tone of the other girl involved is a critical factor in why she became involved in the fight. Kaneka insists it is *because* the girl is light-skinned and has long hair that she believes she can tell the other students what to do. Kaneka is very deliberate about confronting the girl and, therefore, I argue, about symbolically confronting the idea that lighter skin and longer hair confer power and prestige. When Kaneka retaliates after being hit twice, she specifies she aims for the girl's face. Although we cannot know for sure, it is conceivable that Kaneka casts her recompense at what she sees as the root of the other girl's arrogance—lighter skin and more Anglicized facial features and hair.

Still other children describe the flip side of this phenomenon, pointing out situations in which dark-skinned people are assigned lower status or are made to feel inferior. Trisha (fourteen) points out that her little brother is targeted for his darker skin tone. "My brother is darker than me," she says, "and sometimes they call him 'Blackie' at school and stuff like that because he's darker. And

I guess my mom will just tell him, 'You have beautiful skin! Milk chocolate,' and all of that. She calls me 'Caramel' because I'm kind of light." Trisha's story highlights the way in which children must negotiate the sometimes-contrary nature of their conceptualizations of race and their everyday experiences of race. In this case, Trisha's brother must try to reconcile his mother's strong racial socialization messages that no skin tone is better than another with the teasing or bullying he receives from his peers, which suggests the opposite.

Mahogany (fifteen) also reports her parents tell her that skin tone is irrelevant to her racial identity and that dark skin is beautiful. However, she says that she "used to be mad" that her skin tone was "real dark." "When I was younger," she relates, "I used to be mad because I understand that I am black, but the color of my skin was real dark. And [my parents] was like, 'Black is beautiful. Don't let nobody tell you different. Just because you're a little darker than others, you're no blacker. You're all black.' That's what [my father] said back then." Even at a young age, Mahogany formed the opinion that being dark-skinned was something worthy of her resentment. Her parents worked to help Mahogany form a conceptualization of blackness as independent of skin tone, saying of her and her lighter-skinned peers, "You're all black."

"Authentically Black": The Role of Skin Tone and Gender

On the other hand, some of the lightest-skinned children in the study argue that, in Detroit, having light skin is a disadvantage, at least socially. Both Josh (ten), whose father is white, and Elina (thirteen), whose father is described as "black Puerto Rican," posit that light-skinned children in Detroit have to be physically tough. They use this toughness not only to intimidate those who challenge their racial authenticity, but also as a refutation of the challenge itself. Blackness, in general, and black masculinity, in particular, have come in some respects to be defined by "being hard" (Boyd 1997; Orelus 2010). Several boys and girls alike agree with thirteen-year-old Corey's assessment, "You just can't be soft." The children whose racial authenticity is challenged based on their lighter color seem to evoke this idea of hardness in order to assert their blackness. For example, Elina says that she has "to be really tough" because of how much she has been targeted for her skin tone. "Everybody used to make fun of me," she explains, "like, 'Awww, you white!' I'm like, 'I'm not white!' They be like, 'Well, look at your skin color!' I be like, 'I'm not white! I'm black and Puerto Rican.' They be like, 'Oh, my bad.' . . . And some people used to be like so racist. They'd be like, 'Ewww, look at her; she's a Puerto Rican! Uhhhh, look at her! She look white and stuff!' And, as I grew up, I got to be really tough. Every boy in my class used to be so scared of me. . . . But, man, people like to mess with me about it [skin tone]. I'm like, 'I wish you would, because I'll hurt your ass.'" Becoming physically tough is Elina's adaptive strategy for dealing with the stigma placed on her in Detroit for being relatively lighter-skinned.

While she says her skin has become darker over the years, she still retains this toughness.

Josh (ten), the lightest-skinned child in the study and the only participant with one white parent, agrees light-skinned black children have to "act hard" in order to get by in Detroit. Josh spends some weekends with his father in a predominantly white, small city outside of Detroit. Although Josh says he gets teased about his skin color in both places (in his father's town for being black and in Detroit for being light-skinned), he says that he is confronted with more taunting in Detroit.

JOSH: It happens more when I'm here [in Detroit]. Like they'll ask, "Are you Chinese?" Because they say I don't look black or anything.

ERIN: Really? Why do you think that is?

JOSH: I don't know. Because I'm a lighter complexion than them.

ERIN: So there're not any other kids who are light-complected?

JOSH: Not at my school, no. . . . If there are, they probably beat up on kids and say, "I'm so strong, and I'm so tough" and stuff like that. . . .

ERIN: Oh, why is that?

JOSH: . . . [Because other kids] challenge you and say, "You're not really black. You white!" or "You're Chinese!" or "You Asian!" Or judge you, just because that's what they think you are. But you're really not. You have to act hard because you're not black, or—so they'll tease you about it, and seems like you have to try harder than everybody else just because you're a different complexion.

Josh's observations here are rich for analysis. First, he speaks to the importance of place in setting the context for what is seen as "light" or "dark" skin, as well as authentic blackness, saying he is teased and challenged more in Detroit, where there are very few children with light skin at his school. Josh's mother supports this assertion, saying of the other children at his school, "They're not only black, but they're all brown. There's no high-yellows; they're all brown." According to both Josh and Elina, this is so much so that they are not even recognized as black at all; instead, they are called "white" or "Chinese" or "Hispanic" or "Asian" or, Josh says, "white snowflake." The relative homogeny at their schools—not just of race but of skin tone—creates a space in which lighter skin serves to mark them as other. Second, the constant ribbing from his peers seems to have caused Josh to question his own racial identity. In talking about reacting to such taunting, he says one must act a certain way "because you're not black" and then seems to catch himself, saying, "or" before abruptly moving on. So perhaps even Josh himself, who initially identifies himself as black, ultimately slips into the thinking (or at least uses the language) of his classmates, that he is "not black." Finally, Josh speaks to the issue of lighter skin triggering such challenges to racial authenticity—that children with lighter complexions feel compelled to put on a hard façade, to say, "I'm so strong, and I'm so tough," in order to prove their blackness. He concludes, "You have to try harder than everybody else just because you're a different complexion."

Gender, Skin Tone, and Experiencing Racism

This last point—that blackness and physical toughness are closely associated—is an idea mothers and children alike say exists in general but is intensified or mitigated by gender and skin tone. The mothers spoke more clearly to this, with the majority saying they believe that all African American children need to be prepared for racism but that boys need to be especially well prepared. They were asked if their child's gender affected how they taught him or her about racial identity or racism, and while the question posed involved the intersectionality of race and gender—gendered racial identities (i.e., a particular black masculinity or black femininity) and the ways in which racism is gendered (i.e., racist assumptions about black girls and women versus those about black boys and men)—three of the respondents addressed only gender in their answers. These were all mothers of only girls and focused on girls needing special attention in terms of hygiene, sexuality, and personal safety. However, all of the remaining mothers responded by discussing racialized notions of gender or gendered racism.

"White People Are More Threatened": Gendered Racism for Boys
The clear consensus was, as a mother named Gina puts it, "the boy, he's going to be knocked down because they always going to quote-unquote destroy the black man." Michelle agrees, saying, "I think that my [son is] going to deal with [racism] more [than my daughter] just because he's a male," and she says that white people are more threatened by black men than black women: "They just are." The mothers say that this affects the boys in terms of access to opportunities and even physical survival. Desarae, mother of twins Corey and Cara (thirteen), points out, "For a black male, as he gets older—like let's say he gets out of high school—I think it's more of a challenge because black men don't even half of them even make it to twenty-five." As we will see later, mothers of especially light- or dark-skinned children believe gender interconnects not only with race but with skin tone to determine the type of racism their children will face and how it will affect their life outcomes.

The idea that "black women have it better" permeates several interviews. Even mothers who do not have sons of their own think racism affects boys more than girls. Lena, who has two daughters, says, "I guess, historically speaking, black women have had it better, as far as racially—I mean, from what

I hear—than black men because people tend to feel sort of more [threatened]. So, if I had a boy, I would hope that I would have the foresight to mention that." Patrice also does not have any sons but believes black boys are targeted more for racism and that this would require her to prepare them differently. "I don't have [boys]," she says, "but it would be different. I see my friends with boys and they tell them different things from the girls . . . because, boys, I think they, I think they're more different. They'll be harassed more than the girls. I really do think that."

Although scholars agree that racism is gendered and, therefore, experienced differently by women and men, there is certainly not scholarly consensus that this means racism is more debilitating for one gender or the other (Anderson 2008; Essed 1991; Kunjufu 2009; Wingfield 2008). Still, like many other mothers in this study, Audrey believes black men are portrayed as more threatening than black women and that this results in whites having a higher comfort level with black women than black men. As such, she thinks the most powerful way to prepare her sons for gendered racism is for them to see their father successfully confronting it. If they only see her handling interactions with white people, she worries this might teach them to accept or capitulate to misconceptions about black men.

> Because of the—just the dynamics of the black man in America [and] black women in America, I know that women get more mobility than men . . . because we live in a racist society. . . . [My sons] need to have some different tools than black women specifically because of the mobility and the doors that open. . . . One example [of how I'm preparing them], and there are multitudes of them, is for me to be quiet when we're out—like yesterday at the bowling alley—and to make the white male deal with [my husband] instead of me making it easier talking to him [the white male]. Make him [the white male] deal with it. They don't want to deal with that brother; let them deal with the brother. Sit back and be quiet. Make them deal with it.

To be clear, Audrey frequently and actively teaches her sons about confronting racism, and I am confident—based on my experiences with her, her stories, and her robust practice as a trial attorney—she is not a shrinking violet. Here, however, she says it is important for her to "be quiet" and essentially let the men talk. Certainly, black feminist theory critiques the idea that black women should "be quiet" and let men handle the racial struggle (Bambara 1970; Hull et al. 1982; Lorde 1984), but Audrey sees her actions as confronting racism by making life more difficult for its perpetrators. This is something Allan Johnson calls "withdraw[ing] support from paths of least resistance" (2006, 144, emphasis in original). Johnson's argument is that the only way to challenge systems of privilege is to "interrupt the flow of business as usual" by "dar[ing] to make people feel uncomfortable," including oneself (144–145, emphasis in original). Part of Audrey's intent here is to disrupt the "path of least resistance" she sees as condoning white people's discomfort with black men, especially those who have darker complexions; "let them deal with the brother," she says. Audrey's other objective here is for her sons to witness this disruption and see their father confronting racism. Of course, mothers can and do teach their sons how to deal with racism; in fact, the racial socialization literature shows it is mothers who most frequently directly do so (Hughes et al. 2009; McHale et al. 2006; Thornton 1997; Thornton et al. 1990). Nevertheless, Audrey believes her sons will deal with a particular kind of gendered racism and wants them to see their father successfully confronting it.

"Prove You're Different": Dealing with Gendered Racism toward Boys

As a result of the general belief that racism "destroy[s] the black man" while "black women have it better," most mothers report preparing their sons for racism differently than their daughters (although there are exceptions, and we will get to those, too). One way they do so is by encouraging their sons to present themselves in ways that contradict stereotypes. I argue that, while the mothers believe this will mitigate the effects of racism on their sons, their messages could be understood by their children as endorsing those racist stereotypes. Put differently, in instructing their sons to avoid racism by distancing themselves from behaviors or appearances deemed "not respectable," they do not challenge the racist notions themselves. In this way, for example, telling one's son not to wear baggy jeans does not challenge, and may reinforce, the racist perception that black men dressed as such are thugs. If the message received is that some (or many or most) black people fit whites' racist ideas and that the way to deal with this is by distancing oneself from those people, this could potentially motivate children to dissociate themselves from the group or think of themselves as "exceptions to the rule" (Gaertner and Dovidio 2005; Padilla and Perez 2003).

Anita, a mother who has no sons of her own, nevertheless says that she thinks boys heighten the gendered racism directed toward them through their own dress and appearance. She says, "If the boys, if they portray themselves like a thug, that's what people going to think you are: a thug." Mothers Yolanda, Sarah, and Michelle all agree. We heard from Yolanda in chapter 5; she stated that whites (or anyone) would be justified in thinking, "This is a black boy . . . [so] he going to take my stuff," if her sons entered a business with "hair . . . all wild," "acting [a] damn fool, walking around with your pants hanging off your butt, your shoes untied." She teaches her sons the burden is on them to "prove you're different. You have to be hardworking, respectable, clean, and decent." She sees this as a survival skill, saying they will not get by in life if they do not present themselves in a way that counters racist assumptions about black men. This again ties in with Evelyn Higginbotham's concept of a "politics of respectability," discussed in chapter 4, or the historical idea on the part of middle-class African Americans that the way to "earn their people a measure of esteem from white America" was to encourage a particular type of public behavior (1993, 14).

Sarah also focuses on public self-presentation, especially with her son, Elijah (twelve). Her children are learning this partially by watching their older cousin Jeremy, with whom they recently traveled together to Las Vegas.

> When we got to the airport and we were checking our bags, [my sixteen-year-old nephew] got pulled aside by security. And they said, "Come here." And I knew what it was about. It was about his garb, what he had on, and his whole look. And I said to myself, I said, OK, this is a good lesson for him. . . . I said, "Do you know why you got stopped?" He said, "No." I said, "Jeremy, come here, you need to hear this." I said, "You got stopped because of the way you look." I said, "You look like a threat, Jeremy. And you're about as much of a threat as that kid sitting over there." I said, "You are not." And he said, "What do you mean, I look like a threat?" I said, "Look, you're black and you got on the do-rag and the baseball cap. The way you look, people relate that to gang activity or, you know, suspicion." But he said, "Yeah, but they don't even know me! I'm not like that!" I said, "But guess what? Certain things to certain people mean something. . . . And know this: you're an African American male, you're kind of tall, you're kind of dark—you're seen as a threat! And so that's just the reality of it." . . . And so, I told [my children and my nephew] to be prepared . . . based on people's perceptions, that you are going to get certain things. Especially my son, I'm like, "You're tall, and you're dark, and you're going to be big! You're a threat to people. You're going to be a threat." And Elijah is just the sweetest human being.

Michelle, too, has one son and one daughter and says her son, Carlos (ten), will have to pay attention to how he dresses and speaks in a way her daughter will not. "You know," she reflects, "for [Carlos], life is going to—he's going to have to become a lot more aware of how he's dressed and how he's going to speak, who he's speaking to, you know. I mean, those are going to be the things that I instruct him on. You know, it's like, OK, [white people] expect this, but you know what? Flip the script." By telling her son to "flip the script," or do the opposite of what white people expect, Michelle is teaching him to alter his behavior, speech, and appearance around whites in order to counter racist expectations. This gender-specific preparation, which we see from a majority of the mothers with sons, could be interpreted as surrendering to or endorsing the racism from which it is meant to protect the boys. In instructing their sons to avoid racism by distancing themselves from certain behaviors or appearances deemed "not respectable," these mothers do not challenge the racist notions themselves. In this way, for example, Sarah's advice that her nephew change his appearance could be read by her children as not challenging, and perhaps reinforcing, the idea that simply being a black male wearing a do-rag and baseball cap makes one a thug.

This possibility notwithstanding, it would be a mistake for us to read these mothers' messages as carrying this intent. Anita, Yolanda, Sarah, Michelle, Natalie, and Annette, as evidenced in chapter 5, are among the mothers who actively work to teach their children to be critical of racist ideologies. They are caught between a rock and a hard place trying to teach their children to both critique and deflect racism. If they focus entirely on deflecting racism, they run the risk of inadvertently fostering the internalization of some of the racist ideas they are working against. If they encourage their children to critique racist ideas through their self-presentation—much as historian Robin D. G. Kelley argues that working-class African American "race rebels" have over the last century, using clothing, hair, and language to "represent a subversive refusal to be subservient" (1994, 166)—their sons are likely to be even more vulnerable to targeting by police, teachers, potential employers, and others. In compromise, these mothers—specifically those of sons—try to strike a balance, protecting their children as best they know how, while also advocating critical thinking about racism.

Annette also believes her son must be prepared for gendered racism in a way her daughter does not require, but her approach is not about clothing or appearance. Rather, she says, "In terms of Matthew being male, and the way he's looked upon in this society, it has a negative effect. . . . [We have told him] that Matthew has to try much harder than his sister. And that we expect, we have higher, we have expectations. I mean there's expectations for him that he has to surpass to make it. Now Tanya, you know, no. But I think for black and male, I think they've got to do—they have to work harder." Although Annette's son Matthew (thirteen) did not speak to this in his interview, some other children did. For example, Corey (thirteen) reports, "My mother, she say that it's going to be hard being a black male. See, females is—I don't know, but she just said [being a] black male is hard. . . . Like it's going to be hard because it's a lot of, um, negative stuff toward black men. So, it's going to be real hard for me to get a good job or go to college or something . . . from racism."

Elijah (twelve) has developed a similar view of racism as gendered, although he initially did not understand the nuances of this idea and thought his teacher was being "mean" when she talked to him and his peers about it. "[My teacher] keeps saying—she was mean! And she was actually African American, black—she kept saying, she was like, 'Black men in Detroit really don't make it. Everybody, if you get past eighteen, I will be surprised.' I thought that was mean back then, but now I see. . . . When you grow up, you will see; you will soon see that being a black male is pretty hard because of racism and slavery back in the day. And people still, they still hold their grudge against you." At first Elijah was incredulous that his African American teacher would make comments he interpreted as disparaging toward black men, but time and experience brought him to see her remarks as preparing him for gendered racism. Notice his teacher's assertion is also tied to place, perhaps speaking to gendered racism in the United States as whole, but saying specifically that "black men *in Detroit* really don't make it" (emphasis added). Research has indeed shown excess mortality tied not only to race and gender but to place (although certainly not exclusively to Detroit) (Geronimus 1998; Geronimus et al. 2011). Thus, power is enacted and reinforced through place, and this "geography of domination" uses place to artificially naturalize inequity and difference (Gilmore 2002; McKittrick 2006).

Corey (thirteen) ties gendered racism to place as well, although this may be based in the fact he has only ever lived in Detroit. Still, he insists the challenges there are worse for black boys than for girls.

COREY: If you grow up in Detroit, you have to be, like, hard. Because if you soft, you're not going, I mean, it's not going to be a good life for you. You just can't be soft. You can't just walk through Detroit all calm and just regular because, I mean, it's not like that. I don't know. . . . [It is] mainly for boys.

ERIN: OK. So [for] girls, there's not as much pressure to be hard?

COREY: No. They mostly got it all. They got everything.

Unlike Elijah, Corey does not directly cite racism as the reason why, in his opinion, black men face more challenges than black women. However, he does think these challenges are specific to Detroit, where men have to be tough or "hard." Corey's belief that black girls have "got it all" while black boys cannot afford to be "calm and just regular" speaks to his experience of gendered racism in which black boys are forced to be tough and hyper-vigilant in order to survive and succeed.

Although they do not articulate it in the same way, both Elijah and Corey express the idea that black men's lives are more tenuous than black women's. Elijah's sister Trisha (fourteen) says their mother sends messages supporting that idea. "Well," she says, "[our mother] tells my brother to stay good in school because not a lot of black men succeed." This message, that one must work twice as hard as whites to succeed in the face of racism, is common in racial socialization (Hughes and Chen 1999; Peters 1985; Winkler 2008). In this study, however, it was more frequently raised with boys as a tool to prepare them for what is widely considered the heavier burden of racism placed on black men.

"They're Both Going to Have to Deal":
Gender-Neutral Approaches to Racism

Trisha, though, is not sure she agrees. Despite the gender and skin-tone difference between her and her brother, Trisha thinks her mother prepares them both for racism, saying, "I think it's pretty even." A small set of mothers (three out of nineteen) affirms this. While acknowledging that there are indeed gender differences in terms of racial stereotypes placed upon black children, they say the basic preparatory racial socialization should nevertheless be the same. They argue both boys and girls need to be encouraged to know their true history and to combat racist stereotypes about black people through their own actions and examples. Gina, the mother of twins Tyrone and Terri (thirteen), says her son may encounter more racism and her daughter may encounter more sexism, but both can rise above these oppressions if they are educated and prepared.

> I think you really have to prepare both of them. Because the boy, he's going to be knocked down because they always going to quote-unquote destroy the black man. But if he's a educated black man, he don't have too much to worry about. And the girl, she'll deal with the sexism, but if she's educated about racism and sexism, she's not going to let too much get her down. She just going to go through life and that'll be just another thing she has to brush off in life. So I just, I just, I just prepare them about everyday life. And by preparing them by everyday life, you—it's going to be people that like you because of your skin; there's going to be people that dislike you because of your skin. But it's a matter of what you've got in your head that's going to carry you on.

Gina's twins back up their mother's assertion, each saying in separate interviews that their parents teach them the same things in preparation for racism, despite their gender difference. "It's the same stuff," Tyrone says, although he complains, "They just keep covering [it over and over]." Terri agrees. When asked if her parents teach her and her brother different things about racism, she responds, "Mm mmm [no]. They just tell us just to tell them [when we face racism] so they can do something about it instead of us doing something about it because we just kids."

Barbara, who only has daughters, believes she would raise a son in the same way she is raising her daughters. Both genders, she says, need similar preparation: know your history and be conscious of the way you present yourself: "I would raise my son the same way. I think they all—the most important thing— they need to know where they come from and know where they're going. And they need to understand who fought for you to get where you're going, and to never lose that focus. And I also would tell them, like, to me, drugs are slavery.

I would treat my son the way I treat my daughters—that's not good to look like that, to dress like that, because the way you dress is the way somebody would think you are. And when a person first meets you, that is the best and most important encounter with anybody. So the way I raise her is the way I would raise my son."

Sharon acknowledges that others will put gendered, racist expectations on her son and daughter. However, she will not socialize them to worry about countering these notions because, she says, it is not their responsibility to do so.

SHARON: Generally, I kind of stick on the same theme. That there, there are different things that'll confront you because you are a black boy, because you are a black girl. You know, that people perceive, have different notions and perceptions—but that's, you know, going along with, you know, there's always these myths about different cultures and different people. . . . But there are some people out there that feel that way, and they maybe have not been exposed or maybe they had a bad experience. . . .

ERIN: So you sort of stick on the same theme with them, even though you know that the way it's lived for them or the way it manifests itself for them might be different because one's a boy and one's a girl?

SHARON: Yeah, because it's still the same thing. It's still that somebody is putting something on you that's their perceived, their perceptions, because they think, "Oh, she's a black girl." . . . That's *their* perception of you. And you can let them have that perception. You know. So, I try not to tell them that, "Oh, you got to change. You got to be this, or you got to, you know, disprove everybody." No. No. That's not your job. You just let them think that. Whatever they want." So, no, I don't try to because, basically, it's still dealing with the same concept. And they're both going to have to deal with that same concept, just in different manners, because of their gender.

These three mothers are aware that the ways in which racism is perpetuated toward black men and women may take different forms, but they argue that general preparatory racial socialization messages will help protect both boys and girls from the deleterious effects of racism.

"The Lighter You Are, the More Comfortable They Are": Skin Tone and Gendered Racism

Despite the exceptions, a majority of the mothers believe racism is gendered in such a way that it will hurt boys more than girls. A few also mention that skin tone can either exacerbate or mitigate this and say this influences how they prepare their sons for racism. As we read above, Sarah believes her son Elijah's darker skin will impact the already-gendered racism that causes white people to see him as a threat. Julie and Michelle, conversely, feel their sons' lighter skin tones may mitigate some of the effects of stereotypes about black men on their boys. Julie's son, Josh, has a white father. Michelle's son, Carlos, has a father Michelle describes as "black Puerto Rican," adding, "Most people, when they meet him, they assume he's black." Both Josh and Carlos live with their African American mothers, and neither lives in the same city as his father. Michelle does think that her son will have to deal with more racism than her daughter, but she also believes that his skin tone may lessen some of the gendered racism he will face. "I think that he's going to deal with [racism] more [than his sister] just because he's a male," Michele remarks. "For Carlos, what I'm going to teach him is really, really based on how he looks in the years to come because if he grows up like his [black Puerto Rican] father, to look more like him, which he does—the older he gets, the more pronounced I think his ethnicity will become. And, interesting enough, it will be to his advantage because color plays a part, even when you're dealing, interesting enough, even dealing with white people; the lighter you are, the more comfortable they are."

Julie agrees and thinks her son will have less trouble with racism because his lighter skin and curly hair make him "pretty" and, therefore, more accepted by everyone. Plenty of dark-skinned children are also pretty, of course, but this does not free them from the effects of racism. Julie seems to equate the term *pretty* with light skin and loose curls without problematizing this elision. She argues, however, these things put both black and white people at ease.

JULIE: I've always felt like Josh has an excellent advantage because he's pretty. . . . I think, really, black people will be softer to Josh, even if he's not what they wanted him to be, because he's pretty. And white people embrace him, even if they don't really like black people, because he's pretty. . . . I think if he figures out how to flip-flop, he'll be fine. As long as you know how to talk right, that's what my dad told me. I think when I was growing up the lesson was you're a high-yellow, and you know how to talk right, and you're always going to get the front—they're going to hire you. You will always get hired, and you'll get put up front. They'll make sure that you are in a visible position because they will get their coon quota, and you're somebody they can tolerate. They can look at you. So you'll get the job.

ERIN: So you feel the same way?

JULIE: So I think that Josh will get the job.

According to Julie, Josh will find employment easily because white employers need to hire a certain number of African Americans to comply with equal employment laws or not appear racist and they can more easily tolerate light-skinned African Americans. However, she is concerned Josh may not take advantage of this colorism if he does not learn to "flip-flop," or switch codes. As we heard from Julie in chapter 5, she thinks Josh's relatively recent move to Detroit has caused him to adopt African American language (AAL), or Black English, exclusively, much to Julie's chagrin. Here she illustrates her concern through something like a racism vulnerability scale, where Josh's light skin and curly hair lower his vulnerability, but his gender or speech could raise it. In order to mitigate this vulnerability, Julie does not want Josh to invoke blackness too sharply through his speech. On the one hand, this could be seen as teaching her son that anything associated with blackness is negative or lower status. On the other hand, Julie (like many of the mothers) argues against the notion that speech or skin tone is what makes a person black. She says she was taught to play on whites' racism to get ahead, and she is passing that same lesson on to her son.

Speak Up or Pipe Down? Gendered Reactions to Racism

There is some evidence—very limited but worth examining—that children's reactions to racism and mothers' racial socialization follow a distinctly gendered pattern. Specifically, some interviews suggest girls are more likely to speak up in response to racism, while boys are socialized in the opposite manner (*not* to "talk back" when facing racism). First, "having an attitude" or "being loud" is articulated by some girls and mothers as a coping tool that will help girls succeed despite racism. This is consistent with some previous studies that have found "loudness" on the part of African American girls to be an expression of power and resistance and part of how they were raised (Fordham 1993; Lei 2003). Mahogany (fifteen) describes herself as having an "attitude," explaining that this means that she "always [has] something to say back."

ERIN: What do you think your teachers would say about you, and do you agree with them?

MAHOGANY: I would agree with them, but they would say, "Attitude and loud." [*Laughs.*]

ERIN: Why do you think that they would say that?

MAHOGANY: Just because, I don't know. It's like, they say those [things] to me, and then I would be—it's like I try to say something smart, but *I always have something to say back* because I would disagree with what they be saying. I don't agree with what they be saying. When they say I did something, and I be like, "No I didn't." They may call it attitude (emphasis added).

Mahogany sees talking back as a way of standing up for herself when she is unfairly accused. She sees her "attitude" as a tool for correcting what she considers to be small injustices. She also places high value on it. When asked what she likes best about herself, she responds, "I like my attitude." Asked to describe what she means, she says, "[My attitude is] positive, but sometimes it can be negative. Because I try, like, when I'm with my friends, I be trying like mostly to fit in and stuff like that. . . . Because, like, we, the group that we are in, you just got to be hard." So not only is her "attitude" her favorite attribute, but it is common among her friends. She equates her attitude with the ability to be hard and points out that it helps her deal with systemic racism, which she believes can be overcome by standing up for herself. She asserts, "[My mom] said I could do whatever I want to do, be whoever I want to be, no matter where racism come in at. I still can get around it if, you know, *if you stand up for yourself.* You can still make a way because it's a lot of black people that have been through racism, but they still got to where they want to be today" (emphasis added). So Mahogany believes—and her mother clearly stresses in her racial socialization—the only way to succeed in the face of racism is to "stand up for [her]self." Mahogany understands her attitude as the principal means by which she can do this.

Nina (thirteen) also takes pride in her attitude, and, although she does not tie it directly to dealing with racism, she does associate it with "blackness" and sees it as a way of standing up for herself. She explains, "My teachers would describe me as a wild child. . . . They would say that because I'm very outspoken. So if they try to argue with me or try to say something that I disagree with, I will go straight to the, um, straight to my attitude that, um, how you say, the blackness will come out you? Yeah. Kind of come out with the attitude and the finger snapping. And I'll win eventually. [*Laughs.*] Yeah. And I'm going to win." Interestingly, Nina says she only draws on what she describes as her "attitude" when she feels challenged by her teachers, who are clearly in a position of power. While Nina does not specify the races of her teachers or the nature of their disagreements, her comments do suggest that she uses her attitude to stand up to power, as does Mahogany. Moreover, she associates this attitude directly with her blackness, seeing it as a survival skill tied to race. She shows confidence, even in the face of challenges from authority figures, that this attitude will always help her come out on top. However, both Signithia Fordham (1993) and Joy Lei (2003) point out that "loudness" and "attitude" invoked by black girls are not always interpreted in this positive manner by non-black students and teachers and sometimes have negative academic and social consequences when read as consistent with prevalent racist stereotypes.

Michelle, mother of Elina (thirteen) and Carlos (ten), provides further support that teaching daughters to be outspoken or "verbally defensive" is a part of gender-specific racial socialization. Her son, she says, is more likely to be affected by racism because white people are more threatened by black men than by black women. When asked if there are any ways in which "a black girl would be more vulnerable" to racism than a black boy, Michelle thinks for a moment before answering:

> No. . . . Just because, as a black female, [our] concept of self is that we tend to try to think of ourselves as strong and not vulnerable. And, you know, you come with the noise, we're going to give you more noise. And actually, and I really, I kind of think socially, I think, we teach our girls to become—I think because they're girls and they don't have the physical strength of it, I think we teach our girls to be more verbally defensive. Where they can't hurt you with their strength, but look, they're going to bash you to death with their tongues! You will get cussed out; your mama will get talked about really, really bad. So. [*Laughs*.] So, no, I think in terms of that, I think we do tend to try to teach our girls to be more verbally defensive, which is just the way it is.

In contrast to how she teaches her son to deal with racism by essentially placating whites—changing his dress and speech around them—she teaches her daughter to "make noise" and be "verbally defensive" in response to any confrontations or attacks. Michelle made this statement in response to a specific inquiry regarding gendered racism; thus, her answer refers not simply to general confrontations, but specifically to confrontations with racism.

Desarae expresses similar sentiments, commenting that her thirteen-year-old twins respond differently to racism. While she is not worried about Cara's chances of surviving and succeeding, she feels the deck is stacked against Corey. "I think it's more of a challenge [for Corey]," she says, "because black men don't even half of them even make it to twenty-five. . . . With a girl, I think girls tend to be able to get by. Where boys, I think it's going to be harder for him. . . . I don't worry about Cara because I know she's, as I tell her, she's headstrong. She doesn't believe what you tell her unless she can find it out for herself." Desarae's heightened concerns for her son seem to be mostly about societal conditions. Her diminished concerns for her daughter, however, are not simply about a belief that Cara will face less daunting social conditions but that her "headstrong" approach will lead her to question racism. From both the maternal and child perspectives, then, we see some limited evidence that "talking back" is one coping mechanism encouraged for and adopted by girls to deal with racism.

On the flip side, Kenny (thirteen) and his mother, Natalie, both evidence a particular gendered idea that African American boys should react to racism in almost the opposite way as girls. Their interviews reveal the idea that boys should not "fight back" or "mouth off" in response to racism because it puts them in more danger than it would a girl. Natalie tries to prepare Kenny for gendered racism by teaching him to be more humble and less opinionated.

ERIN: So do you think that—because you have a son and three daughters—do you think that the gender of your children affects how you prepare them for dealing with racism or how you tell them about racial identity?

NATALIE: Yes.

ERIN: How so?

NATALIE: Knowing that males, black young males, have a bad rep, I try to prepare my son by not having to have the last word all the time, and always having to have an opinion about something. Me, as his parent, when I tell you to do something and you think that I'm wrong, we'll discuss it after you do what I told you to do. In the classroom, stop arguing with your teacher. And I'm trying to prepare you now for the real world because you're going to get out there on the streets, you're going to say the wrong thing or mouth off at somebody, and they're going to shoot you. Learn how to have self-control and control your mouth. That's why you have one mouth and two ears. Be quick to listen and slow to speak. And if you are to be pulled over by an officer—you could be walking down the street or riding your bike, an officer could stop you—you need to learn how to listen. And for my girls, I really don't tell them that.

In his interview, Kenny confirms, "[My parents] tell me different things [than my sisters, such as,] 'Don't fight unless you have to.'" This is especially important, Natalie says, with authority figures like teachers and police because "in the real world" they often perceive black men as threatening or insubordinate and can act on these presumptions in ways that carry serious consequences. For her girls, she adds, this is not the case. Natalie's message that her son's survival and success rests upon her teaching him not to have to "have the last word all the time" or not to be "always having to have an opinion about something" is in direct opposition to the encouragement of attitude or verbal toughness in girls, of which Mahogany (fifteen), Nina (thirteen), and mothers Michelle and Desarae speak. The difference appears to stem from the concern that authority figures are more likely to see black boys as a threat or as insubordinate, and, thus, attitude and talking back are likely to carry greater consequences for boys, affecting life outcomes like livelihood and longevity in concrete ways.

Keep in mind, however, this evidence is limited, and the issues of attitude and talking back are raised in only a handful of the interviews. At least one mother, Audrey, counters this pattern, saying she and her husband try to model for their three sons that they should always speak up even though white people "don't want to deal with [the] brother." Audrey and her husband, though, take a particularly African-centered approach to raising their son, Toussaint, and often provide exceptions to racial socialization patterns in this sample. Nevertheless, this exception to the gendered pattern of socialization is compelling, and further research is indicated. While the literature is mixed regarding the relationship between gender of child and types of parental racial socialization messages, there is much less evidence as to whether boys and girls adopt gender-specific coping mechanisms to deal with racism (C. Franklin 1999; S. Hill 1999; Hughes et al. 2009; Lesane-Brown 2006; Sanders Thompson 1994; Stevenson et al. 2005; A. Thomas and Speight 1999; T. Williams and Davidson 2009). Future studies should include questions specifically formulated toward the notion of "attitude" as it relates to preparation for racism.

Conclusion

Race, gender, and skin tone converge in complex ways in children's comprehensive racial learning. This is true in relationship to children's developing ideas about racial categories, racial identity, and racial authenticity, as well as in their experiences of and preparation for racism. There are indications, too, that aspects of place—including demographics, place character, and structural racism as enacted through place—may come into play in shaping how skin tone and gender enter into comprehensive racial learning. Certainly, more research is needed, but it is clear that studies of this process can no longer ignore the intersecting influences of gender, skin tone, and place.

7

Conclusion

"I Learn Being Black from Everywhere I Go"

There is a debate among scholars over which sources of information (sometimes called "socializing agents") are most powerful in how children learn about race. The literature falls into two broad camps: those who believe the family is the most critical agent of socialization and those who argue that forces outside the family have more influence. Authors in the first camp claim that the family is primary because it decides "what to filter out, [and] what to promote" (Boykin and Ellison 1995, 124). However, scholars in the second camp argue that socialization about race is controlled by forces outside of the family, such as schools and media. They hold that, although the family does act as an agent in the process, it cannot completely overpower the pervasive negative racial socialization messages communicated by society.

This book argues that the truth lies somewhere in between these two positions and that the nexus of the process is the child. Children, in fact, are pulled in many directions by a wide range of forces—those most often cited in this study were parents, other family members, school (teachers and curriculum), media, peers, church, neighbors, travel, and place. This tug-of-war leaves young people with a puzzle to solve, with multiple conflicting messages to reconcile, and the result often seems to be confusion and ambivalence. The findings presented in this book show that, while the existing literature can tell us much about the sources of messages, we need to reorient the way we look at how children learn about race. Tellingly, there previously was not even a scholarly term to describe how children develop racial identities, attitudes, and strategies, only the general term "socialization," a somewhat passive word— often viewed as something that happens *to* children—or "racial socialization," which refers only to "*parental* practices that communicate messages about ethnicity and race to children" (Hughes et al. 2008, 226, emphasis added). This book introduces the concept of *comprehensive racial learning* to help us rethink the learning process, centering on children and their active learning process rather than on sources or "socializing agents." Using the framework of comprehensive racial learning, *Learning Race, Learning Place* shows the importance of looking at this process from children's points of view and listening to their interpretations of their experiences, which, as we saw, can be quite different from what the adults around them expect or intend. Throughout the chapters we have seen that children's and mothers' assertions of what the children think or experience or feel do not always match. Indeed, the story would have been quite different if only parental perspectives were included. Methodologically, then, this book shows "*how* we study kids affects *what* we learn about them" (Boocock and Scott 2005, 33, emphasis in original). It demonstrates the importance of examining various other actors and influences *at the children's prompting*, of not just studying children, but listening to their voices and letting them tell us where to look.

And in this study, both they and their mothers collectively pointed to place as a primary and overarching factor in the children's comprehensive racial learning. Although I was not asking about (nor even particularly thinking about) the role of place, children and mothers alike raised this issue so repeatedly that it emerged as central to the analysis. Throughout this book, we have seen copious examples of how place directly and indirectly enters into children's comprehensive racial learning—directly through their own experiences with it and indirectly through its impact on their mothers' messages and sometimes those of their peers, teachers, and others. Out of the many hundreds of pages of interview transcripts resulting from this study, one exchange stands out for me as the most concise illustration of this complex and layered influence. It was the exchange I had with Corey (thirteen), who told me he would rather live in Las Vegas than in Detroit.

ERIN: So why would you like [Las Vegas] better than Detroit? What—

COREY: I mean, the black people, they don't act right. . . . I mean, they litter and sell drugs, a lot of stuff like that. In Las Vegas, they don't do a lot of that.

ERIN: Do you think white people litter and sell drugs?

COREY: On TV, but not for real. This far I've never seen it.

When asked why he thinks Las Vegas is different from Detroit in these ways, he responds that the differences are attributable to race, saying, "I mean, Detroit seem like a black neighborhood, black city, I mean. And just Las Vegas seem like just for everybody."

I highlight this exchange because it demonstrates how the many facets of place—in this case, demographic, spatial, material, economic, social, and historical factors—come together to influence Corey's thinking about race. As discussed in detail in chapter 3, there are a myriad complex reasons why

Detroit and Las Vegas are different and why Corey observes different material conditions and human behaviors in each place. In Corey's mind, though, the variations by place boil down to race, not structural racism, but racial differences in behaviors and how people "are." His experiences of place are understood in terms of race, and his understandings of race are shaped by place. While not all of the children in this study would have interpreted the differences between Detroit and Las Vegas in precisely the same terms Corey did, read together, the children's comments and reflections reveal the immense bearing place has upon the ways they experience and think about race and racism. They were growing up in different neighborhoods under different circumstances and attending different schools, yet Detroit's place character held sway over each child's comprehensive racial learning. Perhaps Mahogany (fifteen) put it best when she said, "I learn being black from everywhere I go."

Does this mean African American children's comprehensive racial learning is different in each separate city, suburb, town, or place? Isn't the United States a place, too, with its own place character? The answer to both, I argue, is yes. While children's racial identities, attitudes, and experiences with racism are shaped by national place character, or the broader metanarrative of race in the United States, they are also specific to each particular place, which exerts both direct and indirect influence on children's comprehensive racial learning. It is useful here to look to diaspora theorists, who argue that the identities of people in a diaspora are tied together by a broadly common history, homeland, set of experiences, and cultural production, but that those identities are also grounded in and shaped by the sites in which each diasporic community is located (Clifford 1997; S. Hall 1990; E. Lewis 1999). In other words, there are aspects of identity and experience that tie together members of the African diaspora in Kingston and Dublin and São Paulo and Detroit, but these identities and experiences are also specific in some ways to each location and shaped by the racial and cultural context of each of those places (J. Brown 2009). As this book demonstrates, this understanding should also be applied to African American identities and racialized experiences and attitudes within the United States. In this case, while racial identities and experiences of racism are forged within the United States under a national metanarrative of race, those racial identities, ideas, and experiences are also particular in some ways to each location, shaped by the local place character. Research ignoring place in children's comprehensive racial learning misses a critical and profound piece of the puzzle.

If place occupies this prominent a role in children's comprehensive learning, it is clear that structures, institutions, governments, systems, and cultures have as much influence as parents. Yet we as a society tend to collectively dump all blame for children's racial ideas and attitudes on parents (Van Ausdale and Feagin 2001; Winkler 2009). As the opening page of this book discussed, a recent CNN series called "Kids and Race in America" sparked an unprecedented public response, in which most viewers blamed the children's parents for the children's racial attitudes (CNN 2010a, 2010b). *Learning Race, Learning Place* makes a clear case that children's racial learning outcomes are not merely a reflection of parents' messages nor the sole responsibility of parents, but the result of children's interactions with their broader surroundings. As Debra Van Ausdale and Joe Feagin conclude in their 2001 study of younger children and racial attitudes, "Racist thought and practice remain strong in the United States, and young children cannot avoid participating in and perpetuating them. Racism surrounds us, permeates our ideas and conversations, focuses our relationships with one another, shapes our practices, and drives much of our personal, social, and political lives. There are few social forces so strong. Children are neither immune to it nor unaware of its power. A social reality this mighty is bound to become an integral part of their lives, and thus it endures from generation to generation, perhaps changing somewhat in form but still strong in its impact" (198). All Americans, then, even those who have no direct daily contact with children, are answerable for children's racial learning outcomes, including those of the children in this book.

All the mothers I interviewed want the best for their children. They work to impart healthy racial identities and help their children avoid the crushing effects of racism. But it is simply not possible for parents to do this alone. In some ways, raising their children in Detroit allows these mothers to protect their children from interpersonal and cultural racism through black control of the city and many of its cultural, social, and political institutions. In other ways, Detroit serves as a quintessential manifestation of institutional racism through neglect from larger economic and political institutions and a racialized system of depressed property values, all of which lead to an insufficient tax base and declining schools, employment, services, and standards of living for the people of Detroit. Racial inequity is a *societal* problem, one which "makes the lives and property of some people worth more than the lives and property of others" (Lipsitz 2011, 41). This kind of racism cannot be left for children to manage, families to mitigate, or black spaces like Detroit to buffer or bear. Rather, it is our collective problem, and the onus lies on all of us.

NOTES

CHAPTER 1   COMPREHENSIVE RACIAL LEARNING, GROUNDED IN PLACE

1. A four-part series, "Kids and Race in America," aired on the CNN primetime program *Anderson Cooper 360* from May 17 to May 20, 2010. The study was designed by Margaret Beale Spencer, a developmental psychologist at the University of Chicago. Full results of the study can be found at http://i2.cdn.turner.com/cnn/2010/images/05/13/expanded_results_methods_cnn.pdf.

2. Although the recruitment information for this study made a gender-neutral request for middle-school-aged children and their parents or primary caregivers, all of the interviewed adults were mothers. Some interviews were scheduled with fathers and their children, but these resulted in cancellations or missed appointments.

3. At the time, some literature on racial socialization claimed differences in practices between parents with higher and lower socioeconomic statuses (SES) and levels of education, but the findings were mixed (Caughy et al. 2002; S. Hill 1999; Spencer 1990; Thornton et al. 1990; Thornton 1997). I wondered whether the differences observed by some were due to SES and education or whether those were simply serving as proxies for racial demographics of neighborhood—that the differences might have come from living in a predominantly white area or attending a predominantly white school, not from SES or education itself. Detroit, with its wide range of SES but predominantly black demographics, allows the two to be separated.

4. See note 2.

5. Interviewed mothers were not asked for exact incomes, but rather to place their families within income brackets. Four placed themselves in the "Less than $15,000 per year" category and one placed herself in the $15,000–$25,000 category. The poverty threshold is determined by the size of the family unit and number of related children under the age of eighteen living in the household.

6. National Alliance for Public Charter Schools, "Students by Race and Ethnicity, 2005–2006, MI—Detroit Public Schools," http://dashboard.publiccharters.org/dashboard/students/page/race/district/MI-31/year/2006 (accessed October 15, 2011).

7. These remuneration amounts were decided upon in conjunction with faculty at the University of Michigan School of Social Work, who advised me on the average and appropriate remuneration for interviews of this length at this time in Detroit. Remuneration for participants was made possible through a grant from the Berkeley Center for Working Families.

8. I received a BA in African and African American studies and social science from the University of Michigan, an MA and a PhD in African American studies from the University of California, Berkeley, and spent a year as a postdoctoral fellow in

African American studies at Northwestern University before accepting a position as an assistant professor in the Department of Africology at the University of Wisconsin–Milwaukee.

CHAPTER 2   RHETORIC VERSUS REALITY

1. National Center for Education Statistics, http://nces.ed.gov/ (accessed May 13, 2005).

2. This mirrors the Detroit Public Schools overall, which were about 90 percent African American in 2005.

3. Cara attended a school in which the student body was over 98 percent African American.

CHAPTER 4   PLACE MATTERS

1. Eight Mile Road constitutes the northern border of Detroit, dividing city from suburbs and Wayne County (in which Detroit is located) from Oakland and Macomb Counties. Symbolically, it represents a racial divide, although there are some suburbs with significant black populations on the north side of Eight Mile Road, including Southfield and Oak Park, to name a few (see map 3.1).

CHAPTER 5   COMPETING WITH SOCIETY

1. These interviews were conducted in 2003 and 2004, at a time when MTV and BET still played several hours of music videos per day.

2. At the time of Tanya's admission, the University of Michigan awarded potential undergraduate applicants "a total of 20 points for having an economically disadvantaged background, being an underrepresented minority, attending a high school serving a predominately minority population, or being a scholarship athlete, among others" (University of Michigan, 2003). After the June 2003 Supreme Court decision on the University of Michigan's admissions policies, the point system was altered.

3. Cora is referring to the November 30, 2003, police beating and subsequent death of forty-one-year-old Nathaniel Jones in Cincinnati, Ohio, which was caught on video and shown on national television news (CNN 2003).

CHAPTER 6   BLACK IS BLACK?

1. One child in this study has one white and one black parent. The remaining twenty-seven have two black parents, although two of those have one parent who identifies as black Puerto Rican. All interviewed mothers are African American.

2. The Detroit Public School system listed 4 "Gifted and Talented"/examination schools (out of a total of 268 schools) for the 2003–2004 academic year. These public schools of choice require an examination for entry.

3. See note 2.

4. Among the four types of schools attended by the children in this study, neighborhood schools are the only ones in which all one must do is enroll. Private schools, schools of choice, and charter schools all require one or more of the following: applications, waiting lists, tuition, fees, or entrance exams.

REFERENCES

Aboud, Frances E. 2008. A social-cognitive developmental theory of prejudice. In *Handbook of race, racism, and the developing child*, edited by Stephen M. Quintana and Clark McKown, 55–71. Hoboken, NJ: John Wiley & Sons.

Allen, Bem P. 1976. Race and physical attractiveness as criteria for white subjects' dating choices. *Social Behavior and Personality: An International Journal* 4(2): 289–296.

Anderson, Elijah, ed. 2008. *Against the wall: Poor, young, Black, and male*. Philadelphia: University of Pennsylvania Press.

Anglin, Deidre M., and Arthur L. Whaley. 2006. Racial/ethnic self-labeling in relation to group socialization and identity in African-descended individuals. *Journal of Language and Social Psychology* 25(4): 450–463.

Apfelbaum, Evan P., Kristin Pauker, Samuel R. Sommers, and Nalini Ambady. 2010. In blind pursuit of racial equality? *Psychological Science* 21(11): 1587–1592.

Babson, Steve. 1986. *Working Detroit*. Detroit: Wayne State University Press.

Baker, Wayne, and Andrew Shyrock. 2009. Citizenship and crisis. In *Citizenship and crisis: Arab Detroit after 9/11*, edited by the Detroit Arab American Study Team, 3–32. New York: Russell Sage Foundation.

Balibar, Etienne. 1990. Paradoxes of universality. In *Anatomy of racism*, edited by David Theo Goldberg. Minneapolis: University of Minnesota Press.

Bambara, Toni Cade. 1970. *The Black woman: An anthology*. New York: New American Library.

Bang, Hae-Kyong, and Bonnie B. Reece. 2003. Minorities in children's television commercials: New, improved, and stereotyped. *Journal of Consumer Affairs* 37(1): 42–67.

Bannon, William M., Mary M. McKay, Anil Chacko, James A. Rodriguez, and Mary Cavaleri. 2009. Cultural pride reinforcement as a dimension of racial socialization protective of urban African American child anxiety. *Families in Society* 90(1): 79–86.

Barraclough, Laura R. 2009. South Central farmers and Shadow Hills homeowners: Land use policy and relational racialization in Los Angeles. *Professional Geographer* 61(2): 164–186.

Bell, Ella L. J. Edmondson, and Stella M. Nkomo. 1998. Armoring: Learning to withstand racial oppression. *Journal of Comparative Family Studies* 29(2): 285–295.

Benjamin, Lois. 1991. *The Black elite: Facing the color line in the twilight of the twentieth century*. Chicago: Nelson-Hall Publishers.

Bennett, M. Daniel, Jr. 2006. Culture and context: A study of neighborhood effects on racial socialization and ethnic identity content in a sample of African American adolescents. *Journal of Black Psychology* 32(4): 479–500.

Berry, Gordon L. 1998. Black family life on television and the socialization of the African American child: Images of marginality. *Journal of Comparative Family Studies* 29(2): 233–242.

Billingsley, Andrew. 1992. *Climbing Jacob's ladder*. New York: Simon and Schuster.

Bing, Vanessa M. 2004. Out of the closet but still in hiding: Conflicts and identity issues for a black-white biracial lesbian. *Women and Therapy* 27(1–2): 185–201.

Bishop, Rudine Sims. 1992. Multicultural literature for children: Making informed choices. In *Teaching multicultural literature in grades K–8*, edited by Violet J. Harris, 38–53. Norwood, MA: Christopher-Gordon Publishers.

Blackmun, Harold Andrew. 1978. Separate opinion, *University of California Regents v. Bakke*. 438 US 265.

Blyth, Eric, and Judith Milner. 1996. Black boys excluded from school: Race or masculinity issues? In *Exclusion from school: Inter-professional issues for policy and practice*, edited by Eric Blyth and Judith Milner, 62–75. London: Routledge.

Bogle, Donald. 2001. *Toms, coons, mulattoes, mammies, and bucks: An interpretive history of Blacks in American films*, 4th ed. New York: Continuum International Publishing Group.

Bonilla-Silva, Eduardo. 1999. The essential social fact of race. *American Sociological Review* 64(6): 899–906.

———. 2001. *White supremacy and racism in the post–civil rights era*. Boulder, CO: Lynne Rienner Publishers.

———. 2003. *Racism without racists: Color-blind racism and the persistence of racial inequality in the United States*. Lanham, MD: Rowman & Littlefield.

Boocock, Sarane Spence, and Kimberly Ann Scott. 2005. *Kids in context: The sociological study of children and childhoods*. Lanham, MD: Rowman & Littlefield.

Bowman, Phillip J., and Cleopatra Howard. 1985. Race-related socialization, motivation, and academic achievement: A study of Black youth in three-generation families. *Journal of the American Academy of Child Psychiatry* 24(2): 134–141.

Boyd, Todd. 1997. *Am I Black enough for you? Popular culture from the 'hood and beyond*. Bloomington: Indiana University Press.

Boykin, A. Wade, and Constance M. Ellison. 1995. The multiple ecologies of Black youth socialization: An Afrographic analysis. In *African-American youth: Their social and economic status in the United States*, edited by Ronald L. Taylor, 93–128. Westport, CT: Praeger.

Boykin, A. Wade, and Forrest D. Toms. 1985. Black child socialization: A conceptual framework. In *Black children: Social, educational, and parental environments*, edited by Harriette Pipes McAdoo and John L. McAdoo, 33–51. Beverly Hills, CA: Sage Publications.

Bradsher, Keith. 1999. Plenty of snow in Detroit, but hardly a plow in sight. *New York Times*, January 12.

Bronfenbrenner, Urie. 1979. The *ecology of human development: Experiments by nature and design*. Cambridge, MA: Harvard University Press.

Brooks, Wanda, and Jonda C. McNair. 2009. "But this story of mine is not unique": A review of research on African American children's literature. *Review of Educational Research* 79(1): 125–162.

Brown v. the Board of Education. 347 US 483 (1954).

Brown, Jacqueline Nassy. 2005. *Dropping anchor, setting sail: Geographies of race in Black Liverpool*. Princeton, NJ: Princeton University Press.

———. 2009. Black Europe and the African diaspora: A discourse on location. In *Black Europe and the African diaspora*, edited by Darlene Clark Hine, Trica Danielle Keaton, and Stephen Small, 201–211. Urbana and Chicago: University of Illinois Press.

Brown, Michael K., Martin Carnoy, Elliott Currie, Troy Duster, David B. Oppenheimer, Marjorie M. Shultz, and David Wellman. 2003. *Whitewashing race: The myth of a color-blind society*. Berkeley: University of California Press.

Brown, Tiffany L., Miriam R. Linver, and Melanie Evans. 2010. The role of gender in the racial and ethnic socialization of African American adolescents. *Youth and Society* 41(3): 357–381.

Brown, Tiffany L., Miriam R. Linver, Melanie Evans, and Donna DeGennaro. 2009. African-American parents' racial and ethnic socialization and adolescent grades: Teasing out the role of gender. *Journal of Youth and Adolescence* 38: 214–227.

Brown, Tony N., and Chase L. Lesane-Brown. 2006. Race socialization messages across historical time. *Social Psychology Quarterly* 69(2): 201–213.

Brown, Tony N., Emily E. Tanner-Smith, Chase L. Lesane-Brown, and Michael Ezell. 2007. Child, parent, and situational correlates of familial ethnic/race socialization. *Journal of Marriage and Family* 69(1): 14–25.

Brunsma, David L., David Overfelt, and J. Steven Picou, eds. 2007. *The sociology of Katrina: Perspectives on a modern catastrophe.* Lanham, MD: Rowman & Littlefield.

Buckley, Tamara R., and Robert T. Carter. 2005. Black adolescent girls: Do gender role and racial identity impact their self-esteem? *Sex Roles* 53(9/10): 647–661.

Butsch, Richard. 2003. Ralph, Fred, Archie, and Homer: Why television keeps re-creating the white male working-class buffoon. In *Gender, race, and class in media*, edited by Gail Dines and Jean M. Humez, 575–585. Thousand Oaks, CA: Sage Publications.

Byrd, Christy M., and Tabbye M. Chavous. 2009. Racial identity and academic achievement in the neighborhood context: A multilevel analysis. *Journal of Youth and Adolescence* 38: 544–559.

Caughy, Margaret O'Brien, Saundra Murray Nettles, Patricia J. O'Campo, and Kimberly Fraleigh Lohrfink. 2006. Neighborhood matters: Racial socialization of African American children. *Child Development* 77(5): 1220–1236.

Caughy, Margaret O'Brien, Patricia J. O'Campo, and Carles Muntaner. 2004. Experiences of racism among African American parents and the mental health of their preschool-aged children. *American Journal of Public Health* 94(12): 2118–2124.

Caughy, Margaret O'Brien, Suzanne M. Randolph, and Patricia J. O'Campo. 2002. The Africentric home environment inventory: An observational measure of the racial socialization features of the home environment for African American preschool children. *Journal of Black Psychology* 28(1): 37–52.

Celious, Aaron, and Daphna Oyserman. 2001. Race from the inside: An emerging heterogeneous race model. *Journal of Social Issues* 57(1): 149–165.

Charles, Camille Zubrinsky. 2003. The dynamics of racial residential segregation. *Annual Review of Sociology* 29: 167–207.

Charmaz, Kathy. 2006. *Constructing grounded theory: A practical guide through qualitative analysis.* Thousand Oaks, CA: Sage Publications.

Chavous, Tabbye M., Debra Hilkene Bernat, Karen Schmeelk-Cone, Cleopatra H. Caldwell, Laura Kohn-Wood, and Marc A. Zimmerman. 2003. Racial identity and academic attainment among African-American adolescents. *Child Development* 74(4): 1076–1090.

Christerson, Brad, Korie L. Edwards, and Richard Flory. 2010. *Growing up in America: The power of race in the lives of teens.* Stanford, CA: Stanford University Press.

Clayton, Obie, and Joan Moore. 2006. The effects of crime and imprisonment on family formation. In *Black fathers in contemporary American society: Strengths, weaknesses, and strategies for change*, edited by Obie Clayton, Ronald B. Mincy, and David Blankenhorn, 84–102. New York: Russell Sage Foundation.

Clifford, James. 1997. *Routes: Travel and translation in the late twentieth century.* Cambridge, MA: Harvard University Press.

CNN. 2003. Beating captured on police video. December 3. http://articles.cnn.com/2003–12–01/us/beating.videotape_1_police-officers-squad-car-police-cruiser?_s=PM:US.

———. 2010a. Black or white: Kids on race. Accessed August 10, 2010. http://www.cnn.com/SPECIALS/2010/kids.on.race/.

———. 2010b. Readers: Children learn attitudes about race at home. May 25. http://www.cnn.com/2010/US/05/19/doll.study.reactions/index.html.

Coard, Stephanie I., Scyatta A. Wallace, Howard C. Stevenson, and Laurie M. Brotman. 2004. Towards culturally relevant preventative interventions: The consideration of racial socialization in parent training with African American families. *Journal of Child and Family Studies* 13(3): 277–293.

Coles, Roberta L. 2009. *The best kept secret: Single Black fathers.* Lanham, MD: Rowman & Littlefield.

Collins, Patricia Hill. 1991. *Black feminist thought: Knowledge, consciousness, and the politics of empowerment.* New York: Routledge.

Connolly, Paul. 1998. *Racism, gender identities, and young children: Social relations in a multiethnic, inner-city primary school.* New York: Routledge.

Consoli, John. 2010. Where are the Black TV shows? Roles for minority actors at an all-time high, but programs in decline. *The Today Show*, June 17. http://today.msnbc.msn.com/id/37686988/ns/today-entertainment/.

Constantine, Madonna G., Vanessa L. Alleyne, Barbara C. Wallace, and Deidre C. Franklin-Jackson. 2006. Africentric cultural values: Their relation to positive mental health in African American adolescent girls. *Journal of Black Psychology* 32(2): 141–154.

Constantine, Madonna G., and Sha'kema M. Blackmon. 2002. Black adolescents' racial socialization experiences: Their relations to home, school, and peer self-esteem. *Journal of Black Studies* 32(3): 322–335.

Correll, Joshua, Bernadette Park, Charles M. Judd, Bernd Wittenbrink, Melody S. Sadler, and Tracie Keesee. 2007. Across the thin blue line: Police officers and racial bias in the decision to shoot. *Journal of Personality and Social Psychology* 92(6): 1006–1023.

Crenshaw, Kimberlé W. 1995. Race, reform, and retrenchment: Transformation and legitimation in antidiscrimination law. In *Critical race theory: The key writings that formed the movement*, edited by Kimberlé Crenshaw, Neil Gotanda, Gary Peller, and Kendall Thomas, 103–122. New York: New Press.

———. 1997. Color-blindness, history, and the law. In *The house that race built*, edited by Wahneema Lubiano, 280–288. New York: Vintage Books.

Creswell, John W. 2009. *Research design: Qualitative, quantitative, and mixed methods approaches.* Thousand Oaks, CA: Sage Publications.

Crocker, Jennifer, and Diane Quinn. 1998. Racism and self-esteem. In *Confronting racism: The problem and the response*, edited by Jennifer L. Eberhardt and Susan T. Fiske, 169–187. Thousand Oaks, CA: Sage Publications.

Cross, William E. 1971. The Negro-to-Black conversion experience. *Black World* 20: 13–26.

———. 1991. *Shades of black: Diversity in African American identity.* Philadelphia: Temple University Press.

Crowell, Charlene. 2005. Detroit's public transit stuck in neutral: Under-funding and poor coordination hold back city's renaissance. *Great Lakes Bulletin News Service*, March 9.

Darden, Joe T., Richard Child Hill, June Thomas, and Richard Thomas. 1987. *Detroit: Race and uneven development.* Philadelphia: Temple University Press.

Davidson, Ann Locke. 1996. *Making and molding identity in schools: Student narratives on race, gender, and academic engagement.* Albany: State University of New York Press.

Davis, F. James. 2001. *Who is Black? One nation's definition.* University Park: Pennsylvania State University Press.

Delgado, Richard, and Jean Stefancic. 2001. *Critical race theory: An introduction.* New York: New York University Press.

Demo, David H., and Michael Hughes. 1990. Socialization and racial identity among Black Americans. *Social Psychology Quarterly* 53: 364–374.

Denton, Nancy A., and Douglas S. Massey. 1989. Racial identity among Caribbean Hispanics: The effect of double minority status on residential segregation. *American Sociological Review* 54(5): 790–808.

Detroit Free Press. 2005. Ex-KKK leader's robes bring $6,000 at Howell auction. May 23.

Detroit Public Schools. 2006. African-centered education at the Detroit Public Schools. Accessed February 12, 2007. http://africancentered.detroitk12.org/.

Dixon, Travis L., Cristina Azocar, and Michael Casas. 2003. The portrayal of race and crime on television network news. *Journal of Broadcasting & Electronic Media* 47: 495–520.

Docherty, Sharron, and Margarete Sandelowski. 1999. Focus on qualitative methods: Interviewing children. *Research in Nursing & Health* 22(2): 177–185.

Duncan, James, and Nancy Duncan. 2006. Aesthetics, abjection, and white privilege in suburban New York. In *Landscape and race in the United States,* edited by Richard H. Schein, 157–176. New York: Routledge.

Duneier, Mitchell. 2000. Race and peeing on Sixth Avenue. In *Racing research, researching race: Methodological dilemmas in critical race studies,* edited by France Winddance Twine and Jonathan W. Warren, 215–226. New York: New York University Press.

Durrheim, Kevin, Xoliswa Mtose, and Lyndsay Brown. 2011. *Race trouble: Race, identity, and inequality in post-Apartheid South Africa.* Lanham, MD: Lexington Books.

Eastern Michigan University. 2001. *Student profile.* Institutional Research and Information Management. Ypsilanti, MI. http://irim.emich.edu/datafiles/pdf/student_profile_2001.pdf.

Eder, Donna, and Laura Fingerson. 2001. Interviewing children and adolescents. In *Handbook of interview research,* edited by Jaber F. Gubrium and James A. Holstein, 181–201. Thousand Oaks, CA: Sage Publications.

Edwards, Rosalind. 1993. An education in interviewing: Placing the researcher and the research. In *Researching sensitive topics,* edited by Claire M. Renzetti and Raymond M. Lee, 181–196. Newbury Park, CA: Sage Publications.

Eichstedt, Jennifer L., and Stephen A. Small. 2002. *Race and ideology in southern plantation museums.* Washington, DC: Smithsonian Institution Press.

Ellison, Ralph. (1964) 1995. *An American dilemma:* A review. In *Shadow and act.* New York: Vintage International. Citations refer to the Vintage International edition.

Elton-Chalcraft, Sally. 2009. *"It's not just about black and white, Miss": Children's awareness of race.* Sterling, VA: Trenthan Books Limited.

Essed, Philomena. 1991. *Understanding everyday racism: An interdisciplinary theory.* Newbury Park, CA: Sage Publications.

Farley, Reynolds, Sheldon Danziger, and Harry J. Holzer. 2000. *Detroit divided.* New York: Russell Sage Foundation.

Feagin, Joe R. 2010. *The white racial frame: Centuries of racial framing and counter-framing.* New York: Routledge.

Feagin, Joe R., and Karyn D. McKinney. 2003. *The many costs of racism.* Lanham, MD: Rowman and Littlefield.

Feagin, Joe R., and Melvin P. Sikes. 1995. *Living with racism: The Black middle-class experience.* Boston: Beacon Press.

Feagin, Joe R., Hernán Vera, and Pinar Batur. 2001. *White racism: The basics.* New York: Routledge.

Ferguson, Ann Arnett. 2000. *Bad boys: Public schools in the making of Black masculinity.* Ann Arbor: University of Michigan Press.

Fernandez, Ronald. 2008. *America beyond black and white: How immigrants and fusions are helping us overcome the racial divide.* Ann Arbor: University of Michigan Press.

Figlio, David N. 2005. Names, expectations, and the black-white test score gap. National Bureau of Economic Research working paper number W11195. Cambridge, MA.

Flagg, Barbara J. 1998. *Was blind, but now I see: White race consciousness and the law.* New York: New York University Press.

Fordham, Signithia. 1993. "Those loud Black girls": (Black) women, silence, and gender "passing" in the academy. *Anthropology and Education Quarterly* 24(1): 3–32.

———. 1996. *Blacked out: Dilemmas of race, identity, and success at Capital High.* Chicago: University of Chicago Press.

France, Alan. 2004. Young people. In *Doing research with children and young people,* edited by Sandy Fraser, Vicky Lewis, Sharon Ding, Mary Kellett, and Chris Robinson, 175–190. Thousand Oaks, CA: Sage Publications.

Franklin, Anderson J., and Nancy Boyd-Franklin. 1985. A psychoeducational perspective on Black parenting. In *Black children: Social, educational, and parental environments,* edited by Harriette Pipes McAdoo and John Lewis McAdoo, 194–210. Beverly Hills, CA: Sage Publications.

Franklin, Clyde W., II. 1999. Sex and class differences in the socialization experiences of African American youth. In *The Black family: Essays and studies,* edited by Robert Staples, 248–258. Ontario, Canada: Wadsworth Publishing Company.

Franklin, John Hope, and Alfred A. Moss Jr. 1997. *From slavery to freedom: A history of African Americans.* 7th ed. New York: McGraw-Hill.

Fredrickson, George M. 2002. *Racism: A short history.* Princeton, NJ: Princeton University Press.

Freeman, Michael. 2002. Fewer series feature Black-dominant casts. *Electronic Media* 21(15): 3–4.

Fujioka, Yuki. 1999. Television portrayals and African American stereotypes: Examination of television effects when direct contact is lacking. *Journalism & Mass Communication Quarterly* 76: 52–75.

Funderburg, Lise. 1994. *Black, white, other: Biracial Americans talk about race and identity.* New York: William Morrow and Company.

Gaertner, Samuel L., and John F. Dovidio. 2005. Categorization, recategorization, and intergroup bias. In *On the nature of prejudice: Fifty years after Allport,* edited by John F. Dovidio, Peter Glick, and Laurie A. Budman, 71–88. Malden, MA: Blackwell Publishing.

Gallagher, John. 2009. Detroit's jobless rate hits 26-year high at 22.2%: It tops mark for metro area, Michigan. *Detroit Free Press,* March 20.

———. 2010. *Reimagining Detroit: Opportunities for redefining an American city.* Detroit: Wayne State University Press.

Gavrilovich, Peter, and Bill McGraw, eds. 2000. *The Detroit almanac.* Detroit: Detroit Free Press.

Gaylord-Harden, Noni K., Brian L. Ragsdale, Jelani Mandara, Maryse H. Richards, and Anne C. Petersen. 2007. Perceived support and internalizing symptoms in African American adolescents: Self-esteem and ethnic identity as mediators. *Journal of Youth & Adolescence* 36: 77–88.

Geronimus, Arlene T. 1998. The health of urban African American men: Excess mortality and causes of death. Paper presented at the Aspen Institute's Roundtable on Comprehensive Community Initiatives project on race and community revitalization, November. Queenstown, MD.

Geronimus, Arlene T., John Bound, and Cynthia G. Colen. 2011. Excess black mortality in the United States and in selected black and white high-poverty areas, 1980–2000. *American Journal of Public Health* 101(4): 720–729.

Gibbons, Jeffrey A., Cheryl Taylor, and Janet Phillips. 2005. Minorities as marginalized heroes and prominent villains in the mass media: Music, news, sports, television, and movies. In *Cognitive technology: Essays on the transformation of thought and society*, edited by W. Richard Walker and Douglas J. Herrmann, 149–171. Jefferson, NC: McFarland & Company.

Gieryn, Thomas F. 2000. A space for place in sociology. *Annual Review of Sociology* 26: 463–496.

———. 2002. Give place a chance: Reply to Gans. *City & Community* 1: 341–343.

Gilmore, Ruth Wilson. 2002. Fatal couplings of power and difference: Notes on racism and geography. *Professional Geographer* 54(1): 15–24.

Gilroy, Paul. 1993. *The black Atlantic: Modernity and double consciousness.* Cambridge, MA: Harvard University Press.

Giroux, Henry A., and Grace Pollack. 2010. *The mouse that roared: Disney and the end of innocence.* 2nd ed. Lanham, MD: Rowman and Littlefield.

Golden, Marita. 2004. *Don't play in the sun: One woman's journey through the color complex.* New York: Doubleday.

Goodstein, Renee, and Joseph G. Ponterotto. 1997. Racial and ethnic identity: Their relationship and their contribution to self-esteem. *Journal of Black Psychology* 23(3): 275–293.

Gotanda, Neil. 1995. A critique of 'Our constitution is color-blind.' In *Critical race theory: The key writings that formed the movement*, edited by Kimberlé Crenshaw, Neil Gotanda, Gary Peller, and Kendall Thomas, 257–275. New York: New Press.

Grantham, Tarek C., and Donna Y. Ford. 2003. Beyond self-concept and self-esteem: Racial identity and gifted African American students. *High School Journal* 87(1): 18–29.

Graves, Sherryl Browne. 1993. Television, the portrayal of African Americans, and the development of children's attitudes. In *Children and television: Images in a changing sociocultural world*, edited by Gordon L. Berry and Joy Keiko Asamen, 179–190. Thousand Oaks, CA: Sage Publications.

———. 1999. Television and prejudice reduction: When does television as a vicarious experience make a difference? *Journal of Social Issues* 55(4): 707–727.

Gray, Erika Swarts. 2009. The importance of visibility: Students' and teachers' criteria for selecting African American literature. *Reading Teacher* 62(6): 472–481.

Gray, Steven. 2010. In Detroit, improved 911 response times. *Time.com*, April 19. http://detroit.blogs.time.com/2010/04/19/in-detroit-improved-911-response-times/ #ixzz1WjIeslNp.

Greene, Beverly. 1990. Sturdy bridges: The role of African-American mothers in the socialization of African-American children. *Women and Therapy* 10(1): 205–225.

Gubrium, Jaber F., and Holstein, James A., eds. 2002. *Handbook of interview research: Context & method.* Thousand Oaks, CA: Sage Publications.

Haberman, Maggie. 2011. Conservative group backtracks on marriage pledge slavery language. *Politico*, July 11.

Hagerman, Margaret Ann. 2010. "I like being intervieeeeeeewed!" Kids' perspectives on participating in social research. In *Children and youth speak for themselves*, Sociological

Studies of Children and Youth, vol. 13, edited by Heather Beth Johnson, 61–105. Bingley, UK: Emerald Group Publishing.

Hale-Benson, Janice. 1990. Visions for children: Educating Black children in the context of their culture. In *Going to school: The African-American experience*, edited by Kofi Lomotey, 209–222. Albany: State University of New York Press.

Hall, Ronald E., ed. 2008. *Racism in the twenty-first century: An empirical analysis of skin color.* New York: Springer.

Hall, Schekeva P., and Robert T. Carter. 2006. The relationship between racial identity, ethnic identity, and perceptions of racial discrimination in an Afro-Caribbean descent sample. *Journal of Black Psychology* 32(2): 155–175.

Hall, Stuart. 1990. Cultural identity and diaspora. In *Identity: Community, culture, difference*, edited by Jonathan Rutherford, 222–237. London: Lawrence and Wilson.

Hamm, Jill V. 2001. Barriers and bridges to positive cross-ethnic relations: African American and white parent socialization beliefs and practices. *Youth and Society* 33(1): 62–98.

Hancock, Ange-Marie. 2004. *The politics of disgust: The public identity of the welfare queen.* New York: New York University Press.

Harrell, Camara Jules P. 1999. *Manichean psychology: Racism and the minds of people of African descent.* Washington, DC: Howard University Press.

Harrison, Algea O. 1985. The Black family's socializing environment: Self-esteem and ethnic attitude among Black children. In *Black children: Social, educational, and parental environments*, edited by Harriette Pipes McAdoo and John Lewis McAdoo, 174–193. Beverly Hills, CA: Sage Publications.

Harrison, Algea O., Melvin N. Wilson, Charles J. Pine, Samuel Q. Chan, and Raymond Buriel. 1990. Family ecologies of ethnic minority children. *Child Development* 61: 347–362.

Hartigan, John, Jr. 1999. *Racial situations: Class predicaments of whiteness in Detroit.* Princeton, NJ: Princeton University Press.

Harvey, Richard D., Nicole LaBeach, Ellie Pridgen, and Tammy M. Gocial. 2005. The intra-group stigma of skin tone among Black Americans. *Journal of Black Psychology* 31(3): 237–253.

Henderson, Laretta. 2008. *Ebony Jr! The rise, fall, and return of a Black children's magazine.* Lanham, MD: Scarecrow Press.

Higginbotham, Evelyn Brooks. 1993. *Righteous discontent: The women's movement in the Black Baptist Church, 1880–1920.* Cambridge, MA: Harvard University Press.

Hill, Nancy E., Lea Bromell, Diana F. Tyson, and Roxanne Flint. 2007. Developmental commentary: Ecological perspectives on parental influences during adolescence. *Journal of Clinical Child and Adolescent Psychology* 36(3): 367–377.

Hill, Shirley A. 1999. *African American children: Socialization and development in families.* Thousand Oaks, CA: Sage Publications.

Hine, Darlene Clark. 1989. Rape and the inner lives of Black women in the Middle West: Preliminary thoughts on the culture of dissemblance. *Signs: Journal of Women in Culture and Society* 14(4): 912–920.

Hirschfield, Lawrence A. 2008. Children's developing conceptions of race. In *Handbook of race, racism, and the developing child*, edited by Stephen M. Quintana and Clark McKown, 37–54. Hoboken, NJ: John Wiley & Sons.

Hochschild, Jennifer L., and Vesla Weaver. 2007. The skin color paradox and the American racial order. *Social Forces* 86(2): 643–670.

Holmes, Robyn M. 1995. *How young children perceive race.* Thousand Oaks, CA: Sage Publications.

Holmes, Shannon. 2001. *B-more careful: A novel*. New York: Teri Woods Publishing.

Holtzman, Linda. 2000. *Media messages: What film, television, and popular music teach us about race, class, gender, and sexual orientation*. Armonk, NY: M. E. Sharpe.

hooks, bell. 1992. *Black looks: Race and representation*. Boston: South End Press.

Hughes, Diane. 1997. Racist thinking and thinking about race: What children know but don't say. *Ethos* 25(1): 117–125.

———. 2003. Correlates of African American and Latino parents' messages to children about ethnicity and race: A comparative study of racial socialization. *American Journal of Community Psychology* 31(1–2): 15–33.

Hughes, Diane, and Lisa Chen. 1997. When and what parents tell children about race: An examination of race-related socialization among African American families. *Applied Developmental Science* 1(4): 198–212.

———. 1999. The nature of parents' race-related communications to children: A developmental perspective. In *Child psychology: A handbook of contemporary issues*, edited by Lawrence Balter and Catherine S. Tamis-LeMonda, 467–490. Philadelphia: Psychology Press.

Hughes, Diane, Carolin Hagelskamp, Niobe Way, and Monica D. Foust. 2009. The role of mothers' and adolescents' perceptions of ethnic-racial socialization in shaping ethnic-racial identity among early adolescent boys and girls. *Journal of Youth & Adolescence* 38: 605–626.

Hughes, Diane, and Deborah Johnson. 2001. Correlates in children's experiences of parents' racial socialization behaviors. *Journal of Marriage and Family* 63: 981–995.

Hughes, Diane, Deborah Rivas, Monica Foust, Carolin Hagelskamp, Sarah Gersick, and Niobe Way. 2008. How to catch a moonbeam: A mixed-methods approach to understanding ethnic socialization processes in ethnically diverse families. In *Handbook of race, racism, and the developing child*, edited by Stephen M. Quintana and Clark McKown, 226–276. Hoboken, NJ: John Wiley & Sons.

Hughes, Diane, James Rodriguez, Emilie P. Smith, Deborah J. Johnson, Howard C. Stevenson, and Paul Spicer. 2006. Parents' ethnic-racial socialization practices: A review of research and directions for future study. *Developmental Psychology* 42(5): 747–770.

Hull, Gloria T., Patricia Bell Scott, and Barbara Smith, eds. 1982. *All the women are white, all the Blacks are men, but some of us are brave: Black women's studies*. Old Westbury, NY: Feminist Press.

Irvine, Jacqueline Jordan. 1990. *Black students and school failure: Policies, practices, and prescriptions*. New York: Greenwood Press.

Irvine, Jacqueline Jordan, and Russell W. Irvine. 1995. Black youth in school: Individual achievement and institutional/cultural perspectives. In *African-American youth: Their social and economic status in the United States*, edited by Ronald L. Taylor, 129–142. Westport, CT: Praeger.

Jackson, James S., Wayne R. McCullough, and Gerald Gurin. 1997. Family, socialization environment, and identity development in Black Americans. In *Black families*, edited by Harriette Pipes McAdoo, 251–266. Thousand Oaks, CA: Sage Publications.

Johnson, Allan G. 2006. *Privilege, power, and difference*. 2nd ed. New York: McGraw-Hill.

Johnson, Deborah J. 2001. Parental characteristics, racial stress, and racial socialization processes as predictors of racial coping in middle childhood. In *Forging links: African American children clinical development perspectives*, edited by Angela M. Neal-Barnett, Josefina M. Contreas, and Kathryn A. Kerns, 57–74. Westport, CT: Praeger Publishers.

———. 2005. The ecology of children's racial coping: Family, school, and community influences. In *Discovering successful pathways in children's development: Mixed methods in the study of childhood and family life*, edited by Thomas S. Weisner, 87–109. Chicago: University of Chicago Press.

Johnson, E. Patrick. 2003. *Appropriating blackness: Performance and the politics of authenticity.* Durham, NC: Duke University Press.

Johnson, Heather Beth. 2010. Scholars giving voice so that children and youth can speak for themselves: An introduction to this special volume. In *Children and youth speak for themselves*, Sociological Studies of Children and Youth, vol. 13, edited by Heather Beth Johnson, xii–xv. Bingley, UK: Emerald Group Publishing.

Katz, Judith H. 2003. *White awareness.* 2nd ed. Norman: University of Oklahoma Press.

Katz, Phyllis A. 2003. Racists or tolerant multiculturalists? How do they begin? *American Psychologist* 58(11): 897–909.

Katz, Phyllis A., and Jennifer A. Kofkin. 1997. Race, gender, and young children. In *Developmental psychopathology: Perspectives on adjustment, risk, and disorder*, edited by Suniya S. Luthar, Jacob A. Burack, Dante Cicchetti, and John R. Weisz, 51–74. New York: Cambridge University Press.

Kelley, Robin D. G. 1994. *Race rebels: Culture, politics, and the Black working class.* New York: Free Press.

Kismaric, Carole, and Marvin Heiferman. 1996. *Growing up with Dick and Jane: Learning and living the American dream.* San Francisco: Collins Publishers San Francisco (A Division of HarperCollins Publishers).

Klein, Hugh, and Kenneth S. Shiffman. 2006. Race-related content of animated cartoons. *Howard Journal of Communications* 17: 163–182.

———. 2009. Underrepresentation and symbolic annihilation of socially disenfranchised groups ("out groups") in animated cartoons. *Howard Journal of Communications* 20: 55–72.

Kobayashi, Audrey, and Linda Peake. 2000. Racism out of place: Thoughts on whiteness and an antiracist geography in the new millennium. *Annals of the Association of American Geographers* 90 (2): 392–403.

Kochhar, Rakesh, Richard Fry, and Paul Taylor. 2011. Wealth gaps rise to record highs between whites, Blacks, Hispanics: Twenty-to-one. Washington, DC: Pew Research Center.

Kolb, David A. 1984. *Experiential learning: Experience as the source of learning and development.* Englewood Cliffs, NJ: Prentice-Hall.

Kunjufu, Jawanza. 2002. *Black students, middle-class teachers.* Chicago: African American Images.

———. 2005. *Keeping Black boys out of special education.* Chicago: African American Images.

———. 2009. *State of emergency: We must save African American males.* Chicago: African American Images.

Labov, William, Sharon Ash, and Charles Boberg. 2006. *The atlas of North American English: Phonetics, phonology, and sound change.* Berlin: Mouton/de Gruyter.

Lacy, Karyn R. 2007. *Blue-chip Black: Race, class, and status in the new Black middle class.* Berkeley: University of California Press.

Lacy, Karyn R., and Angel L. Harris. 2008. Breaking the class monolith: Understanding class differences in Black adolescents' attachment to racial identity. In *Social class: How does it work?*, edited by Annette Lareau and Dalton Conley, 152–178. New York: Russell Sage Foundation.

Ladson-Billings, Gloria. 1995. Toward a theory of culturally relevant pedagogy. *American Educational Research Journal* 32(3): 465–491.

LeClair, Thomas. 1994. The language must not sweat: A conversation with Toni Morrison. In *Conversations with Toni Morrison*, edited by Danille Taylor-Guthrie, 119–128. Jackson: University Press of Mississippi.

LeDuff, Charlie. 2010. Detroit paramedics fear they're losing the battle to save lives. *Detroit News*, September 16.

Lefrançois, G. R. 1995. *An introduction to child development.* 8th ed. Belmont, CA: Wadsworth Publishing.

Lei, Joy L. 2003. (Un)necessary toughness? Those "loud Black girls" and those "quiet Asian boys." *Anthropology and Education Quarterly* 34(2): 158–181.

Lesane-Brown, Chase L. 2006. A review of race socialization within Black families. *Developmental Review* 26: 400–426.

Lesane-Brown, Chase L., Tony N. Brown, Cleopatra H. Caldwell, and Robert M. Sellers. 2005. The comprehensive race socialization inventory. *Journal of Black Studies* 36(2): 163–190.

Lewis, Amanda E. 2003. *Race in the schoolyard: Negotiating the color line in classrooms and communities.* New Brunswick, NJ: Rutgers University Press.

Lewis, Earl. 1999. To turn as on a pivot: Writing African Americans into a history of overlapping diasporas. In *Crossing boundaries: Comparative history of Black people in the diaspora*, edited by Darlene Clark Hine and Jacqueline McLeod, 3–32. Bloomington: Indiana University Press.

Lewis, Michael B. 2010. Who is the fairest of them all? Race, attractiveness and skin color sexual dimorphism. *Personality and Individual Differences* 50(2): 159–162.

Lewis, R. L'Heureux. 2010. Speaking the unspeakable: Youth discourses on racial importance in school. In *Children and youth speak for themselves*, Sociological Studies of Children and Youth, vol. 13, edited by Heather Beth Johnson, 401–421. Bingley, UK: Emerald Group Publishing.

Lipsitz, George. 2011. *How racism takes place.* Philadelphia: Temple University Press.

Littlefield, Marci Bounds. 2008. The media as a system of racialization: Exploring images of African American women and the new racism. *American Behavioral Scientist* 51(5): 675–685.

Logan, John R., and Harvey Luskin Molotch. 1987. *Urban fortunes: The political economy of place.* Berkeley: University of California Press.

Logan, John R., Deirdre Oakley, Polly Smith, Jacob Stowell, and Brian Stults. 2001. Separating the children. Report by the Lewis Mumford Center, Albany, NY. http://mumford.albany.edu/census/Under18Pop/U18Preport/page1.html.

Lorde, Audre. 1984. *Sister outsider: Essays and speeches.* Trumansburg, NY: Crossing Press.

Loury, Glenn C. 1995. *One by one from the inside out: Essays and reviews on race and responsibility in America.* New York: Free Press.

Loveman, Mara. 1999. Is "race" essential? *American Sociological Review* 64(6): 891–898.

Lugo-Lugo, Carmen R., and Mary K. Bloodsworth-Lugo. 2009. "Look out new world, here we come"? Race, racialization, and sexuality in four children's animated films by Disney, Pixar, and DreamWorks. *Cultural Studies—Critical Methodologies* 9(2): 166–178.

Lynn, Marvin, and Laurence Parker. 2006. Critical race studies in education: Examining a decade of research on US schools. *Urban Review: Issues and Ideas in Public Education* 38(4): 257–290.

MacEwen, Martin. 2002. *Housing, race and law.* London: Taylor and Francis.

Mandara, Jelani, Carolyn B. Murray, and Toya N. Joyner. 2005. The impact of fathers' absence on African American adolescents' gender role development. *Sex Roles* 53(3/4): 207–220.

Marable, Manning, and Kristen Clarke, eds. 2008. *Seeking higher ground: The Hurricane Katrina crisis, race, and public policy reader.* New York: Palgrave Macmillan.

Marshall, Catherine, and Gretchen B. Rossman. 2010. *Designing qualitative research.* 5th ed. Thousand Oaks, CA: Sage Publications.

Marshall, Sheree. 1995. Ethnic socialization of African American children: Implications for parenting, identity development, and academic achievement. *Journal of Youth and Adolescence* 24(4): 377–396.

Massey, Doreen. 1994. *Space, place, and gender*. Minneapolis: University of Minnesota Press.

McAdoo, Harriette Pipes, Sinead Younge, and Solomon Getahun. 2007. Marriage and family socialization among Black Americans and Caribbean and African immigrants. In *The other African Americans: Contemporary African and Caribbean immigrants in the United States*, edited by Yoku Shaw-Taylor and Steven A. Tuch, 93–116. Lanham, MD: Rowman & Littlefield.

McCrary, Jan. 1993. Effects of listeners' and performers' race on music preferences. *Journal of Research in Music Education* 41(3): 200–211.

McHale, Susan M., Ann C. Crouter, Ji-Yeon Kim, Linda M. Burton, Kelly D. Davis, Aryn M. Dotterer, and Dena P. Swanson. 2006. Mothers' and fathers' racial socialization in African American families: Implications for youth. *Child Development* 77(5): 1387–1402.

McIntosh, Peggy. 1990. White privilege: Unpacking the invisible knapsack. *Independent School* 49(2): 31–36.

McKittrick, Katherine. 2006. *Demonic grounds: Black women and the cartographies of struggle.* Minneapolis: University of Minnesota Press.

Merskin, Debra. 1998. Sending up signals: A survey of Native American media use and representation in the mass media. *Howard Journal of Communications* 9: 333–345.

Mickelson, Roslyn A. 2003. When are racial disparities in education the result of racial discrimination? A social science perspective. *Teachers College Record* 105(6): 1052–1086.

Miller, David B. 1999. Racial socialization and racial identity: Can they promote resiliency for African American adolescents? *Adolescence* 34(135): 491–499.

Miller, David B., and Randall MacIntosh. 1999. Promoting resilience in urban African American adolescents: Racial socialization and identity as protective factors. *Social Work Research* 23(3): 159–169.

Morton-Williams, Jean. 1993. *Interviewer approaches*. Brookfield, VT: Dartmouth Publishing Company.

Moynihan, Daniel Patrick. 1965. *The Negro family: The case for national action*. Washington, DC: US Government Printing Office.

Mukhopadhyay, Carol Chapnick, Rosemary C. Henze, and Yolanda T. Moses. 2007. *How real is race? A sourcebook on race, culture, and biology*. Lanham, MD: Rowman & Littlefield.

Murray, Carolyn Bennett, and Jelani Mandara. 2002. Racial identity development in African American children: Cognitive and experiential antecedents. In *Black children: Social, educational, and parental environments*, edited by Harriette Pipes McAdoo, 73–96. Thousand Oaks, CA: Sage Publications.

Murry, Velma McBride, Gene H. Brody, Ronald L. Simons, Carolyn E. Cutrona, and Frederick X. Gibbons. 2008. Disentangling ethnicity and context as predictors of parenting within rural African American families. *Applied Developmental Science* 12(4): 202–210.

Nagata, Donna K., and Wendy J. Y. Cheng. 2003. Intergenerational communication of race-related trauma by Japanese American former internees. *American Journal of Orthopsychiatry* 73(3): 266–278.

Neblett, Enrique W., Cheri L. Philip, Courtney D. Cogburn, and Robert M. Sellers. 2006. African American adolescents' discrimination experiences and academic achievement: Racial socialization as a cultural compensatory and protective factor. *Journal of Black Psychology* 32(2): 199–218.

Neblett, Enrique W., Ciara P. Smalls, Kahlil R. Ford, Hòa X. Nguyen, and Robert M. Sellers. 2009. Racial socialization and racial identity: African American parents' messages about race as precursors to identity. *Journal of Youth and Adolescence* 38: 189–203.

Noguera, Pedro A. 2008. *The trouble with Black boys . . . and other reflections on race, equity, and the future of public education*. San Francisco: Jossey-Bass.

Norton, Bryan G., and Bruce Hannon. 1997. Environmental values: A place-based theory. *Environmental Ethics* 19: 227–245.

O'Brien, Eileen. 2011. The transformation of the role of "race" in the qualitative interview: Not if race matters, but how? In *Rethinking race and ethnicity in research methods*, edited by John H. Stanfield II, 67–93. Walnut Creek, CA: Left Coast Press.

O'Connor, Lisa A., Jeanne Brooks-Gunn, and Julia Graber. 2000. Black and white girls' racial preferences in media and peer choices and the role of socialization for Black girls. *Journal of Family Psychology* 14(3): 510–521.

O'Donoghue, Margaret. 2005. White mothers negotiating race and ethnicity of biracial, Black-White adolescents. *Journal of Ethnic and Cultural Diversity in Social Work* 14(3/4): 125–156.

Oliver, Melvin L., and Thomas M. Shapiro. 1995. *Black wealth/white wealth: A new perspective on racial inequality*. New York: Routledge.

Omi, Michael. 1997. In living color: Race and American culture. In *Signs of life in the USA: Readings on popular culture for writers*, edited by Sonia Maasik and Jack Solomon, 491–503. Boston: Bedford Books.

Omi, Michael, and Howard Winant. 1994. *Racial formation in the United States: From the 1960s to the 1990s*. New York: Routledge.

Operario, Don, and Susan T. Fiske. 1998. Racism equals power plus prejudice: A social psychological equation for racial oppression. In *Confronting racism: The problem and the response*, edited by Jennifer Lynn Eberhardt and Susan T. Fiske, 33–53. Thousand Oaks, CA: Sage Publications.

Orelus, Pierre W. 2010. *The agony of masculinity: Race, gender, and education in the age of "new" racism and patriarchy*. New York: Peter Lang Publishing.

Orum, Anthony M. 1998. The urban imagination of sociologists: The centrality of place. *Sociological Quarterly* 39: 1–10.

Oyserman, Daphna, Markus Kemmelmeier, Stephanie Fryberg, Hezi Broshi, and Tamera Hart-Johnson. 2003. Racial-ethnic self-schemas. *Social Psychology Quarterly* 66(4): 333–347.

Padilla, Amado M., and William Perez. 2003. Acculturation, social identity, and social cognition: A new perspective. *Hispanic Journal of Behavioral Sciences* 25: 35–55.

Pager, Devah. 2003. The mark of a criminal record. *American Journal of Sociology* 108(5): 937–975.

Pahl, Kerstin, and Niobe Way. 2006. Longitudinal trajectories of ethnic identity among urban Black and Latino adolescents. *Child Development* 77: 1403–1415.

Parham, Thomas A., Joseph L. White, and Adisa Ajamu. 1999. *The psychology of Blacks: An African-centered perspective*. 3rd ed. Upper Saddle River, NJ: Prentice-Hall.

Patterson, Meagan M., and Rebecca S. Bigler. 2006. Preschool children's attention to environmental messages about groups: Social categorization and the origins of intergroup bias. *Child Development* 77(4): 847–860.

Pattillo, Mary. 2007. *Black on the block: The politics of race and class in the city*. Chicago: University of Chicago Press.

Pattillo-McCoy, Mary. 1999. *Black picket fences: Privilege and peril among the Black middle class.* Chicago: University of Chicago Press.

Paulsen, Krista E. 2004. Making character concrete: Empirical strategies for studying place distinction. *City and Community* 3(3): 243–262.

Perry, Imani. 2003. Who(se) am I? The identity and image of women in hip-hop. In *Gender, race, and class in media,* edited by Gail Dines and Jean M. Humez, 136–148. Thousand Oaks, CA: Sage Publications.

———. 2011. *More beautiful and more terrible: The embrace and transcendence of racial inequality in the United States.* New York: New York University Press.

Peters, Marie Ferguson. 1985. Racial socialization of young Black children. In *Black children: Social, educational, and parental environments,* edited by Harriette Pipes McAdoo and John Lewis McAdoo, 159–173. Beverly Hills, CA: Sage Publications.

Pettigrew, Thomas F., and Linda R. Tropp. 2006. A meta-analytic test of intergroup contact theory. *Journal of Personality and Social Psychology* 90: 751–783.

Pulido, Laura. 2000. Rethinking environmental racism: white privilege and urban development in Southern California. *Annals of the Association of American Geographers* 90(1): 12–40.

Quintana, Stephen M., Frances E. Aboud, Ruth K. Chao, Josefina Contreras-Grau, William E. Cross Jr., Cynthia Hudley, Diane Hughes, Lynn S. Liben, Sharon Nelson-Le Gall, and Deborah L. Vietze. 2006. Race, ethnicity, and culture in child development: Contemporary research and future directions. *Child Development* 77(5): 1129–1141.

Ratcliffe, Caroline, and Signe-Mary McKernan. 2010. *Childhood poverty persistence: Facts and consequences.* Washington, DC: The Urban Institute.

Rhodes, Gillian, Kieran Lee, Romina Palermo, Mahi Weiss, Sakiko Yoshikawa, Peter Clissa, Tamsyn Williams, Marianne Peters, Chris Winkler, and Linda Jeffery. 2005. Attractiveness of own-race, other-race, and mixed-race faces. *Perception* 34(3): 319–340.

Richeson, Jennifer A., and Sophie Trawalter. 2005. On the categorization of admired and disliked exemplars of admired and disliked racial groups. *Journal of Personality and Social Psychology* 89(4): 517–530.

Robinson, Jeanene, and Mia Biran. 2006. Discovering self: Relationships between African identity and academic achievement. *Journal of Black Studies* 37: 46–68.

Rockquemore, Kerry, and Tracey A. Laszloffy. 2005. *Raising biracial children.* Lanham, MD: AltaMira Press.

Rondilla, Joanne L., and Paul R. Spickard. 2007. *Is lighter better? Skin tone discrimination among Asian Americans.* Lanham, MD: Rowman & Littlefield.

Rosenbloom, Susan Rakosi. 2010. "They don't wanna get their education": Peers and collective dis-identity in a multiracial urban high school. In *Children and youth speak for themselves,* Sociological Studies of Children and Youth, vol. 13, edited by Heather Beth Johnson, 3–31. Bingley, UK: Emerald Group Publishing.

Rothenberg, Paula S. 2008. *White privilege: Essential readings on the other side of racism.* 3rd ed. New York: Worth Publishers.

Rubin, Herbert J., and Irene S. Rubin. 2005. *Qualitative interviewing: The art of hearing data.* 2nd ed. Thousand Oaks, CA: Sage Publications.

Russell, Kathy, Midge Wilson, and Ronald Hall. 1993. *The color complex: The politics of skin color among African Americans.* New York: Anchor Books.

Said, Edward W. 1978. *Orientalism.* New York: Pantheon Books.

Sanders Thompson, Vetta L. 1994. Socialization to race and its relationship to racial identification among African Americans. *Journal of Black Psychology* 20: 175–188.

Schaefer-McDaniel, Nicole. 2007. "They be doing illegal things": Early adolescents talk about their inner-city neighborhoods. *Journal of Adolescent Research* 22(4): 413–436.

Schopmeyer, Kim. 2000. A demographic portrait of Arab Detroit. In *Arab Detroit: From margin to mainstream*, edited by Nabeel Abraham and Andrew Shyrock, 61–92. Detroit: Wayne State University Press.

Schwarz, Alan. 2011. School discipline study raises fresh questions. *New York Times*, July 19.

Scott, Kimberly Ann. 2003. In girls, out girls, and always Black: African-American girls' friendships. *Sociological Studies of Children and Youth* 9: 179–207.

Scott, Lionel D., Jr. 2003. The relation of racial identity and racial socialization to coping with discrimination among African American adolescents. *Journal of Black Studies* 33(4): 520–538.

Scottham, Krista Maywalt, and Ciara P. Smalls. 2009. Unpacking racial socialization: Considering female African American primary caregivers' racial identity. *Journal of Marriage and Family* 71(4): 807–818.

Seaton, Eleanor K., and Tiffany Yip. 2009. School and neighborhood contexts, perceptions of racial discrimination, and psychological well-being among African American adolescents. *Journal of Youth and Adolescence* 38: 153–163.

Senna, Danzy. 1995. To be real. In *To be real: Telling the truth and changing the face of feminism*, edited by Rebecca Walker, 5–20. New York: Anchor Books.

Shapiro, Thomas. 2005. *The hidden cost of being African American: How wealth perpetuates inequality*. New York: Oxford University Press.

Shelton, Jason E. 2008. The investment in Blackness hypothesis: Toward greater understanding of who teaches what during racial socialization. *Du Bois Review* 5(2): 235–257.

Shyrock, Andrew, and Nabeel Abraham. 2000. On margins and mainstreams. In *Arab Detroit: From margin to mainstream*, edited by Nabeel Abraham and Andrew Shyrock, 15–35. Detroit: Wayne State University Press.

Shyrock, Andrew, and Ann Chih Lin. 2009. Arab American identities in question. In *Citizenship and crisis: Arab Detroit after 9/11*, edited by the Detroit Arab American Study Team, 35–68. New York: Russell Sage Foundation.

Sieber, Joan E. 1993. The ethics and politics of sensitive research. In *Researching sensitive topics*, edited by Claire M. Renzetti and Raymond M. Lee, 14–19. Newbury Park, CA: Sage Publications.

Silverman, David. 1993. *Interpreting qualitative data: Methods for analyzing talk, text, and interaction*. London: Sage Publications.

———. 2010. *Doing qualitative research: A practical handbook*. 3rd ed. Thousand Oaks, CA: Sage Publications.

Small, Stephen A. 2002. Racisms and racialized hostility at the start of the new millennium. In *A companion to racial and ethnic studies*, edited by David Theo Goldberg and John Solomos, 259–281. Malden, MA: Blackwell.

———. 2004a. Mustefinos are white by law: Whites and people of mixed racial origins in historical and comparative perspective. In *Racial thinking in the United States: Uncompleted independence*, edited by Paul Spickard and G. Reginald Daniel, 60–79. Notre Dame, IN: University of Notre Dame Press.

———. 2004b. Researching "mixed-race" experience under slavery: Concepts, methods, and data. In *Researching race and racism*, edited by Martin Bulmer and John Solomos, 78–91. New York: Routledge.

Smalls, Ciara. 2009. African American adolescent engagement in the classroom and beyond: The roles of mother's racial socialization and democratic-involved parenting. *Journal of Youth and Adolescence* 38: 204–213.

Smedley, Audrey, and Brian D. Smedley. 2005. Race as biology is fiction, racism as a social problem is real: Anthropological and historical perspectives on the social construction of race. *American Psychologist* 60(1): 16–26.

Smith, Joel J., and Nathan Hurst. 2007. Grocery closings hit Detroit hard: City shoppers' choices dwindle as last big chain leaves. *Detroit News*, July 5.

Smitherman, Geneva. 1997. "The chain remain the same": Communicative practices in the hip-hop nation. *Journal of Black Studies* 29(1): 3–25.

———. 2000. *Talkin that talk: Language, culture, and education in African America.* New York: Routledge.

———. 2001. Black language and the education of Black children: One mo once. *The Black Scholar* 27(1): 28–35.

Smitherman, Geneva, and John Baugh. 2002. The shot heard from Ann Arbor: Language research and public policy in African America. *Howard Journal of Communications* 13: 5–24.

Sowell, Thomas. 1998. *Race, culture, and equality.* Stanford, CA: Hoover Institution on War, Revolution, and Peace.

Spencer, Margaret Beale. 1990. Parental values transmission: Implications for the development of African American children. In *Black families: Interdisciplinary perspectives*, edited by Harold E. Cheatham and James B. Stewart, 111–130. New Brunswick, NJ: Transaction Books.

Spickard, Paul R., and G. Reginald Daniel, eds. 2004. *Racial thinking in the United States: Uncompleted independence.* Notre Dame, IN: University of Notre Dame Press.

Squires, Gregory D., and Charis E. Kubrin. 2006. *Privileged places: Race, residence, and the structure of opportunity.* Boulder, CO: Lynne Rienner Publishers.

Stack, Carol B., and Linda M. Burton. 1994. Kinscripts: Reflections on family, generation, and culture. In *Mothering: Ideology, experience, and agency*, edited by Evelyn Nakano Glenn, Grace Chang, and Linda Rennie Farcey, 33–44. New York: Routledge.

Staiger, Annegret Daniela. 2005. Recreating Blackness-as-failure through educational reform? A case study of a California Partnership Academy. *Equity & Excellence in Education* 38(1): 35–48.

———. 2006. *Learning difference: Race and schooling in the multiracial metropolis.* Stanford, CA: Stanford University Press.

Stanton-Salazar, Ricardo D. 1997. A social capital framework for understanding the socialization of racial minority children and youths. *Harvard Educational Review* 67(1): 1–40.

Steele, Shelby. 1991. *The content of our character: A new vision of race in America.* New York: HarperPerennial.

Stevenson, Howard C., Jr. 1995. Relationship of adolescent perceptions of racial socialization to racial identity. *Journal of Black Psychology* 21: 49–70.

Stevenson, Howard C., J. Derek McNeil, Teresa Herrero-Taylor, and Gwendolyn Y. Davis. 2005. Influence of perceived neighborhood diversity and racism experience on the racial socialization of Black youth. *Journal of Black Psychology* 31(3): 273–290.

Strauss, Anselm, and Juliet Corbin. 1998. *Basics of qualitative research: Techniques and procedures for developing grounded theory.* Thousand Oaks, CA: Sage Publications.

Stubblefield, Anna. 1995. Racial identity and non-essentialism about race. *Social Theory and Practice* 21(3): 341–368.

Sugrue, Thomas J. 1996. *The origins of urban crisis: Race and inequality in postwar Detroit.* Princeton, NJ: Princeton University Press.

Suizzo, Marie-Anne, Courtney Robinson, and Erin Pahlke. 2008. African American mothers' socialization beliefs and goals with young children. *Journal of Family Issues* 29(3): 287–316.

Supple, Andrew J., Sharon R. Ghazarian, James M. Frabutt, Scott W. Plunkett, and Tovah Sands. 2006. Contextual influences on Latino adolescent ethnic identity and academic outcomes. *Child Development* 77(5): 1427–1433.

Swim, Janet K., and Charles Stangor. 1998. *Prejudice: The target's perspective.* San Diego, CA: Academic Press.

Tatum, Beverly Daniel. 2003. *"Why are all the Black kids sitting together in the cafeteria?" And other conversations about race.* New York: Basic Books.

Thomas, Anita Jones, and Constance T. King. 2007. Gendered racial socialization of African American mothers and daughters. *Family Journal: Counseling and Therapy for Couples and Families* 15(2): 137–142.

Thomas, Anita Jones, and Suzette L. Speight. 1999. Racial identity and racial socialization attitudes of African American parents. *Journal of Black Psychology* 25(2): 152–170.

Thomas, Duane E., Tiffany G. Townsend, and Faye Z. Belgrave. 2003. The influence of cultural and racial identification on the psychosocial adjustment of inner-city African American children in school. *American Journal of Community Psychology* 32: 217–228.

Thomas, June Manning. 1997. *Redevelopment and race: Planning a finer city in postwar Detroit.* Baltimore: The Johns Hopkins University Press.

Thompson, Heather Ann. 2001. *Whose Detroit? Politics, labor, and race in a modern American city.* Ithaca, NY: Cornell University Press.

Thorne, Barrie. 1993. *Gender play: Girls and boys in school.* New Brunswick, NJ: Rutgers University Press.

Thornton, Michael C. 1997. Strategies of racial socialization among Black parents: Mainstream, minority, and cultural messages. In *Family life in Black America*, edited by Robert Joseph Taylor, James S. Jackson, and Linda M. Chatters, 201–215. Thousand Oaks, CA: Sage Publications.

Thornton, Michael C., Linda M. Chatters, Robert Joseph Taylor, and Walter R. Allen. 1990. Sociodemographic and environmental correlates of racial socialization by Black parents. *Child Development* 61: 401–409.

Tickamyer, Ann R. 2000. Space matters! Spatial inequality in future sociology. *Contemporary Sociology* 29: 805–813.

Townsend, Tiffany, and Erin Lanphier. 2007. Family influences on racial identity among African American youth. *Journal of Black Psychology* 33(3): 278–298.

Tuchman, Gaye. 1978. The symbolic annihilation of women by the mass media. In *Hearth and home: Images of women in the mass media*, edited by Gaye Tuchman, Arlene Kaplan Daniels, and James Benét, 3–38. New York: Oxford University Press.

Twine, France Winddance. 2006. Racial logics and (trans)racial identities: A view from Britain. In *Mixed messages: Multiracial identities in the "color-blind" era*, edited by David L. Brunsma, 217–232. Boulder, CO: Lynne Rienner Publishers.

Tyler, Kenneth M., A. Wade Boykin, Christina M. Boelter, and Monica L. Dillihunt. 2005. Examining mainstream and Afro-cultural value socialization in African American households. *Journal of Black Psychology* 31(3): 291–311.

Tyson, Karolyn. 2011. *Integration interrupted: Tracking, Black students, and acting white after Brown.* New York: Oxford University Press.

University of Michigan. 2003. Archived document: Q&A re University of Michigan Former Admissions Policies. Accessed March 10, 2012. http://www.vpcomm.umich.edu/admissions/archivedocs/q&a.html.

Urrieta, Luis, Jr. 2006. Community identity discourse and the heritage academy: Colorblind educational policy and white supremacy. *International Journal of Qualitative Studies in Education* 19(4): 455–476.

US Census Bureau. 1990. Median household income for places with a population of 2,500 to 9,999, ranked within the United States: 1989. Prepared by Income Statistics Branch/Housing and Household Economic Statistics Division. Washington, DC. http://www.census.gov/hhes/www/income/data/1990census/cph1126h.html.

———. 2000a. Table DP-1. Profile of general demographic characteristics: 2000. Ann Arbor city, Michigan. http://factfinder2.census.gov/faces/tableservices/jsf/pages/productview.xhtml?pid=DEC_00_SF1_DP1&prodType=table.

———. 2000b. Table DP-1. Profile of general demographic characteristics: 2000. Bloomfield Hills city, Michigan. http://factfinder2.census.gov/faces/tableservices/jsf/pages/productview.xhtml?pid=DEC_00_SF1_DP1&prodType=table.

———. 2000c. Table DP-1. Profile of general demographic characteristics: 2000. Chicago city, Illinois. http://factfinder2.census.gov/faces/tableservices/jsf/pages/productview.xhtml?pid=DEC_00_SF1_DP1&prodType=table.

———. 2000d. Table DP-1. Profile of general demographic characteristics: 2000. Detroit city, Michigan. http://factfinder2.census.gov/faces/tableservices/jsf/pages/productview.xhtml?pid=DEC_00_SF1_DP1&prodType=table.

———. 2000e. Profile of general demographic characteristics: 2000. Howell city, Michigan. http://factfinder2.census.gov/faces/tableservices/jsf/pages/productview.xhtml?pid=DEC_00_SF1_DP1&prodType=table.

———. 2000f. Table DP-1. Profile of general demographic characteristics: 2000. Las Vegas city, Nevada. http://factfinder2.census.gov/faces/tableservices/jsf/pages/productview.xhtml?pid=DEC_00_SF1_DP1&prodType=table.

———. 2000g. Table DP-1. Profile of general demographic characteristics: 2000. New York City, New York. http://factfinder2.census.gov/faces/tableservices/jsf/pages/productview.xhtml?pid=DEC_00_SF1_DP1&prodType=table.

———. 2000h. Table DP-1. Profile of general demographic characteristics: 2000. Sandusky city, Ohio. http://factfinder2.census.gov/faces/tableservices/jsf/pages/productview.xhtml?pid=DEC_00_SF1_DP1&prodType=table.

———. 2000i. Table DP-1. Profile of general demographic characteristics: 2000. West Bloomfield Township, CDP, Michigan. http://factfinder2.census.gov/faces/tableservices/jsf/pages/productview.xhtml?pid=DEC_00_SF1_DP1&prodType=table.

———. 2001. Majority of African Americans live in 10 states; New York City and Chicago are cities with largest Black populations. Press Release, August 13. http://www.census.gov/newsroom/releases/archives/census_2000/cb01cn176.html.

———. 2003a. *The Arab population 2000: Census 2000 brief,* by G. Patricia de la Cruz and Angela Brittingham. Issued December 2003. http://www.census.gov/prod/2003 pubs/c2kbr-23.pdf.

———. 2003b. *The Black population in the United States: March 2002,* by Jesse McKinnon. Issued April 2003. http://www.census.gov/prod/2003pubs/p20–541.pdf.

———. 2003c. *Married-couple and unmarried-partner households: 2000,* by Tavia Simmons and Martin O'Connell. Issued February 2003. http://www.census.gov/prod/2003pubs/censr-5.pdf.

——. 2006. *Income, earnings, and poverty data from the 2005 American Community Survey*, by Bruce H. Webster Jr. and Alemayehu Bishaw. American Community Survey Reports, ACS-02. Washington, DC: US Government Printing Office. http://www.census.gov/prod/2006pubs/acs-02.pdf.

——. 2008a. *Income, earnings, and poverty data from the 2007 American Community Survey*, by Alemayehu Bishaw and Jessica Semega. American Community Survey Reports, ACS-09. Washington, DC: US Government Printing Office. http://www.census.gov/prod/2008pubs/acs-09.pdf.

——. 2008b. Table *B02001*. RACE—Universe: TOTAL POPULATION. 2008 American Community Survey. http://factfinder2.census.gov/faces/tableservices/jsf/pages/productview.xhtml?pid=ACS_08_1YR_B02001&prodType=table.

US Department of Agriculture. 2005. The story one year later: An after action review. Forest Service, Pacific Southwest Region, R5-PR-015. January 2005. http://www.fs.fed.us/r5/fire/information/story/2004/part_1.pdf.

US Department of Justice. Bureau of Justice Statistics. 2010. Prison inmates at midyear 2009. June 23. http://bjs.ojp.usdoj.gov/index.cfm?ty=pbdetail&iid=2200.

US Department of Labor. Bureau of Labor Statistics. 2009. Metropolitan area employment and unemployment summary. June 14. http://www.bls.gov/news.release/archives/laus_06192009.htm.

Valenzuela, Angela. 1999. *Subtractive schooling: U.S.-Mexican youth and the politics of caring*. Albany: State University of New York Press.

Van Ausdale, Debra, and Joe R. Feagin. 2001. *The first R: How children learn race and racism*. Lanham, MD: Rowman & Littlefield.

Varisco, Daniel Martin. 2007. *Reading Orientalism: Said and the unsaid*. Seattle: University of Washington Press.

Wailoo, Keith, Karen N. O'Neill, Jeffrey Dowd, and Rowland Anglin, eds. 2010. *Katrina's imprint: Race and vulnerability in America*. New Brunswick, NJ: Rutgers University Press.

Wakefield, W. David, and Cynthia Hudley. 2007. Ethnic and racial identity and adolescent well-being. *Theory into Practice* 46(2): 147–154.

Walker, Katrina, Eric Taylor, Angela McElroy, Di-Ann Phillip, and Melvin N. Wilson. 1995. Familial and ecological correlates of self-esteem in African American children. In *African American family life: Its structural and ecological aspects*, edited by Melvin N. Wilson, 23–34. San Francisco: Jossey-Bass.

Wallace, Betty, and William Graves. 1995. *Poisoned apple: The bell curve crisis and how our schools create mediocrity and failure*. New York: St. Martin's Press.

Wang, Wendy. 2012. The rise of intermarriage: Rates, characteristics vary by race and gender. Research report, February 16. Washington, DC: Pew Research Center.

Wayne State University Center for Urban Studies. 2000. Predominant race by 2000 census tract, Metropolitan Detroit Area. Accessed September 20, 2011. www.cus.wayne.edu/content/Maps/Tricounty-tracts-predomrace.pdf.

Welch, Susan, Lee Sigelman, Timothy Bledsoe, and Michael Combs. 2001. *Race and place: Race relations in an American city*. New York: Cambridge University Press.

Wheeler, Mary E., and Susan T. Fiske. 2005. Controlling racial prejudice and stereotyping: Social cognitive goals affect amygdala and stereotype activation. *Psychological Science* 16(1): 56–63.

White, Shane, and Graham White. 1998. *Stylin': African American expressive culture from its beginnings to the zoot suit*. Ithaca, NY: Cornell University Press.

Widick, B. J. 1989. *Detroit: City of race and class violence*. Detroit: Wayne State University Press.

Wiggins, Daphne C. 2005. *Righteous content: Black women's perspectives of church and faith.* New York: New York University Press.

Wilder, JeffriAnne, and Colleen Cain. 2011. Teaching and learning color consciousness in Black families: Exploring family processes and women's experiences with colorism. *Journal of Family Issues* 32(5): 577–604.

Wilkins, Craig L. 2007. *The aesthetics of equity: Notes on race, space, architecture, and music.* Minneapolis: University of Minnesota Press.

Wilkinson, Doris Y. 1995. Disparities in employment status between black and white youth: Explaining the continuing differential. In *African-American youth: Their social and economic status in the United States*, edited by Ronald L. Taylor, 143–154. Westport, CT: Praeger.

Williams, Carmen Braun. 1999. Claiming a biracial identity: Resisting social constructions of race and culture. *Journal of Counseling and Development* 77(1): 32–35.

Williams, Corey. 2008. New Latino wave helps revitalize Detroit. *USA Today*, February 28. http://www.usatoday.com/news/nation/2008-02-28-2962316916_x.htm.

Williams, Tangela L., and Denise Davidson. 2009. Interracial and intra-racial stereotypes and constructive memory in 7- and 9-year-old African-American children. *Journal of Applied Developmental Psychology* 30(3): 366–377.

Wilson, William Julius. 1980. *The declining significance of race: Blacks and changing American institutions.* Chicago: University of Chicago Press.

Winant, Howard. 1994. *Racial conditions: Politics, theory, comparisons.* Minneapolis: University of Minnesota Press.

Wingfield, Adia Harvey. 2008. *Doing business with beauty: Black women, hair salons, and the racial enclave economy.* Lanham, MD: Rowman & Littlefield.

Wingfield, Adia Harvey, and Joe R. Feagin. 2010. *Yes we can? White racial framing and the 2008 presidential campaign.* New York: Routledge.

Winkler, Erin N. 2008. "It's like arming them": African American mothers' views on racial socialization. In *The changing landscape of work and family in the American middle class: Reports from the field*, edited by Elizabeth Rudd and Lara Descartes, 211–241. Lanham, MD: Lexington Books.

———. 2009. Children are not colorblind: How young children learn race. *PACE: Practical Approaches for Continuing Education* 3(3): 1–8.

———. 2010. "I learn being black from everywhere I go": Color blindness, travel, and the formation of racial attitudes among African American adolescents. In *Children and youth speak for themselves*, Sociological Studies of Children and Youth, vol. 13, edited by Heather Beth Johnson, 423–453. Bingley, UK: Emerald Group Publishing.

———. 2011. "My aunt talks about Black people all the time": The significance of extended family networks in the racial socialization of African American adolescents. In *Extended families in Africa and the African diaspora*, edited by Osei-Mensah Aborampah and Niara Sudarkasa, 273–295. Trenton, NJ: Africa World Press.

Wise, Tim J. 2008. *White like me: Reflections on race from a privileged son.* Berkeley, CA: Soft Skull Press.

Worden, Robert E. 1996. The causes of police brutality: Theory and evidence on police use of force. In *Police violence: Understanding and controlling police abuse of force*, edited by William A. Geller and Hans Toch, 23–51. New Haven: Yale University Press.

Young, Alford A., Jr. 2004. Experiences in ethnographic interviewing about race: The inside and outside of it. In *Researching race and racism*, edited by Martin Bulmer and John Solomos, 187–202. New York: Routledge.

Young, Melvina Johnson. 1993. Exploring the WPA narratives: Finding the voices of Black women and men. In *Theorizing Black feminisms: The visionary pragmatism of Black women*, edited by Stanlie M. James and Abena P. A. Busia, 55–74. New York: Routledge.

Zamudio, Margaret, Caskey Russell, Francisco Rios, and Jacquelyn L. Bridgeman, eds. 2011. *Critical race theory matters: Education and ideology*. New York: Routledge.

Zukin, Sharon. 2002. What's space got to do with it? *City & Community* 1: 345–348.

Zwiers, Michael L., and Patrick J. Morrissette. 1999. *Effective interviewing of children: A comprehensive guide for counselors and human service workers*. Philadelphia: Accelerated Development.

INDEX

ABOUT THE AUTHOR

ERIN N. WINKLER is an associate professor of Africology at the University of Wisconsin–Milwaukee. She received her PhD in African American studies from the University of California, Berkeley. Her work on how children develop ideas about race and racism has appeared in a number of books and journals.

CPSIA information can be obtained
at www.ICGtesting.com
Printed in the USA
LVHW052349240820
664146LV00002B/508

9 780813 554297